CompTIA PD Certification

Instructor's Edition

CompTIA PDI+ Certification

Series Product Managers: Charles G. Blum and Adam A. Wilcox
Developmental Editor: Andy LaPage
Technical Editor: Kenneth Wilkinson
Copyeditor: Ken Maher
Keytester: Gail Sandler
Series Designer: Adam A. Wilcox

Photographs provided as a courtesy of Ricoh Americas Corporation

COPYRIGHT © 2008 Axzo Press. All rights reserved.

No part of this work may be reproduced, transcribed, or used in any form or by any means—graphic, electronic, or mechanical, including photocopying, recording, taping, Web distribution, or information storage and retrieval systems—without the prior written permission of the publisher.

For more information, go to www.axzopress.com.

Trademarks

ILT Series is a trademark of Axzo Press.

Some of the product names and company names used in this book have been used for identification purposes only and may be trademarks or registered trademarks of their respective manufacturers and sellers.

Disclaimers

We reserve the right to revise this publication and make changes from time to time in its content without notice.

The logo of the CompTIA Authorized Quality Curriculum (CAQC) program and the status of this or other training material as "Authorized" under the CompTIA Authorized Quality Curriculum program signifies that, in CompTIA's opinion, such training material covers the content of CompTIA's related certification exam.

The contents of this training material were created for the CompTIA PDI+ exam covering CompTIA certification objectives that were current as of December 2007.

CompTIA has not reviewed or approved the accuracy of the contents of this training material and specifically disclaims any warranties of merchantability or fitness for a particular purpose. CompTIA makes no guarantee concerning the success of persons using any such "Authorized" or other training material in order to prepare for any CompTIA certification exam.

ISBN 10: 1-4260-9995-9
ISBN 13: 978-1-4260-9995-3

Printed in the United States of America

1 2 3 4 5 GL 06 05 04 03

Contents

Introduction iii
    Topic A: About the manual... iv
    Topic B: Setting student expectations ix
    Topic C: Classroom setup... xiii
    Topic D: Support... xix

Electromechanical components 1-1
    Topic A: Electromechanical components 1-2
    Topic B: Mechanical components 1-14
    Topic C: Electrical components.. 1-21
    Unit summary: Electromechanical components................................... 1-34

Printing and scanning 2-1
    Topic A: Printing 2-2
    Topic B: Scanning 2-33
    Unit summary: Printing and scanning... 2-40

Connectivity 3-1
    Topic A: Local printing and scanning... 3-2
    Topic B: Network printing and scanning.. 3-22
    Unit summary: Connectivity 3-47

Maintenance and troubleshooting 4-1
    Topic A: Maintenance... 4-2
    Topic B: Troubleshooting... 4-8
    Unit summary: Maintenance and troubleshooting 4-30

Professional conduct 5-1
    Topic A: Communication 5-2
    Topic B: Safety... 5-16
    Unit summary: Professional conduct 5-27

Certification exam objectives map A-1
    Topic A: Comprehensive exam objectives A-2

Course summary S-1
    Topic A: Course summary.. S-2
    Topic B: Continued learning after class S-3

Glossary G-1

Index I-1

Introduction

After reading this introduction, you'll know how to:

A Use ILT Series manuals in general.

B Use prerequisites, a target student description, course objectives, and a skills inventory to set student expectations properly for the course.

C Set up a classroom to teach this course.

D Get support for setting up and teaching this course.

Topic A: About the manual

ILT Series philosophy

Our goal is to make you, the instructor, as successful as possible. To that end, our manuals facilitate student learning by providing structured interaction with the software itself. While we provide text to help you explain difficult concepts, the hands-on activities are the focus of our courses. Leading the students through these activities will teach the skills and concepts effectively.

We believe strongly in the instructor-led class. For many students, having a thinking, feeling instructor in front of them is always the most comfortable way to learn. Because the students' focus should be on you, our manuals are designed and written to facilitate your interaction with the students and not to call attention to manuals themselves.

We believe in the basic approach of setting expectations, then teaching, and providing summary and review afterwards. For this reason, lessons begin with objectives and end with summaries. We also provide overall course objectives and a course summary to provide both an introduction to and closure on the entire course.

Our goal is your success. We encourage your feedback in helping us to improve our manuals continually to meet your needs.

Manual components

The manuals contain these major components:

- Table of contents
- Introduction
- Units
- Appendix
- Course summary
- Quick reference
- Glossary
- Index

Each element is described below.

Table of contents

The table of contents acts as a learning roadmap for you and the students.

Introduction

The introduction contains information about our training philosophy and our manual components, features, and conventions. It contains target student, prerequisite, objective, and setup information for the specific course. Finally, the introduction contains support information.

Units

Units are the largest structural component of the actual course content. A unit begins with a title page that lists objectives for each major subdivision, or topic, within the unit. Within each topic, conceptual and explanatory information alternates with hands-on activities. Units conclude with a summary comprising one paragraph for each topic, and an independent practice activity that gives students an opportunity to practice the skills they've learned.

The conceptual information takes the form of text paragraphs, exhibits, lists, and tables. The activities are structured in two columns, one telling students what to do, the other providing explanations, descriptions, and graphics. Throughout a unit, instructor notes are found in the left margin.

Appendices

Appendix A lists all CompTIA PDI+ exam objectives along with references to corresponding coverage in this manual.

Course summary

This section provides a text summary of the entire course. It's useful for providing closure at the end of the course. The course summary also indicates the next course in this series, if there is one, and lists additional resources students might find useful as they continue to learn about the software.

Quick reference

The quick reference is an at-a-glance job aid summarizing some of the more common features of the software.

Glossary

The glossary provides definitions for all of the key terms used in this course.

Index

The index at the end of this manual makes it easy for you and your students to find information about a particular software component, feature, or concept.

Manual conventions

We've tried to keep the number of elements and the types of formatting to a minimum in the manuals. We think this approach aids in clarity and makes the manuals more elegant looking. But there are some conventions and icons you should know about.

Instructor note/icon

Item	Description
Italic text	In conceptual text, indicates a new term or feature.
Bold text	In unit summaries, indicates a key term or concept. In an independent practice activity, indicates an explicit item that you select, choose, or type.
`Code font`	Indicates code or syntax.
`Longer strings of ▶ code will look ▶ like this.`	In the hands-on activities, any code that's too long to fit on a single line is divided into segments by one or more continuation characters (▶). This code should be entered as a continuous string of text.
	In the left margin, provide tips, hints, and warnings for the instructor.
Select **bold item**	In the left column of hands-on activities, bold sans-serif text indicates an explicit item that you select, choose, or type.
Keycaps like ⏎ ENTER	Indicate a key on the keyboard you must press.

Instructor notes.

⚠ *Warning icon.* — Warnings prepare instructors for potential classroom management problems.

✓ *Tip icon.* — Tips give extra information the instructor can share with students.

Setup icon. — Setup notes provide a realistic business context for instructors to share with students, or indicate additional setup steps required for the current activity.

Projector icon. — Projector notes indicate that there is a PowerPoint slide for the adjacent content.

Hands-on activities

The hands-on activities are the most important parts of our manuals. They're divided into two primary columns. The "Here's how" column gives short directions to the students. The "Here's why" column provides explanations, graphics, and clarifications. To the left, instructor notes provide tips, warnings, setups, and other information for the instructor only. Here's a sample:

Do it!

A-1: Creating a commission formula

Take the time to make sure your students understand this worksheet. We'll be here a while.

Here's how	Here's why
1 Open Sales	This is an oversimplified sales compensation worksheet. It shows sales totals, commissions, and incentives for five sales reps.
2 Observe the contents of cell F4	F4 = =E4*C_Rate The commission rate formulas use the name "C_Rate" instead of a value for the commission rate.

For these activities, we've provided a collection of data files designed to help students learn each skill in a real-world business context. As students work through the activities, they modify and update these files. Of course, students might make a mistake and therefore want to re-key the activity starting from scratch. To make it easy to start over, students rename each data file at the end of the first activity in which the file is modified. Our convention for renaming files is to add the word "My" to the beginning of the file name. In the above activity, for example, students are using a file called "Sales" for the first time. At the end of this activity, they would save the file as "My sales," thus leaving the "Sales" file unchanged. If students make mistakes, they can start over using the original "Sales" file.

In some activities, however, it might not be practical to rename the data file. Such exceptions are indicated with an instructor note. If students want to retry one of these activities, you need to provide a fresh copy of the original data file.

PowerPoint presentations

Each unit in this course has an accompanying PowerPoint presentation. These slide shows are designed to support your classroom instruction while providing students with a visual focus. Each presentation begins with a list of unit objectives and ends with a unit summary slide. We strongly recommend that you run these presentations from the instructor's station as you teach this course. A copy of PowerPoint Viewer is included, so it isn't necessary to have PowerPoint installed on your computer.

The ILT Series PowerPoint add-in

The CD also contains a PowerPoint add-in that enables you to do two things:

- Create slide notes for the class
- Display a control panel for the Flash movies embedded in the presentations

To load the PowerPoint add-in:

1. Copy the Course_ILT.ppa file to a convenient location on your hard drive.
2. Start PowerPoint.
3. Choose Tools, Macro, Security to open the Security dialog box. On the Security Level tab, select Medium (if necessary), and then click OK.
4. Choose Tools, Add-Ins to open the Add-Ins dialog box. Then, click Add New.
5. Browse to and double-click the Course_ILT.ppa file, and then click OK. A message box will appear, warning you that macros can contain viruses.
6. Click Enable Macros. The Course_ILT add-in should now appear in the Available Add-Ins list (in the Add-Ins dialog box). The "x" in front of Course_ILT indicates that the add-in is loaded.
7. Click Close to close the Add-Ins dialog box.

After you complete this procedure, a new toolbar is available at the top of the PowerPoint window. This toolbar contains a single button labeled "Create SlideNotes." Click this button to generate slide-notes files in both text (.txt) and Excel (.xls) format. By default, these files are saved to the folder that contains the presentation. If the PowerPoint file is on a CD-ROM or in some other location to which the slide-notes files can't be saved, you'll be prompted to save the presentation to your hard drive and try again.

When you run a presentation and come to a slide that contains a Flash movie, you see a small control panel in the lower-left corner of the screen. You can use this panel to start, stop, and rewind the movie, or to play it again.

Topic B: Setting student expectations

Properly setting student expectations is essential to your success. This topic will help you do that by providing:

- Prerequisites for this course
- A description of the target student
- A list of the objectives for the course
- A skills assessment for the course

Course prerequisites

Students taking this course should be familiar with personal computers and the use of a keyboard and a mouse. Furthermore, this course assumes that students have user-level experience using Windows XP.

Target student

Students taking this course are entry-level support technicians who want to pass the CompTIA PDI+ exam. In addition, these students plan to support digital print and document-imaging devices in the workplace. Target students might also include current computer support personnel who want to learn more about printers and imaging devices to advance in their current positions.

How to become CompTIA certified

In order to achieve CompTIA PDI+ certification, a student must register for and pass the CompTIA PDI+ exam. In order to become CompTIA certified, students must:

1. Select a certification exam provider. For more information, students should visit: http://certification.comptia.org/resources/registration.aspx
2. Register for and schedule a time to take the CompTIA certification exam(s) at a convenient location.
3. Read and sign the Candidate Agreement, which will be presented at the time of the exam. The complete text of the Candidate Agreement can be found at: http://certification.comptia.org/resources/canidate_agreement.aspx
4. Take and pass the CompTIA certification exam(s).

For more information about CompTIA's certifications, such as its industry acceptance, benefits or program news, students should visit http://certification.comptia.org.

CompTIA is a not-for-profit information technology (IT) trade association. CompTIA's certifications are designed by subject matter experts from across the IT industry. Each CompTIA certification is vendor-neutral, covers multiple technologies and requires demonstration of skills and knowledge widely sought after by the IT industry.

To contact CompTIA with any questions or comments, please call (630) 678-8300 or e-mail questions@comptia.org.

Course objectives

You should share these overall course objectives with your students at the beginning of the day. Doing this gives the students an idea about what to expect, and it helps you identify students who might be misplaced. Students are considered misplaced when they lack the prerequisite knowledge or when they already know most of the subject matter to be covered.

Note: In addition to the general objectives listed below, specific CompTIA PDI+ exam objectives are listed at the beginning of each topic. For a complete mapping of exam objectives to course content, see Appendix A.

After completing this course, students will know how to:

- Identify and explain the function of electromechanical, mechanical, and electrical components.
- Identify and describe the components and processes involved in printing and scanning.
- Connect printers and scanners to a computer, and connect to and use networked printing and imaging devices.
- Troubleshoot printer and scanner problems.
- Communicate effectively with customers and maintain a safe environment.

Introduction

Skills inventory

Use the following form to gauge students' skill levels entering the class (students have copies in the introductions of their student manuals). For each skill listed, have students rate their familiarity from 1 to 5, with five being the most familiar. Emphasize that this isn't a test. Rather, it's intended to provide students with an idea of where they're starting from at the beginning of class. If a student is wholly unfamiliar with all the skills, he or she might not be ready for the class. A student who seems to understand all of the skills, on the other hand, might need to move on to the next course in the series.

Skill	1	2	3	4	5
Examining the characteristics of electricity					
Considering electrical safety					
Identifying electrical components					
Identifying mechanical components					
Measuring electrical values					
Identifying electrical components					
Examining the Windows printing process					
Discussing color theory					
Examining the inkjet print process					
Examining the EP print process					
Examining print media					
Examining the scan process					
Connecting a serial cable					
Connecting a parallel cable					
Connecting a USB cable					
Connecting an IEEE 1394 cable					
Installing an inkjet printer					
Installing a laser printer					
Installing a scanner					
Connecting to the network					
Viewing installed network components					
Using wireless communications technologies					

Skill	1	2	3	4	5
Connecting to a shared printer					
Using ipconfig to display TCP/IP settings					
Testing TCP/IP connectivity					
Using nslookup to verify settings					
Identifying network scanning basics					
Performing inkjet and EP printer maintenance					
Performing scanner maintenance					
Troubleshooting problems					
Using Microsoft Knowledge Base to research a problem					
Tracking problems and resolutions					
Troubleshooting printer problems					
Troubleshooting scanner and multifunction device problems					
Using effective verbal communication					
Using non-verbal communication effectively					
Maintaining professionalism					
Ensuring customer satisfaction					
Identifying typical off and computer-related hazards					
Reading a material safety data sheet					
Selecting the proper methods for equipment disposal					

Topic C: Classroom setup

All our courses assume that each student has a personal computer to use during the class. Our hands-on approach to learning requires that they do. This topic gives information on how to set up the classroom to teach this course. It includes minimum requirements for the students' personal computers, setup information for the first time you teach the class, and setup information for each time that you teach after the first time you set up the classroom.

Hardware requirements

Each student's personal computer should have:

- Intel Pentium II or Intel-compatible processor, running at 400 MHz or higher (Pentium III strongly recommended)
- At least 512 MB RAM
- SVGA display adapter, supporting at least 256 colors and 800×600 resolution
- Keyboard and mouse
- 10/100 Mbps network card (NIC), plus associated cabling
- 10 GB hard drive
- 1.44 MB 3.5" floppy disk drive
- CD/DVD drive
- Sound card
- Modem card
- An infrared port
- Serial port, parallel port, USB port, IEEE 1394 port and cables. Optional: Cables with mini-parallel (mini-Centronics) and SCSI connectors.

In addition to the requirements for each computer, you need the following hardware and components in the classroom for demonstration and activities during class.

- At least one laser printer and one ink dispersion printer that the instructor and students can use to take apart to examine the different components. These can be nonworking printers that are used only for parts examination.
- At least one laser printer and one ink dispersion printer that the instructor and students can connect to their computers. Students need printers to connect directly to their computers and a network printer to which they can connect to complete activities in Unit 3. You must have the manufacturer's documentation for each printer.
- Multifunction device with scanner, fax modem, and printer, and the manufacturer's documentation.
- Inkjet printer with SD card or Compact Flash card slots along with a variety of SD and Compact Flash cards pre-loaded with files for students to print.
- Maintenance kits for each laser printer to be used in class.
- A variety of papers, such as inkjet paper and laser printer paper of various weights, card stock, and cover stock, transparences, envelopes, and paper with preprinted letterhead. The paper should be in a variety of textures and a variety of brightness levels.

- A scanner test chart, and a variety of pictures, documents, and objects for the instructor and students to scan, including documents that include security and anti-counterfeiting measures.
- Cleaning supplies, including cleaning solutions, soft cloths, cotton swabs, denatured alcohol, rubbing alcohol, mild spray cleaners, toner rags, and a toner vacuum, and any other cleaning supplies recommended by the manufacturers of the printers you're using in class.
- STP, UTP, fiber optic, crossover cables and associated network cards. Cables with RJ-45 and RJ-11 connectors.
- Bluetooth devices to complete Activity B-3 in Unit 3.
- The following electromechanical components for demonstration during class and independent practice activities. If you don't have individual parts available, you can demonstrate the parts to students in place on working or nonworking printers, scanners, and other devices.
    - Clutches
    - Solenoids
    - Motors, including AC/DC motors and stepping motors
    - Relays
    - Sensors, including photo-reflective sensors, photo-interrupters, and optical encoders
    - Switches, including micro switches and magnetic switches
    - Gears, bearings, bushings, and belts
    - Rollers, including rubber, Teflon, and steel rollers
    - Cams
    - Cables
    - Pulleys and idlers
    - Springs
    - Power supplies, both low- and high-voltage
    - Fuses
    - Thermistors
    - Thermal switches and fuses
    - Lamps, including halogens, Xenons, and LEDs
    - Grounding components, including screws, shields, points, straps, mats, and wires
    - Cables, including copper wire harnesses, flat/ribbon, and fiber optic
    - Connectors, including ZIF sockets, Molex, Ultrex, spade, pin, and spring contacts
    - EEPROM and EPROM
    - Memory modules
    - PCBs, including logic boards, fax cards, and network cards
    - Lockout/tagout equipment

- The following tools for demonstration and use during class and independent practice activities (follow manufacturers' guidelines):
    - Multimeter
    - Polarity tester
    - AC line monitor
    - Toner vacuum and toner rags
    - Service documentation for each printer or device in class, including theories of operation, block diagrams, and wiring/circuit diagrams
    - Lubricants and cleaning solutions
    - Scanner test chart
    - Chip puller/EEPROM puller

Software requirements

You need the following software:
- Windows XP Professional

Network requirements

- Internet access, for the following purposes:
    - Downloading the latest critical updates and service packs from www.windowsupdate.com
    - Completing activities throughout the course
- Analog phone line for faxing

First-time setup instructions

Instructor and student computers

The first time you teach this course, you need to perform the following steps to set up the instructor and each student computer.

1 Install Windows XP Professional on at least a 5 GB partition according to the software manufacturer's instructions using the following variables.
   - Format the partition to NTFS.
   - Set regional settings appropriate for your environment.
   - Enter a name and organization appropriate for your environment.
   - Name the instructor's computer **PDI00**; name each student computer **PDI##**, where ## is a unique number assigned to each student starting with **01**.
   - Use an Administrator password of **Pa$$321**.
   - Set the Date, Time, and Time Zones for your area.

- Use Custom network settings to configure the computer to use IP address information appropriate to your environment. (This can be a static IP address with subnet mask, gateway address, and DNS server address or obtained from a DHCP server.)
  Note: If Setup doesn't detect your network card during installation, you need to install the network card manually and configure networking after setup is complete.
- Make the computer a member of the **PDIPLUS** workgroup.

During the initial setup phase on Windows XP Professional with SP2:

- Turn off Automatic Updates.
- Activate Windows XP Professional.
- Create a **PDIADMIN##** user on the computer. Use the ## that matches the computer number.

Note: If your copy of Windows XP Professional doesn't include SP2, you need to complete the above steps after Windows XP starts.

2 Use Control Panel, User Accounts to:
   - Verify the PDIADMIN## user is a computer administrator.
   - Set the password to **Pa$$321**.
   - If prompted, don't make files and folders private.

3 If your copy of Windows XP Professional doesn't include SP2, install SP2 now.

4 After the installation process is complete, use Device Manager to ensure that all devices are functioning correctly. You might have to download and install drivers for devices listed with a yellow question mark.

5 Open the Display Properties dialog box and apply the following settings:
   - Theme — Windows XP
   - Screen resolution — 1024 by 768 pixels
   - Color quality — High (24 bit) or higher

6 Configure Windows Firewall:
   a In Control Panel, click Security Center.
   b Under "Manage security settings for," click Windows Firewall.
   c In the Windows Firewall dialog box, on the Exceptions tab, check File and Printer Sharing.
   d Click OK.
   e Close Windows Security Center and Control Panel.

Setup instructions for every class

Every time you teach this course, including the first time, you need to reinstall the operating system according to the steps above.

Troubleshooting lab setup suggestions

The "Maintenance and troubleshooting" unit in this course includes troubleshooting activities in which students are asked to solve problems related to the material in that unit and based on the knowledge they've acquired throughout the course. The following section presents ideas for problems you can implement.

We suggest two possible means for implementing these problems:
- Send students off on a break while you induce these problems in their computers, or
- Divide students into two groups. Both groups would implement problems in a set of printers. The groups would switch places and solve the problems that the other group created.

When determining which problems to implement, make sure you consider the technical proficiency of your students.

Unit 4: Maintenance and troubleshooting

For the Topic B activity, entitled "Troubleshooting printer problems," you could implement one or more of these problems:
- Replace the ink cartridges with empty ones or ones that produce poor output.
- Install a printer that prints stray marks on output.
- Disconnect or loosely connect the interface cable.
- Disconnect or loosely connect the power cord.
- Leave the cover or door open, off, or slightly ajar.
- Plug the printer into the power strip, but turn off the strip.
- Create a paper jam.
- Remove the printer driver.
- Install the wrong printer driver.
- Remove the ink cartridge(s).
- Turn the printer off midway through a cleaning cycle or while printing.
- Provide the wrong interface cable, power cord, and/or drivers.
- In the BIOS, disable the port to which the printer connects.
- Add paper that is either very static-laden or humid (to produce poor images and possibly printer jams).
- Replace the toner cartridge with an empty one or one that produces poor output.
- Remove the toner cartridge(s).
- If the printer requires setup on the printer, change the settings to use a different interface, or other settings. (For example, on a LaserJet printer, use the menu on the printer to specify that it's connected via the serial port, while it's actually connected via parallel port.)

For the Topic B activity entitled "Troubleshooting scanner problems," you could implement one or more of these problems:
- Install a defective scanner.
- Provide the wrong interface cable, power cord, and/or drivers.
- Install the wrong scanner driver.
- Disconnect or loosely connect the interface cable.
- Disconnect or loosely connect the power cord.

For the independent practice activity, choose from any of the problems above, or come up with additional ones as appropriate to students' levels of understanding of the troubleshooting process and the equipment.

Downloading the PowerPoint presentations

If you don't have the CD that came with this manual, you can download the PowerPoint presentations for this course. Here's what you do:

1. Connect to www.axzopress.com.
2. Under Downloads, click Instructor-Led Training.
3. Browse the subject categories to locate your course. Then click the course title to display a list of available downloads. (You can also access these downloads through our Catalog listings.)
4. Click the link(s) for downloading the PowerPoint presentations, and follow the instructions that appear on your screen.

CertBlaster software

CertBlaster pre- and post-assessment software is available for this course. To download and install this free software, students should complete the following steps:

1. Go to www.axzopress.com.
2. Under Downloads, click CertBlaster.
3. Click the link for CompTIA PDI+.
4. Save the .EXE file to a folder on your hard drive. (**Note**: If you skip this step, the CertBlaster software will not install correctly.)
5. Click Start and choose Run.
6. Click Browse and then navigate to the folder that contains the .EXE file.
7. Select the .EXE file and click Open.
8. Click OK and follow the on-screen instructions. When prompted for the password, enter **c_pdi+**.

Topic D: Support

Your success is our primary concern. If you need help setting up this class or teaching a particular unit, topic, or activity, please don't hesitate to get in touch with us.

Contacting us

Please contact us through our Web site, www.axzopress.com. You will need to provide the name of the course, and be as specific as possible about the kind of help you need.

Instructor's tools

Our Web site provides several instructor's tools for each course, including course outlines and answers to frequently asked questions. To download these files, go to www.axzopress.com. Then, under Downloads, click Instructor-Led Training and browse our subject categories.

Unit 1
Electromechanical components

Unit time: 120 minutes

Complete this unit, and you'll know how to:

A Identify and explain the function of electromechanical components.

B Identify and explain the function of mechanical components.

C Identify and explain the function of electrical components.

Topic A: Electromechanical components

This topic covers the following CompTIA PDI+ exam objectives.

#	Objective
4.1	**Identify and explain the function of electromechanical components** • Clutches • Solenoids • Motors (ie: stepper motors, AC/DC motors) • Relays • Sensors (ie: photo reflective, encoders, photo interrupters) • Switches (ie: micro switches, magnetic switches)
8.1	**Demonstrate and apply safety procedures** • Use proper ESD (Electrostatic Discharge) practices and proper grounding techniques • Wrist straps, static mats, unplugging / lockout / tagout

Characteristics of electricity

Electricity is the flow of electrons, which are one of the fundamental building blocks of all matter. In some materials, electrons flow easily, while in others, electrons are tightly bound to their atoms and hardly flow at all.

A *conductor* is a material that permits the flow of electricity. An *insulator* is a material that inhibits the flow of electricity. Most metals, some plastics, and some liquids are conductors. Most ceramics, plastics, and gases are insulators.

Voltage

Voltage is analogous to water pressure.

Voltage is the force of electricity caused by a difference in charge, or electrical potential, at two locations. This value, measured in *volts*, is also called the *potential* or *potential difference*. The abbreviation for volts is officially an uppercase "V," though a lowercase "v" is commonly used.

Electricity flows to equalize potential. More electricity flows when there's a greater difference in potential than when there's a smaller difference. Thus, more energy can be drawn from a high-voltage system than from a low-voltage system.

Electrical systems in typical buildings operate at 110 volts (actually, within a range of 90–135 V). Household devices, such as light bulbs, are designed to work at this power level. Sensitive electronics inside computers, televisions, and other devices use a much lower voltage. Computer components use either 5 V or 12 V.

Current

Current is a measure of the flow of electrons past a given point. It's measured in amperes, or *amps*, which constitutes essentially a count of electrons passing per second.

For current to flow, there must be a complete *circuit*, or path, from the source, through any intervening devices, and back to ground. A complete circuit is called *closed*; an incomplete circuit is called *open*.

Any interruption in the circuit causes the current to stop. This is the principle behind a switch, which is simply a device with which you can open a circuit to stop the flow of current.

Alternating and direct current

Current that flows in a single direction at a constant voltage through a circuit is called *direct current* (DC). Batteries provide this sort of current, and it's the type required by most electronic components. (Especially in nontechnical usage, "component" is sometimes used to mean a whole device, such as an MP3 player, monitor, and so forth. However, in this case, components are circuit boards, chips, and other internal devices.)

Current that flows repeatedly back and forth through the circuit at a constantly varying voltage level is called *alternating current* (AC). A building's electrical service is an AC system, and most household devices require AC to operate.

AC systems complete a full cycle—voltage change from zero, through maximum voltage, minimum voltage, and back to zero—many times a second. In the United States, Canada, and elsewhere, AC operates at 60 cycles per second (60 *hertz*, or Hz). Europe and other countries use 50 Hz AC electricity.

Resistance and impedance

Resistance is a force that opposes the flow of DC through a conductor. *Impedance* is like resistance but applies to AC instead. When resistance or impedance is present, electrical energy is converted to heat or some other form of energy. All conductors possess some resistance or impedance, though considerably less than that possessed by insulators.

Resistance and impedance are measured in *ohms*. This quantity is written using the Greek letter omega (Ω). One ohm (1Ω) is defined as the resistance of a system in which 1 volt maintains a current of 1 amp.

Electrical power and energy

Electrical power, measured in *watts* (W), is a derived quantity that you can calculate by multiplying the voltage by the current. It's a measure of the energy delivered by the flow of electricity.

Consumption estimate from the US National Renewable Energy Laboratory (www.nrel.gov).

Power supplies are rated according to the watts of electrical power they can supply. A power supply rated at 450 W promises to deliver 450 watts of power, though, in practice, it might deliver a bit more or less than that value.

Electrical energy is electrical power delivered over time. For example, one *kilowatt-hour* (kWh) is the flow of one kilowatt (1000 W) delivered for a one-hour period. The average home in the US consumes about 800 kWh of electrical energy per month.

1–4 CompTIA PDI+ Certification

Do it!

A-1: Examining the characteristics of electricity

Questions and answers

1 Which delivers more power: a 500 W power supply or a 1 kilowatt power supply?

1 kilowatt equals 1000 watts, so it's the more powerful power supply.

2 Why might you be concerned about the output power rating of a power supply?

Power supplies with a higher power rating can supply power to more components and peripherals than power supplies with lower ratings can.

3 Of the various properties of electricity, which will concern you as a PC technician?

You might be concerned with any of them at one time or another. Certainly, you'll work with volts when you connect components inside the PC, so you can connect devices to the correct power supply connector. You'll encounter watts as a power supply rating.

4 Given what you've learned about electricity, particularly voltage and current, speculate on the purpose of a PC's power supply.

A power supply converts the 110 V AC electricity delivered at the outlet to the 5 V and 12 V DC electricity required by the computer's components.

Electricity

Explanation

Electricity is the source of energy for electronic equipment, including personal computers, monitors, printers, and multifunction devices. Electricity can be dangerous. If you don't follow proper safety precautions, electricity can kill you.

Current, not voltage, is what causes the danger. Even a small amount of current passing through your heart can be sufficient to cause ventricular fibrillation or stop your heart entirely. A dangerous level of current is possible, even with low voltage sources, such as a 9 V battery.

Some sources indicate that 70 mA is sufficient to cause death.

The *1-10-100 rule* states that you can feel 1 mA (1 milliamp, or 1/1000 amp) of current through your body, 10 mA is sufficient to make your muscles contract to the point where you can't let go of a power source, and 100 mA is sufficient to stop your heart. This is a rule you should learn and respect.

Calculating current

Voltage, current, and resistance are related through the following formula:

```
V = i * r
```

In this formula, V is voltage in volts, i is the current in amps, and r is the resistance in ohms (Ω). At a given voltage, current increases as resistance drops. A dangerous level of current can be reached if resistance is reduced sufficiently.

Resistance of the human body

Visit www.allaboutcircuits.com/vol_1/chpt_3/4.html for more detailed information about the resistance of the human body and dangers from electricity.

The human body has a resistance of about 500 KΩ (500,000 Ω). This value is a somewhat ideal figure for contact with a small area of dry skin. Moisture and sweat on your skin lowers the resistance to a value nearer 5000 Ω. Contact with a greater area of skin, for example, gripping a wire between your fingers or grasping a pipe, further reduces resistance. If you were to immerse your hand or foot, or puncture the skin so the electrical connection is made with your more-conductive blood and tissue, the resistance could be as low as 100 Ω.

Death isn't likely if electricity passes from finger to finger through your body, along your arm, and so forth. However, your heart and brain are considerably more sensitive. Current that passes from hand to hand or through your head is much more likely to cause death. Electricity passing elsewhere through your body could cause an electrical burn.

Safety precautions

You should always follow common sense safety precautions to avoid electric shock. These precautions include:

- Don't touch exposed electrical contacts with any part of your skin.
- Touch only insulated handles and parts of tools, probes, cords, etc.
- Leave covers on equipment, unless you need to access their internal components.
- Work one-handed. If you use only one hand, electricity is less likely to flow through your body (specifically your heart or head) and cause injury or death.
- Never insert anything into a wall outlet other than a power cord.
- Rings, watches, and jewelry can cause unintended contact with electrified components. Furthermore, these metallic items can increase the surface area that's in contact with an electrical source and thus lower your body's resistance. Remove jewelry when working around electricity.
- Keep your hands clean and dry.
- Don't work with electricity in wet surroundings, especially wet floors.
- Be sure the device you're working on is turned off and unplugged before beginning to make repairs. Use *lockout* procedures to prevent the device from being re-energized while you're still working on it and *tagout* procedures to warn others of potential electrical hazards with plastic and paper warning tags. For more information, see the Occupational Safety and Health Administration (OSHA) Web site at www.osha.gov/SLTC/controlhazardousenergy/index.html.

Static electricity

Explanation

Static electricity is a phenomenon that occurs when the charges on separate objects are unequal, which means one object has an excess positive or negative charge when compared to the other object. Typically, the objects are made of an insulating material (one that doesn't transmit electricity easily) or a conductive material that's insulated from ground.

The charge imbalance creates an electric field that can cause objects to attract or repel each other—such as when a static field makes your hair stand on end. When the objects are brought into contact with each other, a current will flow between them to balance their charges. This current flow, called an *electrostatic discharge (ESD)*, is characterized by a high voltage, but low amperage.

While static discharges aren't dangerous to humans, even though the voltage in the system can measure in the range of thousands of volts, they're potentially harmful to electronics. To feel a static shock, you experience a discharge of approximately 3,000 volts or more. Discharges of more than roughly 8,000 volts might generate a visible spark. Walking across a carpet on a dry day can generate a charge of as much as 35,000 volts. Yet electronics can be damaged by a 1,000-volt discharge or less—a third or less than the minimum discharge you can feel.

Static prevention

There are two ways to prevent problems from static: prevent the buildup of static charges and prevent discharges or discharge the charge safely.

To prevent or reduce the buildup of static charges:

- Don't shuffle your feet as you walk.
- Increase the humidity in the room or building—static charges can dissipate before growing large if the humidity level is sufficiently high.
- Keep yourself grounded as you work and move around, using the tools found in a typical ESD kit, such as wrist straps and mats.
- Wear cotton clothing, which is less likely to generate static charges than many synthetic materials.
- Remove carpeting from rooms where you service computers and from computer rooms.
- Use an air ionization system to build up an opposite, and thus neutralizing, charge in the air.

To prevent or reduce static discharges:

- Equalize the charge safely—unplug the equipment, then touch a metal portion of its chassis.
- If you must move around as you work, keep yourself grounded (with an antistatic wrist strap) so that charges can't build up.

Tell students that, while some guides do recommend leaving the computer plugged in, doing so is a dangerous practice, and they shouldn't follow it.

It isn't important to be at equal potential with ground, only with the device you're servicing.

To prevent damaging discharge, your goal is to be at equal charge potential with the device you're servicing, not with ground. You shouldn't leave the computer plugged in while servicing it.

If there were a fault in the building's wiring system, full wall current could be flowing through the ground wire. You can be injured or killed if you come into contact with the ground.

Do it!

⚠️ *These are thought exercises. Don't let students attempt to carry these out as actual experiments.*

A-2: Considering electrical safety

Questions and answers

1. Which is more dangerous, exposed leads in a 500 W power supply or a 12 V automotive battery?

   Both can be dangerous or even lethal. Keep in mind that it's the current, and not the voltage or power of a system, that causes the danger.

2. Could you feel the current generated if you were to wet your fingers and touch both terminals of a 9 V battery?

   *9 V = i * 5000 or i = 9 / 5000, thus i = 0.0018 or 1.8 milliamps. Yes, you could feel the shock.*

3. Is a shock from an electrical outlet sufficient to cause pain, contract your muscles, or kill you?

   It would depend greatly on how you received the shock, whether good contact was made, and over what area of your body.

   Assuming a relatively high resistance of 5000 Ω, a 110 V source would deliver about 22 milliamps. You would feel the pain, and the current would cause your muscles to contract. If you were to grasp the wires between your fingers or with your whole hand, it's likely that your resistance would be much lower. A lethal shock would be delivered if the resistance of your skin were lowered to approximately 1500 Ω.

4. What are two general ways to prevent damage from static electricity?

   Prevent the buildup of static charges and prevent discharges or discharge the charge safely.

Electromechanical components

Display the components or pass them around as you teach this topic.

When you click Print, it's an intricate Web of electrical and mechanical components that produces the printed page that eventually emerges from the machine. The same is true for fax machines, scanners, and multifunction units: dozens of pieces working in harmony to produce the end result.

If you work with these machines, it's important to understand what's going on under the hood, and that starts with knowing and understanding the function of each part.

Electromechanical components

The following sections contain descriptions of important electromechanical components.

Exhibit 1-1: A magnetic clutch and gears

- *Clutches* synchronize rotation and link gears to transmit various rates of rotation to aligned shafts. Clutches can be engaged and disengaged by the device, as needed. They're used mostly for paper pickup from paper trays and cassettes. There are many types of clutches, including timing roller clutches, paper feed clutches, and pickup clutches. Registration assemblies also contain a clutch. Improperly engaged clutches produce grinding noises and prevent paper loading and carriage movement.

Electromechanical components 1-9

Exhibit 1-2: Solenoid

- A *solenoid* is a device that uses electromagnetic force to create motion. In a solenoid, an electromagnetic coil is wrapped around a core that contains a moveable component, called an *armature* or *plunger*. When electricity is applied to the coil, it creates a magnetic field, which forces the armature out of the core, creating force that's used to drive other mechanical components inside the printer, including print heads in older impact (dot-matrix or daisy wheel) printers and pickup rollers in laser printers. Solenoids are typically very reliable devices.

Exhibit 1-3: DC servo motors

- *Motors* convert AC and DC electrical sources into mechanical energy, usually a rotating mechanical force. Motors are used to power rollers or gears and pulleys, and are an integral part of a printer's mechanics. Like solenoids, motors have electrical wires that create a magnetic field that causes an armature move. Unlike solenoids, the armatures in motors rotate rather than thrust.

Exhibit 1-4: Stepping motor with gears

- *Stepper motor*s or *stepping motors* are brushless, synchronous motors, with toothed electromagnets around the central gear. The teeth allow the motor to turn at precise angles (hence "steps"). Stepper motors are AC but perform like a hybrid DC motor-solenoid. Stepper motors allow for a fine range of motion, which is crucial for feed systems and other parts of the mechanism that handle positioning of paper and print heads.

Exhibit 1-5: Relays

- *Relays* are electromechanical devices that either open or close when they're energized by an electromagnetic field. Relays that are normally open are closed when the electrical coil on the relay is energized. Relays that are normally closed open when the relay coil is energized. When the coil is no longer energized, the relay returns to its normal state, either by gravity or by a mechanical force, such as a small spring.

Exhibit 1-6: Photo-reflective sensor

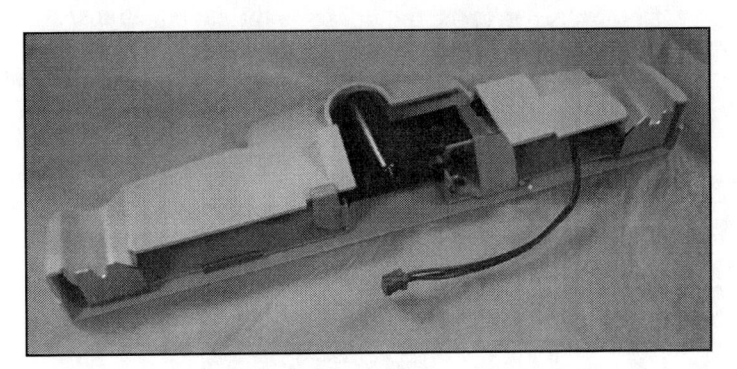

Exhibit 1-7: Photo-interrupter sensor

- *Sensors* are used to transmit real-time information to the printer, to tell it, among other things, the position of the paper inside the machine or the current position of the print head.
    - *Photo-reflective sensors*, an example of which is shown in Exhibit 1-6, relay a continuous wavelength of light from a light source that's reflected off a target, such as a stack of paper in a paper tray, onto a *photosensitive transistor* (receiver), which you can think of as the "eye." When the light beam is broken, because it isn't reflecting off its target, the printer knows the target object is missing and generates a message or error code, or take corrective action without user input.
    - *Photo-interrupters*, an example of which is shown in Exhibit 1-7, work similarly, but instead of using reflected light, they use a direct beam of light from the light source to the photosensitive transistor. A photo interrupter sensor is activated when the beam of light is broken.

Exhibit 1-8: Optical encoder

- An *optical encoder*, as shown in Exhibit 1-8, uses a rotating plastic or metal disk with a pattern of clear and opaque sectors and at least one light source/receiver pair. The disk is connected to a motor or a print head carriage, and as it rotates in response to the motor or carriage motion, the sensors detect the light passing through the transparent sectors or being interrupted by the opaque sectors of the disk. The printer uses these light pulses to determine location, direction, or both, depending on whether there are one or two light sensor pairs.

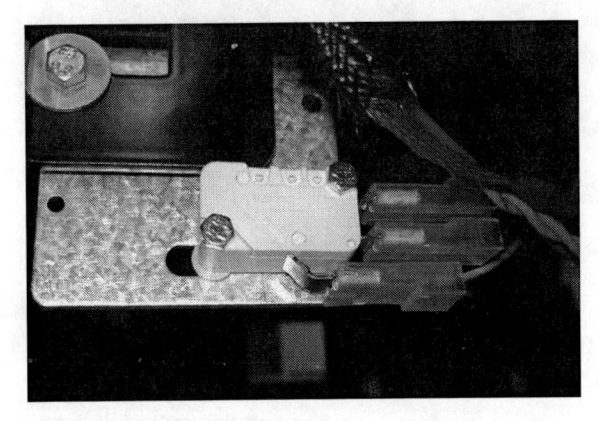

Exhibit 1-9: Micro switch

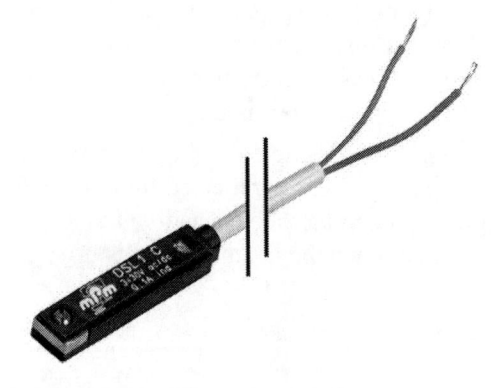

Exhibit 1-10: Magnetic switch

Electromechanical components **1-13**

- A *switch* is a device used to change the flow of an electrical current. At its most basic, a switch has two contacts and an actuator. When the contacts are brought together by the force of the actuator, electric current flows through the switch. This electric current can power just about any printer component and even the printer itself. A *micro switch*, as shown in Exhibit 1-9, is generally just a switch small enough to be placed just about anywhere inside a printer or multifunction device. A micro switch is actuated by physical motion, where a *magnetic switch*, as shown in Exhibit 1-10, is actuated by a magnetic field. Switches can be used to power internal components or even to detect improperly inserted toner cartridges and interlock errors, which are caused by printer doors and paper trays that aren't completely closed.

Do it!

A-3: Identifying electromechanical components

Here's how	Here's why

1 _____ convert AC and DC electricity into mechanical energy, typically a rotating mechanical force.

Motors

2 A _____ is used to change the flow of an electrical current.

switch

3 Compare and contrast photo-reflective sensors and photo-interrupters.

Both sensors rely on a beam of light transmitted to a photosensitive transistor. Photoreflective sensors reflect the light off a target, while photo-interrupters transmit the beam of light directly to the transistor.

4 A _____ is a device with an electromagnet coil wrapped around a central core that contains an armature. When electrified, the coil creates a magnetic field that forces the armature out of the core.

solenoid

5 _____ synchronize rotation and link gears to transmit various rates of rotation to aligned shafts.

Clutches

6 What kind of motors have toothed electromagnets around the central gear, which allow the motor to turn at precise angles?

Stepper or stepping motor

7 _____ are electromechanical devices that either open or close when energized by an electromagnetic field: those that are normally open are closed, while those that are normally closed are opened.

Relays

Topic B: Mechanical components

This topic covers the following CompTIA PDI+ exam objective.

#	Objective

4.2	Identify and explain the function of mechanical components
	• Drive components
	    • Gears (ie: one way, gear trains)
	    • Bearings
	    • Bushings
	    • Belts
	• Rollers (ie: rubber, teflon, steel, etc)
	• Cams
	• Cables
	• Pulleys / Idler
	• Springs

Mechanical components

Display the components or pass them around as you teach this topic.

The following sections contain descriptions of important mechanical components.

Exhibit 1-11: Gears

Electromechanical components **1-15**

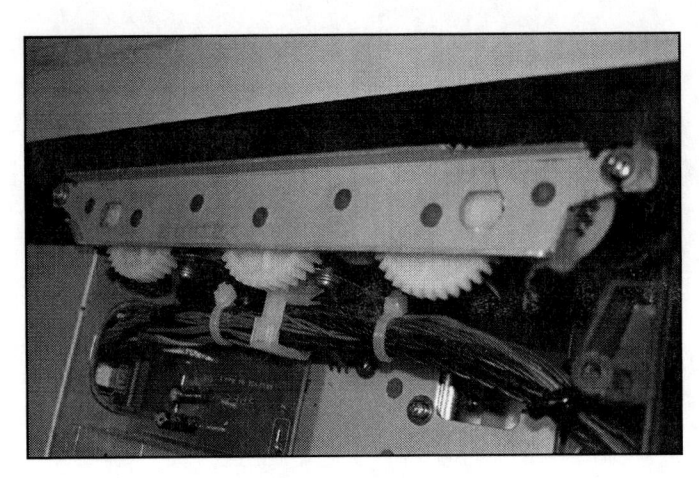

Exhibit 1-12: Gear train assembly

- A printer has a complex system of components to transport paper through the machine and apply the printed image to the paper.
    - *Gears*, shown in Exhibit 1-11, are used to transfer rotation from one rotating shaft to another. Typically a *gear box* contains a motor to produce rotation, and gears transfer that rotation from the primary shaft in the motor to other shafts, known as *secondary shafts*. Gears can connect one rotating shaft to another, causing the other shaft to rotate in one way or one direction; or, multiple gears, called gear trains, as shown in Exhibit 1-12, can cause multiple shafts to rotate in one direction or multiple directions, at the same or different speeds, depending on the relative sizes and positions of the gears.

Exhibit 1-13: Bearings

- *Bearings*, as shown in Exhibit 1-13, are small steel balls that support rotating shafts and reduce friction between the shaft and any surface with which it comes into contact. Typically, bearings are contained within a bearing case and are lubricated with oil to keep friction at a minimum.

Exhibit 1-14: Bushings

- *Bushings* also support rotating shafts and reduce friction but are made of a disposable material that gradually wears away, requiring them to be replaced. Typically, bushings are used in lower-stress locations in place of bearings.

Exhibit 1-15: Drive belts

Electromechanical components   **1-17**

Exhibit 1-16: Drive belts; pulley and idler

- *Belts* and *cables* transmit rotation between nonadjacent rotating shafts, as shown in Exhibit 1-15. Belts are often used to connect pulleys, connecting the motor-driven drive pulley with a secondary pulley, or *idler*. Pulleys can be used to move print heads in printers, optical encoders, as shown in Exhibit 1-16, and image sensors in scanners.

Exhibit 1-17: Pickup roller

Exhibit 1-18: Steel roller

- *Rollers* are smooth, axle-fitted cylinders that serve several functions, including moving paper through a printer. You find rollers at the beginning of the path, pulling paper from the tray and into the printer, and at the end of the path, helping fuse the final image onto the paper. Rollers that aren't exposed to high temperatures are usually made of rubber, while those that are exposed to high temperatures are usually made of steel. Teflon-coated rollers are used in the fuser assembly because of their resistance to heat and their non-stick properties. Some rollers are driven by motors, such as pickup rollers, and some are idle and just guide paper out (in larger machines).

Exhibit 1-19: Cams

- A *cam* is a mechanical component that converts rotation into a push or a reciprocating (back-and-forth) motion. Cams are employed in a variety of situations:
  - Paper/media feed to pick up, raise, and lower media as it passes through the print device.
  - Paper release levers operate a cam that lowers in order to relieve pressure on the media, so it can be pulled out.
  - Cams are sometimes fitted to lift paper inside trays.
  - Cams can also lock into various parts, such as toner cartridges, when doors are closed, because some types of cartridge require motion from motors.
  - Cams can be attached to certain shafts in order to close/open photo-interrupter switches.

Electromechanical components   **1-19**

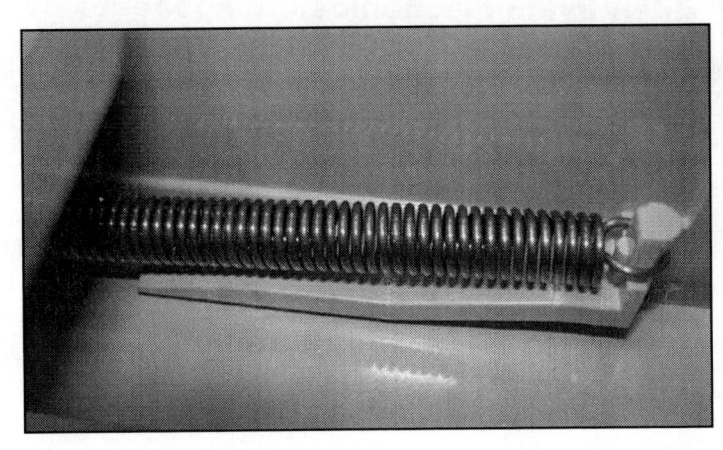

Exhibit 1-20: Springs

- *Springs* are metal coils that are used for a variety of purposes, including returning moving parts to their home locations and ensuring that paper is loaded tightly in the tray and ready to be pulled into the printer.

Do it!

B-1: Identifying mechanical components

Here's how	Here's why

1 What device is used to transfer rotation from one rotating shaft to another?

   A gear

2 _____ transmit rotation between nonadjacent rotating shafts.

   Belts and cables

3 _____ convert rotation into a push or a reciprocating motion.

   Cams

4 _____ are small steel balls used to support rotating shafts and reduce friction.

   Bearings

5 _____ support rotating shafts like bearings, but are made of disposable material that gradually wears away.

   Bushings

6 _____ are smooth, axel-fitted cylinders that move paper through the printer.

   Rollers

7 A _____ is a motor-driven shaft that's connected by a belt or cable to an idler.

   pulley

8 Small metal coils, called _____, are sometimes used to return moving components to their home location.

   springs

Topic C: Electrical components

This topic covers the following CompTIA PDI+ exam objectives.

#	Objective
4.3	**Identify and explain the function of electrical components** • Power supplies (ie: low and high voltage) • Fuses • Thermistors • Thermal switches/fuses • Lamps (ie: halogen, xenon, LED) • Grounding components (ie: screws, shields, points, straps, wires) • Cables (ie: copper wire harnesses, flat cable, fiber optics) • Connectors (ie: ZIF sockets, Molex, Ultrex, spade, pin connectors, spring contacts) • EEPROM and EPROM (ie: NVRAM) • Memory • Control PCBs (Printed Circuit Boards) (ie: I/O boards, drivers boards, logic boards, fax board, network card)
4.4	**Demonstrate the proper and safe use of tools** • Multimeter • Polarity tester • AC line monitors
8.1	**Demonstrate and apply safety procedures** • Use proper ESD (Electrostatic Discharge) practices and proper grounding techniques • Wrist straps, static mats, unplugging / lockout / tagout

Power supplies

Explanation

A *power supply*, as shown in Exhibit 1-21, is the internal component that converts wall voltage (110 V or 220 V) to the various DC voltages used by a computer's other components. Inkjet and laser printers both have internal DC power supplies to provide power to their various internal components, such as the motors and pulleys. But while inkjet printers have just one DC power supply, laser printers have both a *low-voltage power supply (LVPS)* and a *high-voltage power supply (HVPS)*, the latter of which converts 120 volt, 60 Hz AC current into high-voltage electricity. It's the HVPS that powers the primary corona.

Exhibit 1-21: DC high-voltage power supply

Measuring electrical values

When troubleshooting power supply problems, you might need to measure some aspect of electricity, such as the voltage level output of the power supply. You measure electrical properties using a device called a *multimeter*. Multimeters are available in digital and analog models. Digital multimeters, as shown in Exhibit 1-22, output discrete numeric values on an LED or LCD screen. Analog multimeters, the older type shown in Exhibit 1-23, display their output using a needle and dial.

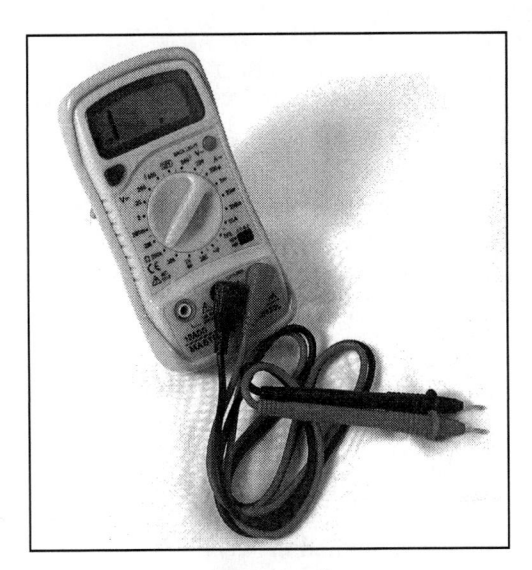

Exhibit 1-22: A digital multimeter

Exhibit 1-23: An analog multimeter

Before taking a measurement with a multimeter, you must set options with a dial, button, or other means to indicate what you're about to measure. For example, if you're using a meter, as shown in Exhibit 1-22, you press the appropriate buttons to indicate which electrical property (voltage range) you're going to read.

Measuring resistance

To measure resistance:

1. Turn off and disconnect the device you're measuring from its power source. You can damage your meter if you leave the device connected to the power source.
2. Additionally, you might need to disconnect the device from its circuit. If it remains connected and multiple paths through the circuit exist, you'll get misleading readings. These readings can be high or low depending on the circuit.
3. Set the multimeter to read resistance. On most meters, you must indicate the resistance range that you expect to be reading.
4. Touch the two leads of the multimeter together. The meter zeros out and provides an indication that the meter is functioning properly in the resistance mode.
5. Touch the black and red probes to either side of the circuit to be measured and read the resistance from the meter's display.

Note: If you're using an analog meter and the needle moves very little or moves all the way to its maximum, you need to choose another resistance scale. Full scale deflection could indicate a short.

Measuring voltage

⚠ You must exercise care when taking voltage readings while a device is powered up.

To measure voltage:

1. The power supply must be on.
2. Set your multimeter to read either DC or AC voltage. On most meters, you must also indicate the voltage range that you expect to be reading.
3. Touch the black probe to the ground and the red probe to the spot where you want to measure the voltage.

   If you're using an analog meter, the needle might attempt to swing backward. This indicates that you have the red probe on the ground. Reverse your contact points to take the reading. A digital meter indicates a negative voltage, for example -55V.

Note: The device must be connected to its power source and turned on while you measure voltage.

Measuring current

To measure current, you must break the circuit and insert the meter into the break. The current in the circuit then flows through the meter, which by design, should offer little disruption and not change the reading appreciably.

A device specifically made for measuring current is called an *ammeter*. A special form of ammeter, called a clamp-on ammeter, clamps around a single wire to measure the current flow. Such a meter doesn't require you to break the circuit. Clamp ammeters are often used by electricians to measure current flow in 110 V and higher circuits.

Measuring continuity

You can determine if a fuse is good or a wire is whole by measuring continuity. You might also use this technique to determine which pins on one end of a cable are connected to which pins on the other end.

To measure continuity, you can either set your multimeter to display resistance (ohms) and look for circuits with zero resistance, or if your multimeter includes it, you can use your meter's continuity mode. In this mode, the multimeter sounds a tone whenever it detects a closed (unbroken) circuit.

Testing polarity and line status

Improperly wired outlets can easily damage laser printers. Two simple devices can help determine whether an outlet is safe for connecting expensive electronic devices:

- *Polarity tester*: Many multimeters include an automatic polarity test function. When you apply the probes, the multimeter's display indicates normal or reversed polarity. You can find polarity testers in other multifunction testing devices, many of which plug into a wall outlet and display results using LEDs or a small LED screen.
- *AC line monitor*: This type of monitor plugs into a wall outlet and determines the integrity of the AC line.

Consult with a licensed electrician to repair damaged or improperly wired outlets.

Do it!

C-1: Measuring electrical values

⚠ *Make sure students follow proper electrical safety during this activity.*

Provide students with batteries, power adapters, good and bad network cables, and so forth to measure.

Assist students and show them the proper procedures.

Here's how	Here's why
1 Using a multimeter, determine the voltage output of the various devices provided by your instructor	Your instructor will provide you with devices, such as a battery or power adapter, that you can use to determine output voltages.
2 Determine the resistance of the various components provided by your instructor	Your instructor will provide you with cables and other components for you to measure.
3 Use a polarity tester/AC line monitor to test various wall outlets in the classroom	
4 Unplug one of the laser printers in the classroom, and use proper ESD and safety procedures to open the laser printer	
Identify the power supplies inside	To locate the potentially dangerous electricity sources are inside a laser printer. Be sure to follow safety precautions.
Work with your instructor to apply lockout and tagout equipment	To protect against electrical hazards.
5 Remove lockout and tagout equipment	
Close the printer	

Electrical components

The following sections contain descriptions of important electrical components.

Display the components or pass them around as you teach this topic.

Exhibit 1-24: Fuses

- A *fuse* is a disposable, single-use component that protects an electrical circuit from current overload. The fuse is placed into the circuit, so the electricity flows through it. If the current in the circuit exceeds the fuse's rating, a wire in the fuse melts, opening the circuit and protecting it from overload. Fuses help protect printer components and prevent against the threat of fire. An example of a fuse is shown in Exhibit 1-24.

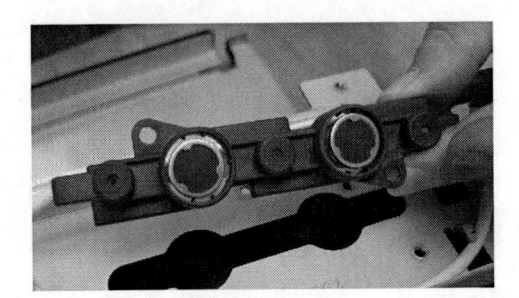

Exhibit 1-25: Thermal switch

- *Thermal fuses* and *thermal switches* are similar to fuses, except that they operate to protect components from excessive heat. Unlike fuses, they don't respond to current overload. Thermal fuses are good for one use and then must be replaced; thermal switches, designed for multiple uses, interrupt power to a heating element if the heat is too high but restore the flow of power when the heat has returned to an acceptable level.

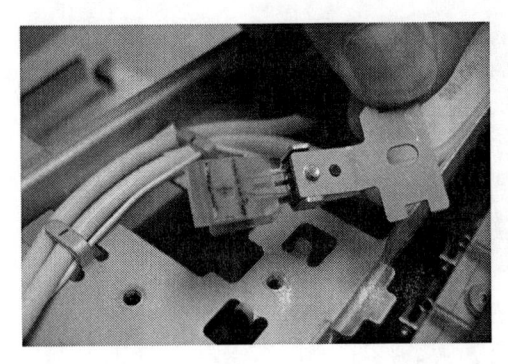

Exhibit 1-26: Thermistor

- A *thermistor* (*thermal resistor*) is an electrical device that can be used to measure temperature, such as in the fuser, where correct temperature is critical. The thermistor's temperature measurement determines how much power needs to be passed on to the fuser to ensure its proper operation.

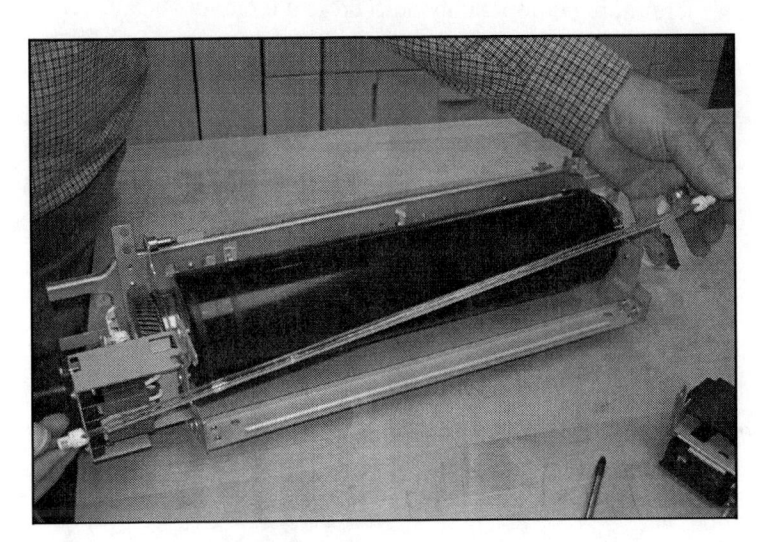

Exhibit 1-27: Lamp from a fuser

- *Lamps* convert electricity into light and have a variety of applications in printing and scanning. *Light Emitting Diodes (LEDs)* can provide users with information, such as printer or scanner settings, device power state, and error and warning messages. LEDs are also used in the print process itself, to create images on the photosensitive drum. LEDs provide a cheaper alterative to laser printers but don't necessarily produce the same quality output. *Halogen lamps* are used in the fusing process to fix the toner to the paper and complete the printing process. *Xenon lamps* are used in scanners to illuminate the image source during the scanning process.

Exhibit 1-28: Grounding plate

- Grounding components help protect technicians and sensitive printer components from ESD and electrical charges by dissipating electricity. Some grounding components include:
    - *Ground wires* and *ground plates*, which dissipate electricity by connecting sensitive components to ground, as shown in Exhibit 1-28. Grounding screws secure a grounding conductor in place.
    - *Ground shields*, such as copper strand braiding, which eliminate *radio frequency (RF) interference* by running it to ground, preventing noise in the circuit. Ground shielding stops *crosstalk* and reduces the possibility of ESD hopping between sensitive components.

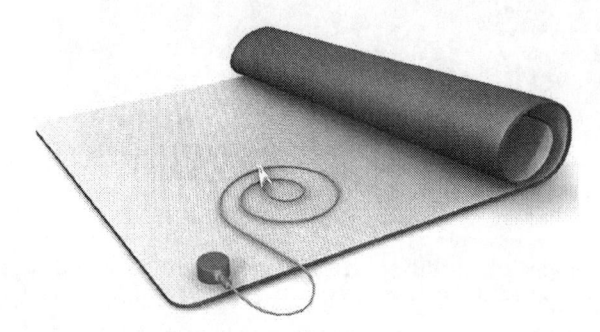

Exhibit 1-29: Static mat

- *Static mats*, as shown in Exhibit 1-29, which allow excess static to run away from components and safely to ground, can be used on floors or work surfaces. A *grounding point* connects static mats to ground by a wire.

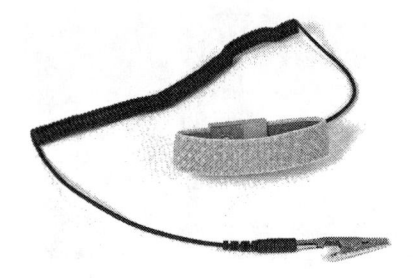

Exhibit 1-30: Wrist strap

- *Grounding wrist straps*, as shown in Exhibit 1-30, and heel straps are worn by technicians while they're working on internal components. They help run excess static to ground. Wrist straps normally have a 1-4 mega ohm *resistor*, a component that limits the amount of electricity that can flow through it. Wrist straps are grounded to a workbench by a clip or similar attachment.

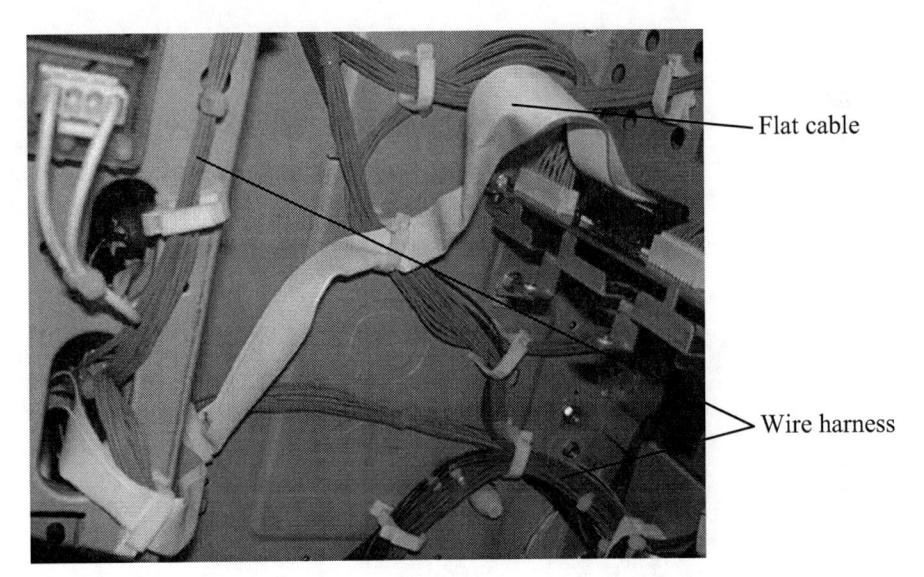

Exhibit 1-31: Flat cable and wire harnesses

- A variety of cables connect components within a printer or scanner. For visual convenience, accessibility, and general organization, insulated wires are bundled together inside devices, such as plastic ties or cords, forming what's known as a *wire harness*, several of which are shown in Exhibit 1-31. Often, wires are bundled in sets and, sometimes, sets of sets. In printers, wire harnesses typically secure the wires that connect boards to other boards.
  - *Flat cable*, or *ribbon cable*, as shown in Exhibit 1-31, so named because the individual signal wires are side by side. Ribbon cable is normally found inside a device, connecting internal components or connecting external ports to the logic board.
  - *Fiber optic* cabling, which carries data on a beam of light, is used to connect high-end networked printers to the local area network. Fiber optic provides the fastest network speeds available today. At this time, fiber optic interfaces aren't commonly found on printers.

Exhibit 1-32: ZIF socket

- You find several types of *connectors* inside printers, scanners, and multifunction devices:
    - *Zero insertion force (ZIF)* sockets are designed to make it easy to connect memory and other chips and integrated circuits on a circuit board without the risk of damaging them in the process. ZIF sockets have a lever that you can use to loosen or tighten the connection, without having to push or pull on the chip you're trying to insert or remove.

Exhibit 1-33: Molex

   - *Molex* connectors, an example of which is shown in Exhibit 1-33, are 4-pin DC power connectors.
   - An *Ultrex* connector is a block-shaped circuit-board connector. Ultrex connectors are used to connect the PCB to sensors or even other PCBs.
   - *Spade* connectors have a forked end, which is clamped down under a connecting screw to ensure secure contact.
   - *Pin* connectors are exactly what the name implies: the connection is made by inserting the pins on the male end of the connector into the corresponding sockets on the female end.

Electromechanical components **1–31**

- *Spring contacts* are often used in doors and trays, where the spring forces them to return to their home position when the load against them is removed. Their home position is usually a circuit-open state, which prevents operation until the necessary doors are shut, pushing the contacts into the circuit closed state. Spring contacts are also used to ensure that components, such as toner cartridges, are properly installed.

Exhibit 1-34: Memory modules

- Printers, like computers, have memory chips to hold print jobs as they're sent from a computer. Some printers have a standard *Random Access Memory (RAM)* chip, such as the one shown in Exhibit 1-34. This type of memory is considered volatile because its contents are lost when the power supply is turned off.
- *Erasable Programmable Read Only Memory (EPROM)* is a type of nonvolatile RAM (NVRAM) that doesn't lose its contents when the power is removed. You erase the contents of an EPROM by exposing its glass window to ultraviolet light.

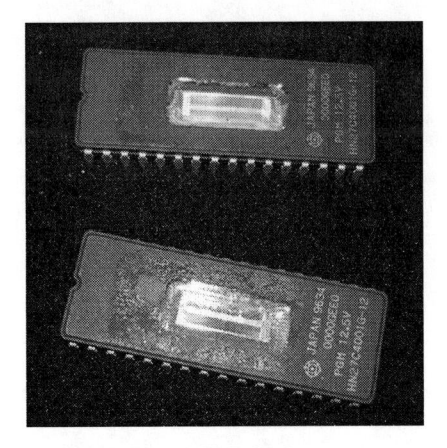

Exhibit 1-35: EEPROM

- *Electronically Erasable Programmable Read Only Memory (EEPROM)*, as shown in Exhibit 1-35, is another type of NVRAM that doesn't lose its contents when the power is removed.

Exhibit 1-36: PCB

- A *printed circuit board (PCB)* is a thin plate into which circuits are printed, using a thin layer of copper. PCBs also contain memory chips and other necessary components. PCBs perform all types of input/output (I/O) functions required to operate a printer or multifunction device, as well as specialized functions, such as fax and network interface capabilities. A single printer can have multiple PCBs.

Do it!

C-2: Identifying electrical components

Here's how	Here's why

1 Specialized mats and wrist straps help protect electronic components from _____.

ESD or static electricity

2 What device is used to monitor temperature in the fuser assembly in a laser printer?

Thermistor

3 _____ bundle wires to help keep them organized inside electronic devices.

Harnesses

4 _____ convert electricity into light.

Lamps

5 _____ are disposable, single-use components that protect electrical circuits from current overload.

Fuses

6 _____ temporarily interrupt the flow of electricity to heating elements when temperatures exceed a predetermined threshold.

Thermal switches

7 Describe the various types of connectors you might encounter inside a printer or scanner.

Answers include: ZIF sockets; Molex, Ultrex, spade, and pin connectors; and spring contacts.

8 Name two types of nonvolatile memory.

EPROM and EEPROM

9 _____ perform all types of I/O functions inside a printer.

PCBs

Unit summary: Electromechanical components

Topic A In this topic, you learned to identify and describe **electromechanical** components, such as **solenoids**, **motors**, **relays**, and **sensors**.

Topic B In this topic, you learned to identify and describe **mechanical** components, such as **gears**, **rollers**, **cams**, and **pulleys**.

Topic C In this topic, you learned to identify and describe **electrical** components, such as **fuses**, **thermistors**, **lamps**, **memory**, and **PCBs**.

Review questions

1 _____ is the force of electricity caused by a difference in electrical potential at two locations.

   Voltage

2 In the United States, electrical systems in office buildings typically operate at what voltage?

   A 85

   B 110

   C 145

   D 210

3 Which of the following is a measure of the flow of electrons past a given point?

   A Voltage

   B Amps

   C Ohms

   D Current

4 Current is measured in _____.

   Amps or amperes

5 True or false? Current that flows in a single direction at a constant voltage through a circuit is called direct current.

   True

6 True or false? Direct current is the type of electrical current supplied by a typical office building's electrical system.

   False

7 Which of the following describes the force that opposes the flow of AC through a conductor?

   A Resistance

   B Wattage

   C Voltage

   D Impedance

8 Which of the following describes the force that opposes the flow of DC through a conductor?

   A Resistance

   B Wattage

   C Voltage

   D Impedance

9 True or false? It takes more than 10,000 volts of static electricity to damage electronic components in most modern devices.

False

10 _____ are typically used to engage rollers for paper pickup from paper trays and cassettes.

Clutches

11 True or false? Stepper motors allow for a finer range of motion than typical DC motors.

True

12 Relays that are normally open will _____ when energized by an electromagnetic field.

close

13 Which of the following powers the primary corona?

   A HVPS

   B LVPS

   C Stepper motor

   D Clutch

14 _____ encoders are used to determine location, direction, or both.

Optical

15 A _____ switch is actuated by a physical motion, whereas a magnetic switch is actuated by a magnetic field.

micro

16 _____ are used to reduce friction in place of bearings.

Bushings

17 True or false? Rollers can be made of both steel and rubber.

True

18 Which of the following are used to convert rotation into a reciprocating motion?

   A Gears

   B Bushings

   C Cams

   D Pulleys

19 Which of the following is used to monitor temperature?

   A HVPS

   B Multimeter

   C Thermistor

   D Corona

20 You use a _____ to measure electrical properties.

multimeter

21 Which of the following lamps is often used in scanners as a light source during the scanning process?

   A Xenon

   B HVPS

   C Halogen

   D Diodes

22 _____ helps protect sensitive electronic components from ESD.

Grounding

23 True or false? Ribbon cable is used to connect networked printers to the local network.

False

24 Which of the following connectors has a forked end that's secured under a tightened screw?

   A Molex

   B Ultrex

   C Spade

   D Pin

Independent practice activity

In this activity, you'll identify electromechanical components. (Note: Be sure the devices you use are NOT connected to a power supply. Be sure to follow proper electrical safety and ESD procedures.)

1. Use the printer provided to you to identify the electromechanical components you learned about in this unit. Make notes detailing the name and location of each component you were able to identify. If necessary, make a quick sketch of the component and its location in the printer, and describe its function. You might not be able to find every component listed in this unit.

Unit 2
Printing and scanning

Unit time: 150 minutes

Complete this unit, and you'll know how to:

A Identify and describe the steps and components involved in ink dispersion and electrophotographic printing.

B Identify and describe the steps and components involved in scanning.

Topic A: Printing

This topic covers the following CompTIA PDI+ exam objectives.

#	Objective

1.1	**Define, describe and demonstrate an understanding of the following commonly used printing processes:**
	• Identify and describe basic steps of laser / LED printing
	   • Photoconductor preparation, charging, writing, developing, transferring, fusing
	      • Photoconductor preparation
	         • Removal of residual toner by cleaning blade, brush or roller
	         • Removal of residual charge by light or electrical charge
	      • Charging
	         • Supply uniform charge to the photoconductor surface by charge corona or charge roller
	      • Writing
	         • Laser or LED creates a latent image by discharging the appropriate areas of the photoconductor
	      • Developing
	         • Toner is attracted to the latent image
	      • Transferring
	         • Toner is transferred from the photoconductor to the media by using electrostatic charges
	      • Fusing
	         • Toner is fixed/fused to the media with heat and pressure
	• Identify and describe basic steps of Ink dispersion printing
	   • Purging, ink delivery, image application to media
	      • Purging
	         • Cleaning the heads and nozzles
	      • Ink delivery
	         • Ink is moved from reservoir to print head
	         • Unidirectional and Bi-directional printing
	      • Image application to media
	         • Ink is delivered through the nozzles (print head) directly to media via heat/charge

#	Objective
1.2	**Identify and describe print process components and their functions**

- Laser or LED image formation components
    - Photoconductor
    - Laser Unit (beam detector, polygon mirror / motor, laser diode, toner shield) or LED unit
    - Developer Unit (toner supply, mono component, vs. dual component)
    - Charge assembly
    - Cleaning Unit (residual toner removal)
    - High Voltage Power Supply
    - Low Voltage Power Supply
    - Transfer / separation
- Device fuser components
    - Heat roller / belt, pressure roller, lamps / heaters, thermistor, fuser cleaning components, pawls, thermal protection
- Ink dispersion image formation components
    - Print head, IDS (ink delivery system), carriage, carriage belt, ink supply, purge unit, absorption pads.
- Media transport/feed components
    - Pickup roller, feed roller, separate roller/pad, torque limiter, transport rollers, registration assembly, sensors, media guides, exit rollers, gates/diverters/deflectors, static brushes
- Ventilation components
    - Fans, ozone filters, dust filters, ducts
- Accessories
    - Finishers, sorters, large capacity paper source, document feeders, stapler, duplexers, punch units, folders cutters, binders, stackers, inserter.

#	Objective
1.3	**Describe the purpose of firmware**
1.4	**Identify and describe print data flow and job processing**

- Demonstrate awareness of the interaction between software application, driver, printer control languages, raster image processing, printing and image creation.
- Identify the impact of memory on the printer

#	Objective
1.5	**Identify media types and explain their impact on print process, quality and device performance**

- Use appropriate media types based on device specifications
- Identify and recognize paper weights, sizes and standards
- Identify and recognize paper textures, brightness, grain, coatings
- Identify and recognize other media types (ie: transparencies, envelopes, labels, card stock, raised letterhead, recycled paper)
- Describe adverse affects of improper media storage on device performance

#	Objective
6.1	**Identify and describe the basics of color theory**
	• Differentiate between additive and subtractive color (RGB vs. CMYK)
	• Describe color gamut and its relationship to device limitations
	• Explain perception of color and what affects perception
	• Light, media, contrast, the observer
6.2	**Define and explain basic color management**
	• Identify how color adjustments affects the quality of image output
	• Describe the need for color calibration

Windows print process

Before a printer powers up and puts toner or ink to paper, a computer must send data to the printer, either through a cable between the printer and the computer or across a network. The print process in Windows XP (and earlier) has been upgraded in Windows Vista (although Windows Vista also supports the Windows XP print process for printers that don't meet the new specifications). You'll learn about both in the following sections.

Windows XP

The Windows XP print process can be broken down into the following steps:

1. A user prints from within a *Win32 application*, and a new print job is created. A Win32 application is an application developed using the Windows *application programming interface (API)*, which is a set of rules and constructs that developers use to create Windows applications. Typically, almost any modern application you use on a Windows 2000 or later computer is a Win32 application.
2. The application calls the *Graphics Device Interface (GDI)*. The GDI is a Windows operating system component that renders graphics for output on a printer or a monitor. GDI enables the computer to handle most of the print job processing.
3. The GDI either renders the print job independently, as an *enhanced metafile (EMF)*, or it calls the GDI-based *printer driver* to determine how to render the print job for the selected printer. The printer driver also determines if the printer is online and ready to print.
4. The GDI sends the print job to the *spooler*.
5. The spooler components work together to further refine the print job by providing layout information and formatting it for the selected printer. The spooler also inserts print job instructions into the data stream it sends to the printer.
6. The spooler sends the print job to the printer, which could be either a local or network printer. The printer stores some of the print job in a *RAM buffer*, which is a temporary data store that allows the printer to accept a print job and begin printing without having to wait for the computer to release the job one page at a time.

GDI printers don't require the computer to communicate using a printer control language (PCL), such as *PostScript* or *Print Command Language (*also known as *PCL)*. A GDI print device uses the *raster image*, or dot pattern, that represents the final printed image, from the computer, rather than compiling the raster image itself.

Some devices, such as some laser printers, compile the raster image themselves in the onboard *Raster Image Processor (RIP)*. Because much of the processing for these print jobs is done on the printers, the printers must have a sufficient amount of RAM to process all the pages in the print job. More complicated images or those with high resolutions might require a larger amount of RAM than a printer has installed, which event can cause the printer to generate memory errors. You can work around these memory errors by reconfiguring the print job (e.g., reducing the resolution or dividing the job into smaller jobs) or installing additional memory in the printer.

Windows Vista

Windows Vista supports a new print specification called *XML Paper Specification (XPS)*. While Windows Vista still provides backward support for GDI print devices and Win32 applications, newer XPS print devices and Windows Presentation Foundation (WPF) applications use a different print process from those used in Windows XP and earlier Windows operating systems. In this new process, the WPF applications call on WPF support functions to spool the document to the spooler in XPS format. If the printer supports XPS and has an XPSDrv printer driver, the spooler sends the spooled XPS file to the XPSDrv printer driver for output to the printer. However, if the printer has a GDI-based driver, the spooler sends the XPS print job to the GDI Conversion Module to be converted to an EMF file.

Do it!

A-1: Examining the Windows printing process

Questions and answers

1 What's different about the Windows XP and Windows Vista print processes?

   Windows Vista supports a print process that uses the new XPS specification, although it still supports the same process that's found on Windows XP computers.

2 Describe the function of the GDI.

   The GDI is a Windows component that renders graphics for output to a monitor or printer. The GDI is responsible for taking the print job from the applications, processing it using the print driver, if necessary, and handing the print job off to the spooler.

3 Describe the function of the spooler.

   The spooler takes the print job from the GDI, further refines it, as necessary, by adding layout information and print instructions, and sends the print job to the printer.

4 Where's the raster image created?

   Either on the computer, where it's then sent to the printer, or on the printer itself using the onboard RIP.

5 What happens on a Windows Vista computer when you print to a non-XPS compliant printer?

   The XPS print job is sent to the GDI Conversion Module for processing.

Color theory

Explanation

Color printing has become widespread with the introduction of inexpensive color inkjet printers. Even color laser printers are becoming more common, as their price drops in relation to monochrome (black-and-white) laser printers. As a technician, you're expected to understand the basics of color theory and how color printers create colored text and graphics on the printed page.

Each ray of light is composed of waves that vibrate at various speeds. How the human eye responds to each wavelength determines how we perceive color. When light passes through a prism, the light is bent, or refracted, and the various wavelengths can be seen separately when reflected off a white surface. The colors we see in the refracted light are known as the spectrum, which is composed of the following colors:

- Red
- Orange
- Yellow
- Green
- Blue
- Indigo (or blue-violet)
- Violet

All these wavelengths together create white light. Mixed separately in various combinations, they create various hues, or colors in the spectrum.

In the science of color mixing, there are two models: *additive color*, the method of creating color by mixing colored lights, and *subtractive color*, the method of creating color by using light reflected off pigment in paint or ink.

Additive color

Additive color process is the method of creating the color spectrum by mixing colored light. The resulting color combinations come not from a property of the light itself but instead from how the eye perceives color. This color model is also known as *RGB* for the three main colors used: red, green, and blue, also known as *additive primaries*. When these three colored lights are projected together, they create white light. When combined in pairs they create the *additive secondaries* of cyan (blue+green), magenta (red+blue), and yellow (red+green).

Because the additive color model uses light rays to create colors, there must be a light source. Additive color is used to create a wide range of colors in color monitors and color projectors. Newer monitors and video adapters can produce millions of colors using this color model.

Subtractive color

The subtractive color process is the method of creating the color spectrum using pigment. White paper reflects all light wavelengths back to the viewer, but when pigment is applied, some of the light isn't reflected. Light that isn't reflected is absorbed by the pigment and is said to be subtracted from the light that's reflected. The wavelength subtracted from the reflected light—the wavelength absorbed by the pigment—is perceived as color by the human eye. It's this method that printing technologies use for creating color.

In printers, the pigment is contained in ink (ink dispersion printers) or toner (electrophotographic printers). The subtractive color model is also known as *CMYK* for the four main colors used: cyan, magenta, yellow, and black. The letters CMYK are used rather than CMYB so that the B isn't misunderstood to mean blue. The K is from the last letter of "black," although experts in color printing technologies will tell you that K is for "key," which refers to a component in traditional color printing that uses black ink.

A combination of the CMY is used to create the color spectrum, and all three colors together create black. A separate black source (ink or toner) is used, because black is the most heavily used color, especially for text, and a separate black pigment reduces waste.

Color printing

Color printing presents some additional challenges not found in monochromatic printing. While some devices can print in color, not all devices provide the same quality color output. *Color gamut* is the term used to describe the entire range of colors a printing device can produce. Typically printers with better monochromatic print quality produce better color pages when printing with color ink or toner, resulting mostly from the printer's ability to create high-resolution text and graphics, measured in *dots per inch (DPI)*. However, this isn't always true. And while a photograph or other graphic image might be rendered brilliantly on a monitor, the device's limitations might prevent it from being rendered on paper with comparable clarity. A device with a larger color gamut produces a greater number of colors and thus produces a printed page that more closely resembles the onscreen image.

In addition, the perception of color on the printed page is affected by a number of factors, including the viewer's vision and ability to perceive color, ambient light, the type of paper or other media on which the text and graphics are printed, and the contrast between the printed text and graphics and the background. Bright light can make colors appear deeper and more saturated, while low light can make colors appear muted. Different colored paper, even paper that's white as opposed to "bright white," can affect the clarity and brilliance of color, mostly a function of the contrast between the background and the pigment. And of course, a viewer with poor vision or impaired ability to perceive color finds printed colors less vivid than a viewer without such impairments, regardless of a printer's ability to reproduce color, the type of media, or the ambient light. Even two people with excellent eyesight perceive color differently.

Color printers also require careful calibration to ensure that all the colors are properly aligned on the page. Registration errors occur when colors are misaligned, producing blurry and out-of-focus images. Color printers usually provide a test function that lets you print a test page and adjust or realign print heads or other printer components to ensure that colors appear properly aligned on the printed page.

Do it!

A-2: Discussing color theory

Here's how

1 Describe the additive color process.

   Additive color process is the method of creating the color spectrum by mixing colored light.

2 What are the additive primaries?

   Red, green, and blue.

3 Describe the subtractive color process.

   The subtractive color process is the method of creating the color spectrum using pigment on a white background. Light absorbed by the pigment isn't reflected, so the resulting color is said to have been subtracted from the reflected light.

4 What colors are used in the subtractive color process?

   Cyan, magenta, yellow, and black.

5 What's a device's color gamut?

   The entire range of colors a device can produce.

6 Name several factors that affect color perception. Why is calibration important?

   Answers include ambient light, media, contrast between pigment and background, and the viewer's ability to perceive colors. Calibration ensures colors are properly aligned on the printed page so images are crisp and in focus.

Inkjet print process

Explanation

Inkjet printers, also known as *ink dispersion* printing technology, produce images by forcing ink through tiny *nozzles* and onto the paper. Each nozzle is approximately 50 to 60 *microns* in diameter. Most inkjet printers are designed to be everyday printers for a variety of documents from text to graphics, while some inkjet printers are designed just for printing photos. These are often small printers, as shown in Exhibit 2-1, that can print 4 x 6-inch or smaller photos on specialty paper.

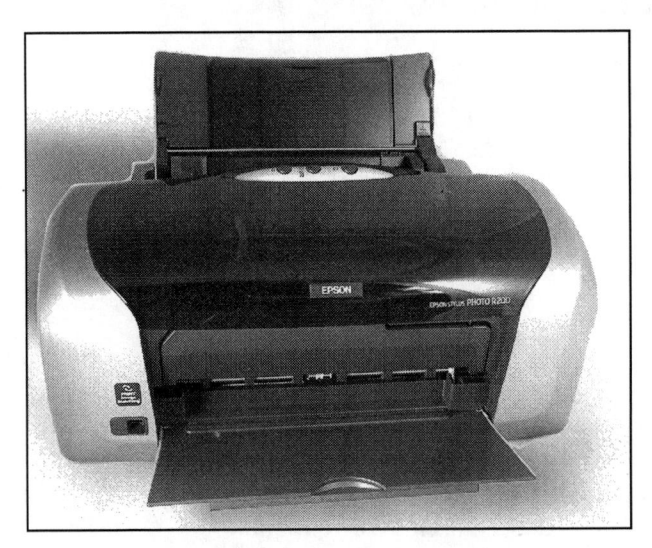

Exhibit 2-1: Inkjet printer

The printer is controlled by a PCB, also known as a *logic board*. The logic board contains the memory chips that hold the page information while the print job is processed, and the firmware, which is the onboard software that controls the printer's functions. Firmware controls not just the print process but all aspects of the printer's operation, including communication with an attached computer and any built-in networking or communication capabilities, especially in multifunction units.

The inkjet print process is less complicated than the electrophotographic (EP) print process and contains fewer components. There are three main stages to the inkjet print process:

1. Purging
2. Ink delivery
3. Image application to media

Exhibit 2-2: Inkjet print head

Purging

The first step in the inkjet print process is purging. In this step, the print enters a short cycle, during which the print heads are cleaned. Each print head, an example of which is shown in Exhibit 2-2, contains hundreds of minute openings, or nozzles, through which ink droplets are sprayed during the inkjet print process. The print head on an inkjet printer is usually part of the ink cartridge. Because this part typically wears out the soonest, having it replaced each time you replace the ink means you always have a good print head.

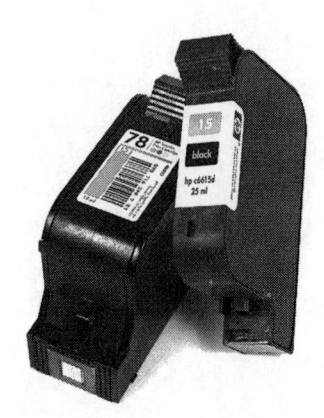

Exhibit 2-3: Ink cartridges

Each nozzle is connected to a channel that runs directly to the ink cartridge. Ink cartridges are the reservoirs that hold ink for inkjet printers. The number of cartridges varies from printer to printer, but most inkjet printers have a black cartridge and a color cartridge, with compartments for cyan, magenta, and yellow. Some printers have separately replaceable cartridges for each color. Some printers have more colors than these basic ones. Some inexpensive printers don't have a separate black cartridge. Instead, when black is required, they mix all three colors together to produce a dark color. Exhibit 2-3 shows examples of inkjet cartridges: a single color cartridge that contains the cyan, yellow, and magenta inks, and a separate black-ink cartridge, which holds black ink or black and color inks for color inkjet printers.

The ink is always in the channels and at the ready in each nozzle. Two things keep the ink from dripping out:

- *Viscosity*, a property of liquids that describes their ability to flow. The higher the viscosity of a liquid, the less likely the liquid will flow; conversely, the lower the viscosity, the more likely the liquid will flow.
- *Surface tension*, another property of liquids that's used to describe the elasticity of an unbroken liquid surface.

Because the ink in each nozzle is exposed to air, it evaporates and its viscosity increases, causing it to harden and eventually clog the nozzles. During the purging cycle, a small amount of ink is forced through the channels and out of the nozzles and onto a small sponge or absorbent pad in a component sometimes known as a *purge unit*. This ensures that the nozzles are clean and ready to use in the next step of the inkjet print process. In some inkjet printers, the print head is also cleaned using a sponge or pad and a wiping or blotting movement created by the motion of the carriage assembly.

The ink cartridges, print head, and associated parts are known collectively as the *ink delivery system (IDS)*.

Ink delivery

After the purge cycle, the motor that controls the pickup rollers engages and draws a sheet of paper into the paper path. Some inkjet printers have a paper tray behind the printer and pull the paper through the printer on a straight-through paper path using a set of feed rollers. This setup leads to fewer paper jams and is good for heavy paper stock. Exhibit 2-4 shows a straight-through paper path in an inkjet printer.

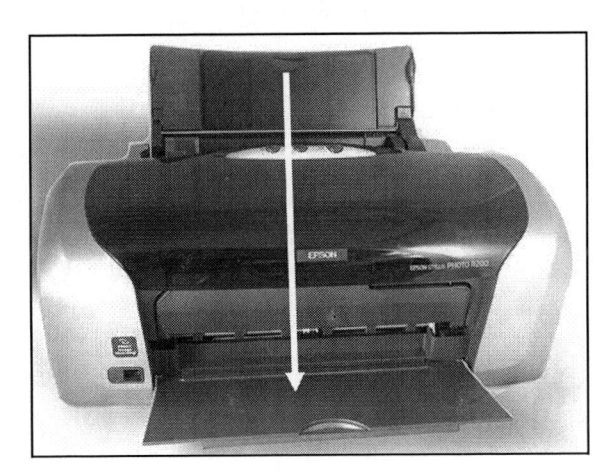

Exhibit 2-4: Straight-through paper path

Other printers store the paper in a tray below and to the front of the printer then pull the paper up through feed rollers and under the print head. Printers using this technology pull the paper up through an S-curve or a U-curve. Exhibit 2-5 shows a curved paper path in an inkjet printer. In both types of paper tray, simple switches detect the presence of paper and can alert you if the paper runs out using a small LED warning.

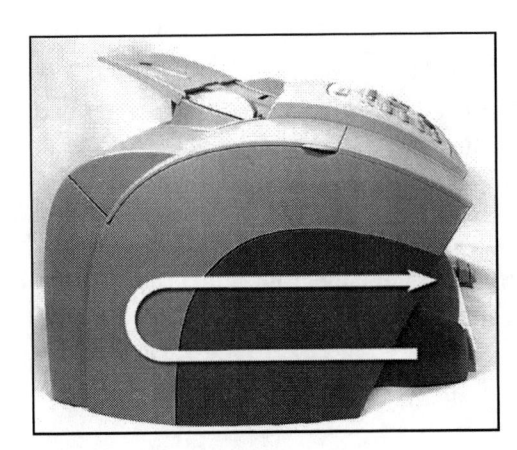

Exhibit 2-5: Curved paper path

Because the nozzles have been purged, fresh ink is now moved into position at each nozzle on the print head in a process known as *priming*. When printing begins in the next step of the process, some inkjet printers print on both passes across the page: left to right and right to left. Other printers print in only one direction, either right to left or left to right. The first type of printer is said to be *bidirectional*; the second type of printer is said to be *unidirectional*.

Image application to media

There are two methods of forcing ink through the nozzles: thermal bubble and piezoelectric bubble.

- *Thermal bubble technology* heats the ink until it vaporizes, creating a bubble. The bubble protrudes out through the nozzle and sprays onto the paper. When the bubble bursts, it creates a vacuum, which draws more ink from the cartridge into the print head, readying it to create the next dot.
- *Piezoelectric technology* creates a bubble using a *piezo crystal* behind each nozzle. An electrical current sent to the crystal causes it to vibrate. When it vibrates inward, it releases ink onto the paper; when it vibrates outward, it pulls ink from the cartridge.

The stepping motor drives the belt that moves the carriage containing the print head across the page, stopping for a fraction of a second for the ink droplets to be sprayed onto the paper. The motion of the stepping motor is so fluid that it isn't visible to the naked eye. Depending on the type of printer, one of three things happens:

- the print head makes another pass at the same line
- the paper advances and the print head starts back in the other direction, printing a new line as it goes, as with bidirectional printers
- the print head returns, the paper advances, and the print head starts on a new line, as with unidirectional printers

When printing is complete, the stepping motor that has been advancing the paper ejects the printed page, and the print head returns to its home position. Most inkjet printers use a fast drying ink, so the page is safe to touch after it's been ejected. Some photo printers or images on paper that contain a lot of ink might take a few seconds or a few minutes to dry before they're safe to touch.

Do it!

A-3: Examining the inkjet print process

Here's how	Here's why
1 Observe the inkjet printers at your instructor's work station	Be sure to follow standard ESD and electrical safety procedures.
2 Work with your instructor and other students to identify as many of the printer's components as you can	Refer to the book, if necessary.
3 Watch as your instructor prints several test pages and explains the inkjet print process	
4 Work with your instructor to identify the various steps as each page is printing	

Be sure to have working and non-working inkjet printers ready before starting this activity. The working inkjet printer should be connected to your computer and ready to print.

Open the cover and point to various parts. Ask students to identify each part you point to.

As you print several pages, walk students through the steps in the inkjet print process. You might need to print several pages. Discuss both the software and hardware aspect of the process.

Exhibit 2-6: Laser printer

Electrophotographic print process

Explanation

EP printers (laser and LED) provide the standard level of quality to which other printers are measured. EP printers can create high-quality documents in a high-volume printing environment, but as you might expect, the EP print process is more complicated than the inkjet print process. Most EP printers produce black-and-white output, but color EP printers are widely available. Exhibit 2-6 shows an example of a laser printer.

Like those of an inkjet printer, an EP printer's functions are controlled by the logic board. To store their firmware, laser printer logic boards typically contain much more RAM and EPROM or EEPROM chips than inkjet printer logic boards.

The EP print process consists of the following steps:
1. Photoconductor preparation
2. Charging
3. Writing
4. Developing
5. Transferring
6. Fusing

Printing and scanning **2-15**

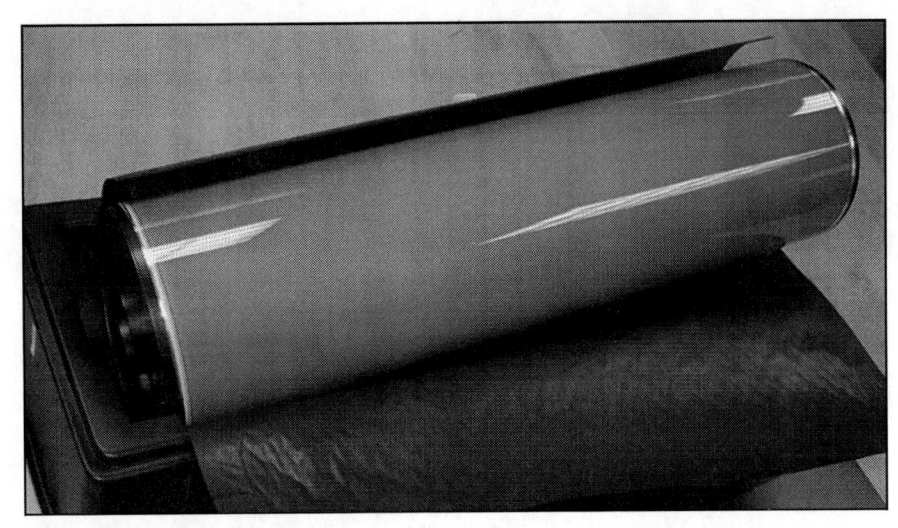

Exhibit 2-7: A drum exposed

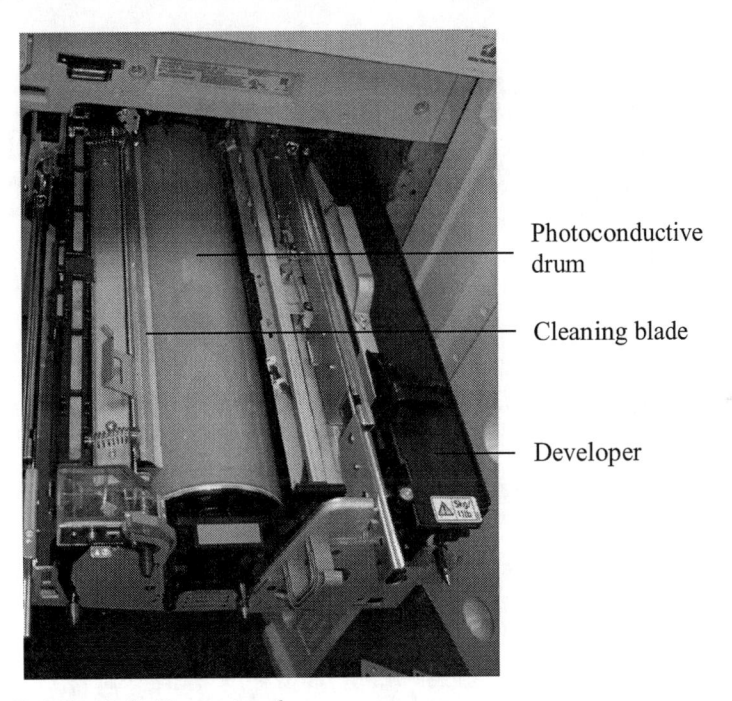

Exhibit 2-8: Drum in place

Photoconductor preparation

Display any components you have in the classroom as you discuss them in the following sections.

The *photoconductor*, or *drum*, as shown in Exhibit 2-7 and Exhibit 2-8, is an aluminum cylinder that's coated with a photoconductive material. The material is said to be photoconductive, because it conducts electricity when it's exposed to light, in this case a laser beam or an array of LEDs. The drum is grounded to the power supply, but the photosensitive coating isn't, so any charge the aluminum drum receives bleeds away into the grounding. However, the coating remains conductive.

Exhibit 2-9: Cleaning unit

Because the drum is so integral to the process, it must be clean and free of any toner residue or electric charge. A rubber cleaning blade or brush, as shown in Exhibit 2-8 and Exhibit 2-9, removes any toner from the surface of the drum. The toner is scraped back into the original toner supply or into a collection chamber that's part of the developer unit, so it's disposed of when you remove and replace the unit. If the toner isn't removed from the drum, residual toner appears on subsequent pages as small spots and flecks.

The drum is also exposed to erasure or discharge lamps to ensure that any charges written to the drum's photosensitive surface by the laser or LED array are removed or reversed. This process prevents phantom images from making their way onto subsequent pages.

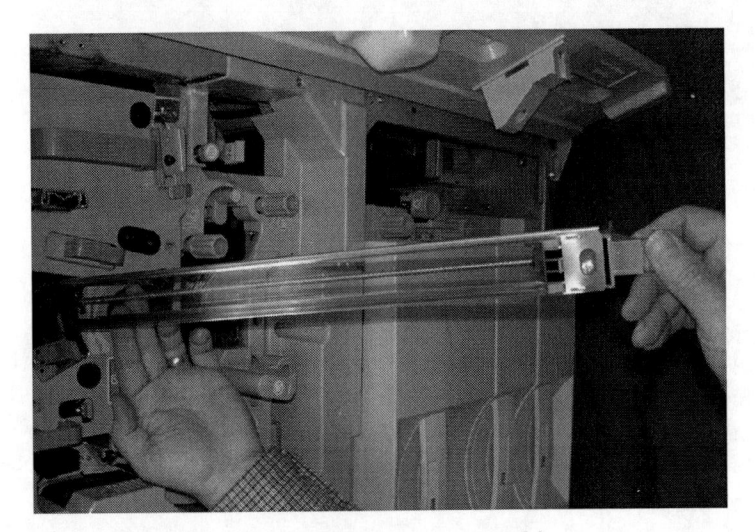

Exhibit 2-10: Primary charge corona assembly

Charging

After the drum is prepared, it's charged by the *primary corona*, as shown in Exhibit 2-10, or the *charge roller*, as shown in Exhibit 2-11. A printer has either one or the other, and it's connected to the high-voltage power supply (HVPS). (A low-voltage power supply powers other printer components.) This step is also called *conditioning*.

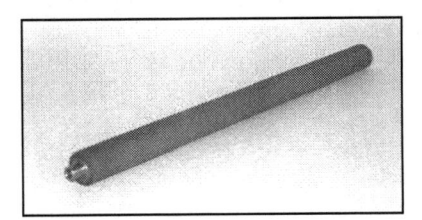

Exhibit 2-11: Charge roller

Both the corona and roller apply a negative charge of around -600V to the surface of the drum, the corona by creating an electrical field between it and the drum, and the charge roller by direct contact. The electrical field generated by the primary corona changes the air between it and the drum into ozone, so printers with a corona always have an ozone filter and exhaust component.

Writing

After the drum has been charged, it's ready for the next step: the laser or LED array writes the image to be printed onto the surface of the drum by removing the negative charge—in effect, cutting out the patterns of the letters and graphics that make up the final printed page. By exposing areas of the drum to precise beams of light, the printer creates an image on the surface of the drum by discharging the -600V charge to about -100V. It's this discharged image, which is basically a series of dots, that attracts the negatively charged toner in the next step where the image is positively charged in relation to the stronger negative charge on the rest of the drum.

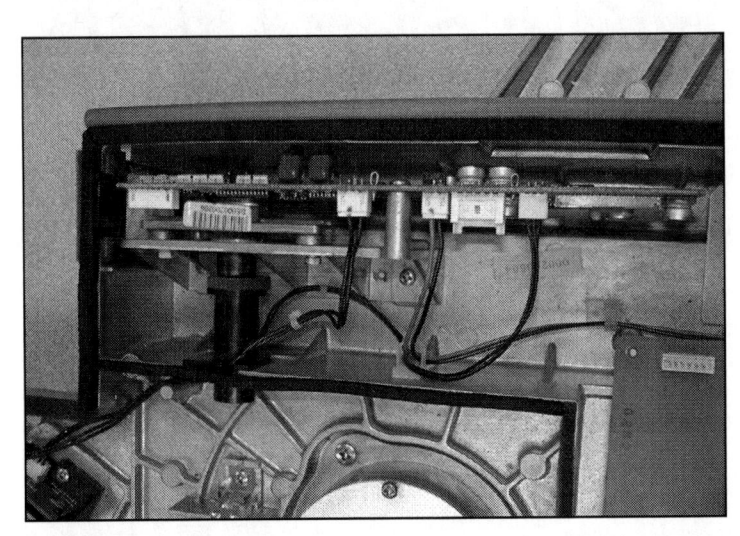

Exhibit 2-12: Laser unit

In a laser printer, the laser unit, as shown in Exhibit 2-12, is responsible for writing the image onto the drum. The laser is emitted from a laser diode, which is a tiny eye (aperture) that measures at most only a few millimeters in diameter.

Designs vary, but a typical diode is set in a metal, cylindrical mounting. Some are set directly in the wall of the laser unit.

The laser is focused through a lens and reflected off a motorized polygon mirror to expose, and as a result discharge, a single row of dots. The drum is stopped while each row is discharged and advanced when each row is completed. The beam detector is responsible for tracking the location of the laser beam. The stopping and starting is coordinated with the motion of the laser beam and is virtually imperceptible. A *toner shield* protects the integrity of laser beam by preventing toner from entering the laser's line of travel or touching the lens or diode.

In an LED printer, a strip of LEDs replaces the laser unit. The LED array doesn't require a mirror assembly; instead each LED fires on cue to create the image on the drum. Typically LED printers are less expensive than laser printers but don't produce output of comparable quality. However, as LED technology improves, the quality will eventually approach that of laser printers.

Exhibit 2-13: Developer unit

Developing

After the invisible image is etched into the electrical charge on the surface of the drum, it must be developed and made visible. The *developer unit*, as shown in Exhibit 2-13, contains the toner supply, which is the "ink" of an EP printer. Toner is a fine powder made of pigment, either black alone or CMYK, bound to minute plastic beads, and often superfine metallic particles. There are two types of toner:

Exhibit 2-14: Dual-component toner

- *Dual-component* toner uses a separate metallic medium to transfer the pigment to paper. The metallic particles are drawn out of the toner supply, bonding to the pigment as they move. Exhibit 2-14 shows a package of dual-component developer that contains an iron oxide mixture and carbon black toner.
- *Mono-component* toner has the pigment and metallic medium already bound in the same particle.

The toner is kept in a trough in the developer unit, and is exposed to the drum using a magnetic transfer roller that lifts the toner out of the trough in a thin layer with the help of a *doctor blade* (or *skimming blade* or *metering blade*), which scrapes the toner into a single layer on the roller. The negatively charged toner is repelled by most of the drum, except for the areas that were discharged by the light—the areas that contain the text and graphics on the printed page. The toner is attracted to these areas and fills them in, creating the page's image on the surface of the drum. (You could actually see the image on the drum if you were to stop it and remove it from the printer during the print process.)

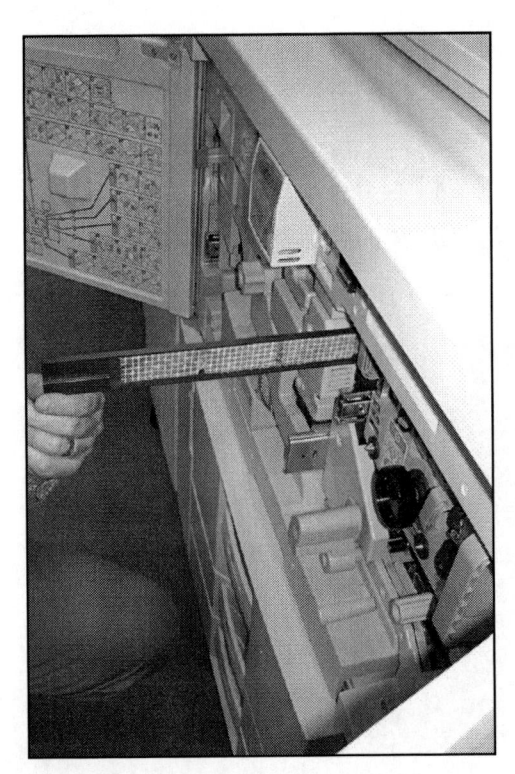

Exhibit 2-15: Dust filter

Paper, especially fibrous paper, generates dust, and this, along with particulate matter carried in on paper surfaces, collects inside the machine. The high temperatures involved in EP processes exacerbate dust problems, so dust filters are built into locations where dust is most likely to accumulate. Filters can be removed, cleaned, and then reinserted. They must be routinely checked and cleaned. Some are replaceable, because after several reuses, their ability to retain dust deteriorates, especially if printing is continuous, and dusty paper is used.

Transferring

At this stage, the developed image on the drum must be transferred to paper. But to transfer the toner to the paper, the printer must attract it away from the charged drum and onto the surface of the paper. To accomplish this task, the paper is pulled into the printer and given a positive charge by the *transfer corona*. This charge is strong enough to attract the negatively charged toner off the surface of the drum and onto the surface of the paper. Remember, not all the toner is transferred to the paper, which is why the drum must be cleaned and prepared before it's given another charge to start this process all over again.

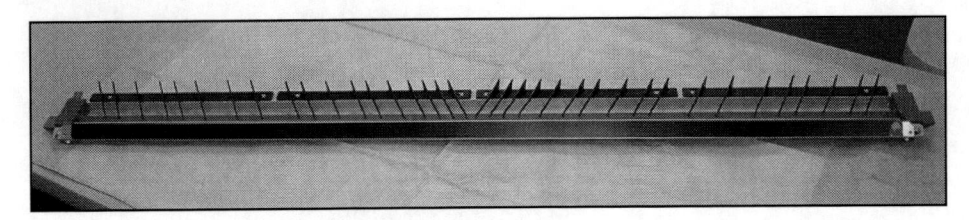

Exhibit 2-16: Transfer corona assembly with pawls

To help prevent the positively charged paper from sticking to the negatively charged drum and wrapping around it, the charge on the paper is removed by a static charge eliminator right after the toner is transferred to the paper. *Pawls*, claw-like metal components, in the transfer assembly, such as those shown in Exhibit 2-16, help guide the paper away from the drum. The paper is then ready for the next step in the process.

Exhibit 2-17: Fuser assembly

Fusing

At this point, the toner is sitting loosely on the surface of the paper, and it's ready to be permanently bonded (fused) to the paper. The paper is fed through the *fuser assembly* and sandwiched between two rollers: a heated, non-stick roller on top, and a pressure roller on the bottom, which is indicated in Exhibit 2-17 (the heated roller being above it). Often the nonstick roller is coated with Teflon. As the paper is squeezed between the two rollers, the toner is melted and forced into the paper, fixing the image permanently. Pawls guide the paper away from the heated roller and toward the delivery or exit rollers. A cleaning unit scrubs the surface of the heated roller to ensure the heated roller is free of any residual toner.

The heated roller is heated by a lamp, such as a quartz or halogen lamp, or by a heating coil, to raise its temperature to around 350 degrees Fahrenheit, or 180 degrees Celsius. Examples of a heating lamp are shown in Exhibit 2-18 and Exhibit 2-19. A thermistor is used to monitor and maintain the proper temperature by regulating electrical current to the heating lamps. A thermal switch protects against any spikes in temperature by cutting the electrical current if the temperature is too high. Fans, such as the one in Exhibit 2-20, and air ducts help keep air circulating through the printer to help maintain proper temperature in not just the fuser assembly but also throughout the machine.

Exhibit 2-18: Fusing lamps inside the roller

Exhibit 2-19: Fusing lamp exposed

The heated roller is heated by a lamp, such as a quartz or halogen lamp, or by a heating coil, to raise its temperature to around 350 degrees Fahrenheit, or 180 degrees Celsius. A thermistor is used to monitor and maintain the proper temperature by regulating electrical current to the heating lamps. A thermal switch protects against any spikes in temperature by cutting the electrical current if the temperature is too high. Fans and air ducts keep air circulating through the printer to help maintain proper temperature not just in the fuser assembly but also throughout the machine.

Printing and scanning   **2-23**

Exhibit 2-20: Fan

After the paper exits the fuser assembly, it's pushed out of the printer and into a waiting tray (or into a finisher for further processing). This process repeats until the entire document submitted for printing is completed.

Exhibit 2-21: Transfer belt

Color laser printers

Color laser printers use one of the following processes to produce the colored text and graphics on the page:

- The printer has four separate developer units, one for each color of toner (usually CMYK). The drum is discharged once for each color, and successive layers of colored toner are applied to the drum and then the paper, one color at a time, to produce the final printed page.
- The printer contains a belt or plate that's the size of a sheet of paper. To build the image, four different colors of toner are applied, one after the other, to the belt, a sample of which is shown in Exhibit 2-21, or plate. The combined toner is then applied to the page as a single image. The toner is then fused to the page as in the normal monochrome process.
- The printer has separate print process components for each color: a drum, developer, and fuser. The final printed page is put through all four processes before finally exiting the printer.

Color printers require more memory than monochrome printers, because each the page must be rasterized in each color and stored in memory.

Paper path

The path the paper takes through a laser printer must be precisely controlled in order to produce the final printed copy. A slight deviation from the correct path can result in a paper jam, damage to internal printer components, and misprinted or blank pages. Photo-interrupt and photo-reflective sensors help ensure that the paper is properly positioned throughout its path through the printer. Sensors also trigger errors if paper isn't where it should be or if a jam occurs.

Exhibit 2-22: Pickup roller and separation pad

The following components are responsible for keeping paper on the correct path.

- *Pickup rollers* (often wedge-shaped and powered by a motor and clutch or solenoid), in contact with the top of the paper stack, push a single sheet forward into the closely fitting *feed roller* (the upper roller) and *separation roller* or *separation pad* (the lower roller). The separation roller knocks away any excess sheets that have traveled beneath the sheet that was pushed by the pickup roller. The feed roller pushes or pulls the sheet into the printing area of the device. The edge of the paper that enters the printer first is called the *lead edge* or *leading edge*.
- A *torque limiter* in the separation roller helps keep sheets straight by providing *back-feed pressure* to sheets as they're feeding through the paper path. Torque limiters might also be fitted to feed rollers to limit excess rotation from the drive. Torque limiters attached to roller shafts might resemble two cylinders or thick washers. These cylinders are magnetic and, between them, is a cushion of iron filings. It's this cushion that neutralizes the torque. Depending on the printer model, torque limiters can also be found integrated into clutch assemblies.
- The *Registration assembly* is a series of rollers that keep the paper flat as it's drawn into the printer and ensure that it's properly positioned.
- *Transport rollers* provide a fluid, rolling surface to facilitate paper movement through the paper path.
- *Media guides* ensure that the paper is straight and properly oriented in the paper path.

Exhibit 2-23: Gates

- *Gates* provide a transition from one assembly to another.
- *Diverters* and *deflectors* help steer paper in one direction or another.
- *Delivery* or *exit rollers* move (deliver) the paper to the printer's exit tray.
- *Static brushes* remove any residual static electricity from printed sheets.

Printer accessories

After the print process, the printed page is usually delivered to a tray where you can pick it up. Many larger printers have a wide range of add-on accessories that you can use to assemble printed pages in almost any format imaginable. Not all printers support all the available add-ons.

Exhibit 2-24: Duplexer

- Duplexers allow a printer to print on both sides of a sheet of paper, creating double-sided pages. After the print process is complete on the first side, the paper is put through the process again for the second side.
- Finishers are add-on units that take the printed pages and complete a job using any or all of the following features:
    - Staplers.
    - Punch units, to punch holes so that you can put the finished pages in a binder.
    - Folders.
    - Cutters, to cut paper into sizes other than what was fed into the printer; for example, you can cut pages in half or into quarters if printing tickets or flyers.
    - Binders, such as comb or spiral wire binders.
    - Inserters, to insert blank or preprinted pages, such as covers, in collated print jobs.

Printing and scanning   **2–27**

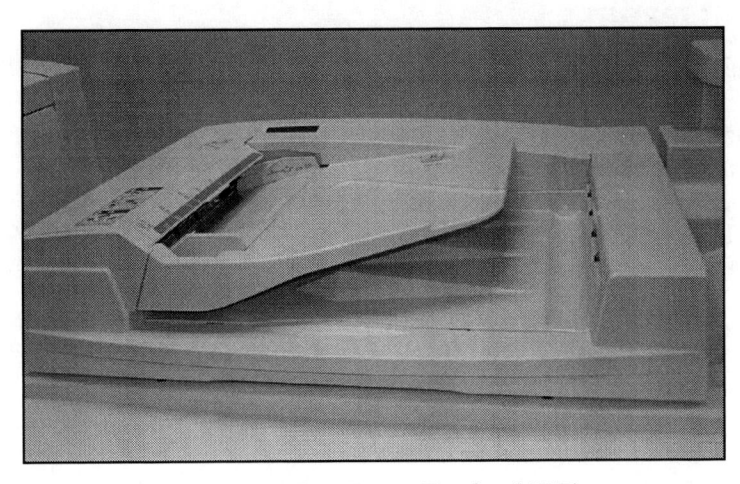

Exhibit 2-25: Automatic Document Feeder (ADF)

- Sorters and stackers collate finished pages into separate piles that correspond to the document that was printed or copied (on multifunction printers). You can feed multipage documents into copiers and multifunction printers using an *automatic document feeder (ADF)* such as the one shown in Exhibit 2-25.

Do it!

A-4: Examining the EP print process

Here's how	Here's why
1 Observe the printers at your instructor's workstation	Be sure to follow standard ESD and electrical safety procedures.
2 Work with your instructor and other students to identify as many of the printer components as you can	Refer to the book, if necessary.
3 Watch as your instructor prints several test pages and explains the EP print process	
4 Work with your instructor to identify the different steps as each page is printing	

Be sure to have working and nonworking EP printers ready before starting this activity. The working EP printer should be connected to your computer and ready to print.

Open the cover and point to various parts. Ask students to identify each part as you point to it.

As you print several pages, walk students through the steps in the EP print process, discussing both the hardware and software aspects.

Print media

Paper is the most widely used print medium, although most inkjet and laser printers with the right software can print on mailing labels, envelopes, CDs, DVDs, and transparencies. Paper is loaded into paper trays on the sides, the front, the back, or under the printer. The trays can be exposed or hidden in drawers or cabinets. Paper can also be loaded into *cassettes*, which are closed containers loaded with paper and inserted into a printer. Large capacity paper sources can hold thousands of sheets of paper. This is especially important for large print jobs, so that users don't have to replenish the paper supply constantly.

Most printers can accommodate a variety of paper sizes, weights, and types. However, the best advice for choosing the proper paper is to check the printer's documentation and use the paper recommended by the manufacturer.

Paper grain

A paper's *grain* is the direction in which most of the paper's fibers lie. *Grain long* is paper with the grain parallel to the long side, while *grain short* is paper with the grain parallel to the short side. The paper should be inserted such that the grain of the paper is parallel to the lead edge. Check the paper packaging to see how the paper manufacturer recommends that you insert the paper.

Paper weights

Paper is available in a variety of weights. The weight of a given paper is stated in pounds (lbs) of an uncut *basis ream* (500 sheets) of that paper. From the basis ream, the paper is cut to size and finished before being packaged. So while a basis ream of a 20lbs paper would weigh twenty pounds, the ream of 20lb paper you buy at the store isn't 20lbs. (It's actually closer to 5.)

General-purpose paper is usually 20lb or 24lb paper. Other general use paper can range up to 32lbs. You can determine the paper weight by examining its packaging. With experience, you can gauge paper weight by feeling its thickness and checking its translucency. A 20lb paper feels thinner and lighter, and it generally allows more light to pass through it when held up to a light source than does a 24lb or heavier paper.

Cover stock is paper from 65lb to 68lb. Its name implies its general purpose, although it can be used for flyers, signs, or handouts. Card stock is generally 110lb and likely the heaviest paper you use in a typical printer. You need to check the documentation, however, to see how it should be loaded into the printer, if it can be used at all.

Some more expensive papers have a higher cotton content, so their texture feels heavier and rougher. These papers are sometimes called *linen* or *vellum* to denote the higher cotton content and quality. Rougher papers tend to have reduced text and graphic quality, because they don't accept the ink and toner as well as smoother papers. Thicker papers, especially, should be fed into the printer with the lead edge parallel to the grain. Not all papers are suitable for all printers, so checking the printer documentation is crucial for success with special papers.

Paper sizes

The paper used most often for general printing in North America measures 8.5 by 11 inches. This size paper is called *letter size*. Paper that measures 11 by 17 is called *legal size*. Most printers can handle both types of paper and have paper trays or cassettes than can accommodate either. You might need to make adjustments in the application you're printing from to accommodate a paper size different from its normal setting.

Outside of North America, you might see letter-sized paper designated at *A4* and legal-sized paper as *A3*. A4 paper measures 210mm x 297mm (8.27in x 11.69in), which makes it longer and narrower than North American letter paper. A1 paper measures A1 594mm x 841mm.

Paper color and brightness

Paper comes in a variety of colors, and this variety can add interest to printed copies. Keep in mind that dark paper makes black text difficult to see, because it reduces the contrast between the text and the background. Black text on lighter colored paper also has a reduced contrast when compared with standard white paper. But for many uses, such as signs, handouts, or report covers, colored paper is a good choice.

Colored paper has a negative impact on the appearance of text and graphics printed in color. Remember, the subtractive color method relies on a white background. So when printing pages with colored ink, you should use white paper.

A paper's brightness indicates the amount of light reflected from it on a scale of 1 to 100. Newsprint has a brightness level in the 50s, while standard copy and printer paper has brightness levels ranging from the upper 80s to the lower 90s. Glossy photo paper can have brightness levels in the upper 90s. Brighter paper renders very crisp text and graphics, although lighter colors on colored pages might appear to be slightly washed out. Darker colors appear very dark.

Coatings

Generally, paper coatings range from *matte*, a rough, unpolished appearance, to a smooth, glossy finish. Rougher papers can cause ink and toner to bleed slightly, which can reduce the crispness of text and graphics. Very glossy papers, on the other hand, might cause ink or toner to smear if the pages aren't given ample time to dry (several minutes in extreme cases). Specialty photo papers are very glossy and, when used with inkjet photo printers, can produce a near darkroom-quality photograph.

Recycled papers

Companies are increasingly becoming "greener," that is, using recycled paper products, banning incandescent light bulbs, and encouraging workers to use public transportation or share rides. From time to time, you'll encounter recycled printer and copier paper that's fine for most general-purpose print jobs. However, common complaints concern the bits and specks in the recycled paper that, of course, show up on final printed pages. While the quality of recycled paper is improving, you can still find papers that have small specks of matter pressed into the paper grain. Saving higher quality paper for special print jobs, especially those seen by clients and others outside the business, is a good strategy, since it's important to make good impressions but to incorporate recycled products at the same time.

Inkjet papers

Regular copier paper doesn't produce as clear an image as specially coated inkjet paper does. The ink bleeds out on regular paper, creating fuzzy edges of characters and images. Coated inkjet paper has a layer of clay that the ink sits on, thus preventing bleed-out.

Attempting to print on a shiny surface, such as a transparency, can also prove difficult, if the wrong type of transparency plastic is used. The ink might not dry properly and could smudge on the kind of transparency that's meant to be written on with pens and markers. Transparency sheets with a special textured coating allow the printer ink to adhere and dry properly.

The ink in most inkjet cartridges is water-soluble, which can be a problem if your printouts get wet. Being caught in the rain with a poster containing images printed from an inkjet printer can result in the ink running down the page. You can purchase waterproof inks for some inkjet printers.

Other media

Most modern inkjet and EP printers can handle a variety of media, even if the media must be fed into the one unit at a time. Check your printer's documentation to see which media are appropriate, and then check the medium itself to ensure that it's appropriate to use with your printer. Sometimes you can select different media types by using the settings on your printer, while other times you need a software program to print on special media.

Other media types include:

- Transparencies, for use with an overhead projector.
- Envelopes and mailing labels for single unit or mass mailings.
- Photo paper is the best choice for printing high-quality images from a digital camera or scanned photos. Printing such items on regular paper or even coated inkjet paper results in lower-quality photos.
- Paper with preprinted, raised letterhead, that's inserted into a printer a page at a time for special documents or kept in the paper tray for everyday use. You must ensure that the paper is properly seated in the paper tray or cassette such that the text is printed on the correct side of the paper and with the correct orientation.
- CDs and DVDs can have professional quality labels printed directly on the top surface of the disc. Exhibit 2-26 shows an example of a photo printer printing on a CD.

Exhibit 2-26: Printing directly onto a CD

Media storage

Paper should be stored on a flat surface, and away from humidity, moisture, and sunlight. Paper that isn't flat is likely to jam on its way through the printer. Paper that has absorbed moisture is also likely to jam and might not bind properly with ink or toner. A dry, cool cabinet or closet with plenty of shelving is the best location for storing paper or any other media that's used in a printer.

Do it!

A-5: Examining print media

Here's how	Here's why

1 What's paper grain? Describe the difference between grain long and grain short paper.

Grain is the direction in which the paper's fibers lie. Grain long is paper with the grain parallel to the long side, and grain short is paper with the grain parallel to the short side.

2 What's a paper cassette?

A closed container into which you load paper. The container is then inserted into the printer.

3 Which is thicker: 20lb paper or 65lb paper?

65lb paper

4 How are letter-sized paper and A4 size paper related?

Letter-sized paper is 8.5 by 11 inches. A4 paper is slightly smaller. A4 is the paper size recognized outside North America.

5 Which is brighter: a paper rated 95 or a paper rated 75?

A paper rated 95.

6 Describe media types other than 20lb paper that you can use with a printer.

Answers might include labels, envelopes, transparencies, CDs, DVDs, photo paper, cover stock, and card stock.

7 Explain the importance of proper paper storage.

Paper that isn't stored properly can jam inside the printer or produce printed pages that aren't crisp. Excessively dry (particularly very thin) paper can carry an electrostatic charge that can severely disrupt the EP process. This is a risk in regions of high temperature and very low humidity.

Topic B: Scanning

This topic covers the following CompTIA PDI+ exam objectives.

#	Objective
2.1	**Identify and describe common hardware scanner components** • Lamps, mirrors, CCD, CIS, CMOS, lens, glass, analog to digital converter, color filters. • Differentiate between ADF (Automatic Document Feeder) and flatbed component

2.2	**Describe and summarize image capture in relation to scanning technologies**
	• Identify and describe common scanner technologies such as TWAIN and network scanning methods
	• Identify the effects of using different image formats (ie: PDF, JPG, GIF, TIFF)
	   • Impact on file size, quality, scan time, network bandwidth, storage, resolution, color, depth, reduction, enlargement, compression
	• Define the image capture process
	   • Light exposure, reflection, focus, filter, capture (CCD), Analog to Digital conversion, image processing.
	• Recognize the reasons for and potential impact of security and anti-counterfeiting features

Scanners

Scanners convert pictures or text on paper to digital data. You can use scanners to create electronic images of just about anything that fits in or on a scanner, such as documents, books, pictures, and even three-dimensional objects, although the latter choice isn't recommended. However, some documents, such as some business and personal checks and currency, have built-in security features to protect against unlawful copying, theft, counterfeiting, and identity fraud. These features include watermarks, reflective seals, and threads that appear only when illuminated, such as by the lamp of a scanner or copier. If a document containing such features is scanned, the resulting image can easily be distinguished as a scanned and copied document rather than an original.

Scanners can be standalone devices or part of a multifunction device. Most standalone desktop scanners are flatbed scanners, an example of which is shown in Exhibit 2-27. With this type of scanner, you place the document or picture to be scanned on a glass surface under a cover, much as you would on a photocopier.

Exhibit 2-27: Flatbed scanner

Multifunction scanners, such as the one shown in Exhibit 2-28, usually have an *automatic document feeder (ADF)* that can hold several pages at once and insert each page one at a time. Some multifunction units also have a flatbed for scanning or copying. Some scanners have a built-in network card, so they can be networked as a printer can.

Exhibit 2-28: Multifunction scanner

If you're supporting older equipment, you might also encounter handheld scanners. These devices are dragged across the paper to scan the page. Early scanners had to be dragged at a uniform speed over the page, or the resulting image would be distorted. Later models used gears or sensors to match the scanning speed to the drag speed, so that you didn't have to be so precise when dragging it.

Scanner components

The following sections describe important scanner components.

- Lamps are used to illuminate fully the document or photo being scanned. Most newer scanners use a Xenon lamp or a *cold cathode fluorescent lamp (CCFL)*. Some older scanners might have a plain fluorescent lamp.

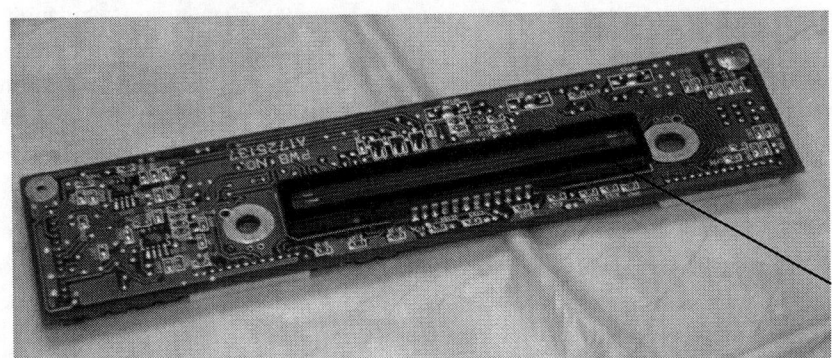

Exhibit 2-29: CCD

- A *charge-coupled device (CCD)*, as shown in Exhibit 2-29, is a silicon-based integrated circuit that converts light energy into electric charges, which are stored as pixels and transferred to the computer after the scan pass is complete. A CCD scanner uses either two or three mirrors and a lens to focus the light onto the CCD. A CCD scanner also contains an analog-to-digital converter (ADC) to convert the light (analog signal) into a digital signal that can be stored and manipulated on a computer. Some CCD scanners use three passes, each pass scanning through a different color filter. However, most scanners use a single pass, and the lens divides the scan image into three smaller images, each of which passes through a separate color filter.

Exhibit 2-30: CIS with fluorescent exposure lamp

- A *contact image sensor (CIS)* is a newer form of image sensor. Unlike the CCD image sensor, the CIS doesn't use mirrors and a lens to focus the image on a stationary sensor. Instead, the CIS uses red, green, and blue LEDs on a moveable unit to illuminate the item being scanned. The reflected light is absorbed by an array of sensors just under the scanner glass on the same unit as the LEDs. Like the CCD image sensor, the CIS contains an ADC to convert the light into a digital signal. CIS devices are cheaper than CCD sensors and require less power to operate. However, sometimes the quality from a CIS is lower than that from a CCD image sensor.

- A *complimentary metal-oxide semiconductor (CMOS)* image sensor is the third type of image sensor. It works like a CCD in that an illuminated image is reflected onto its surface, but it processes the image differently using transistors built directly into its chip. CMOS sensors consume up to 10 times less power than CCDs. Although the quality of CMOS sensors is constantly improving, CCDs are still the best choice for high-end scanners because, compared to CCDs, CMOS sensors are less light-sensitive and provide lower resolution.

TWAIN, other drivers, and software

TWAIN is a standard protocol and API that defines and controls communications between a scanner or other image-capture device (such as digital cameras) and the applications on a computer. TWAIN isn't an acronym but derives its name from a line in the Rudyard Kipling poem, "The Ballad of East and West": "Oh, East is East, and West is West, and never the twain shall meet…" The name was used as a metaphor to describe the often difficult prospect of getting a scanner to communicate with a computer.

TWAIN provides a standard for communication between applications and scanners. TWAIN scanners (scanners with a TWAIN-compliant driver) are compatible with any application that supports TWAIN. Because just about every scanner has a TWAIN driver, just about any TWAIN application can communicate with any scanner. TWAIN provides a minimum level of features that you can use with each scanner.

In addition to TWAIN, there are a couple of other drivers you might encounter:

- *Windows Image Acquisition (WIA)*: This is Microsoft's driver model for image-capture devices. First implemented in Windows Me, it's available for Windows XP and Windows Vista. Most newer scanners provide WIA-compliant drivers, which provide basic functions only. WIA can be made accessible through TWAIN. Devices using TWAIN drivers are usually incapable of scanning at higher than the maximum hardware resolution (performing interpolation), because WIA supports only the actual optical resolution of a scanner. To provide interpolation (application-enhanced resolution), a third party application is required. WIA is easy to write scripts for, but setting the scanning DPI (resolution) can be problematic.

- *Image and Scanner Interface Specification (ISIS)*: ISIS is an open-standard image and scanner interface specification, the only imaging solution that lets users take full advantage of a scanner's specifications. The architecture is based on modules, so users of network scanners get a standard interface regardless of the scanner model they're using. This makes it good for large-scale imaging solutions.

- *Scanner Access Now Easy (SANE)*: An open standard that's commonly used on Linux computers. Unlike TWAIN, SANE is separated into front ends (user applications) and back ends (drivers). SANE makes network scanning relatively simple, and it supports batch scanning.

Most scanners also come with their own specific software. Such software is typically more fully featured than what's provided through the TWAIN interface alone.

The functions available in the software vary but usually include features that allow you to configure the following items:

Feature	Description
Image type	Optimizes scanning based on the type of image (grayscale, color, or line art).
Scan mode	Allows you to select high-speed or high-quality.
Scan resolution	Specifies the resolution (DPI) at which the image is scanned.
Image format	Selects the file format of the scanned image. Typically, you can choose from PNG, BMP, PDF, JPG, GIF, and TIF.
Scaling	Specifies whether the image is the same size as the original or is enlarged or reduced from the size of the original.
Image control	Allows you to invert the image (change black to white, etc. – also referred to as a "negative image"), to enable color balancing, to control the brightness and contrast of the image, to rotate the image, and to produce a mirror reflection of the image.
Preview features	Allows you to zoom in and out on the scan area without affecting the scanned image, so you can preview the scanned image. The preview area usually has a feature for selecting a specific area of the scanned image to scan to a file or printer.

Feature	Description
Scan	Performs the scan and sends the scanned image file to the destination specified in the application.
Print	Sends the scanned image file directly to a printer (either a separate attached printer or the printer that's integrated into the same multifunction unit as the scanner.
E-mail	E-mails the scanned images using the specified e-mail program.
Network sharing	Saves scan data as an image file in a specified network location. This feature is generally available only on network-connected scanners or on scanners that have a network card and the appropriate software. You can use this setting to save scanned images to a central file server, which can then share the images among multiple users.

File formats

When you scan a document, you can choose the file type, color setting (color, monochrome, grayscale), and the resolution. *Color depth*, or *bit depth*, refers to the number of colors a scanner can reproduce from the original. Not all scanners can scan at the same color depth, although some have the ability to produce a greater color depth by adding pixels to the final output. When choosing file types and other settings, here are some tips to keep in mind:

- Higher-quality, higher-resolution image files, such as some TIF files, can quickly fill up hard drive space and use more bandwidth when using network scanning or transferring across the network or though e-mail.
- Color files are larger than monochrome and grayscale files.
- If you choose to create a color file, it takes longer to scan than a monochrome or grayscale file.

File sizes and image quality depend on the settings you choose for the scan, including color, resolution, and whether the image should be reduced or enlarged. When an image of any format is enlarged beyond its original size at capture, the application is forced to introduce pixels to fill in the gaps. This process reduces overall quality dramatically. Enlargement requires more pixels so that images in formats that support great pixel density show fewer flaws when enlarged. However, enlargement beyond the original size always reduces image quality, on paper or screen (unless you are viewing from a proportionately increasing distance).

Reducing the size of images also reduces quality, but since they're smaller, the loss is practically imperceptible. Reducing (compressing) file sizes, of course, creates images that are of lower quality than they were before compression. The greater the compression, the greater the loss of resolution.

The following describes some widely used file formats for scanned image files.

File format	Description
Tagged Image File Format (TIFF or TIF)	This ISO standard format represents documents as virtual photocopies of their originals. It can be used for bi-tonal, grayscale, and color documents. It is the optimal choice for black and white. TIFF 6.0 is the most common version. Text search for content isn't possible post conversion. Although it can be compressed, it isn't the best choice for reduction or enlargement.
Portable Document Format (PDF)	Because Adobe Acrobat Reader is free, PDF is now approaching universal acceptance. It's a graphical format that represents documents as replicas of the original (raster with text or vector for Postscript). Layout is preserved, and text is stored as characters. This makes it different from most other formats and allows smaller file sizes than graphical formats. Newer Acrobat versions support XML, and PDF is a good choice for e-forms linked to databases. It's best for text or text with graphics, such as magazines. It isn't optimal if the image needs to be edited by an application and isn't an ISO standard.
Joint Photographic Experts Group (JPG or JPEG)	JPEG is an ISO-standard graphical format and compression method combined. JPEG averages fields of color to reduce variants of data, but it loses quality with compression. There are many types, including JPEG2000, an emerging standard). JPEG is best for photos, because sharp edges aren't a problem as they would be with logos, etc.. JPEG is lossy, which means it has some loss of quality due to compression, but it's the best choice for photos, paintings, and other gradient-rich images.
Graphics Interchange Format (GIF)	This is the Compuserve standard for digitized color raster images, but it's now losing ground to other formats. It allows line art to be displayed on a variety of graphics hardware and was designed as an exchange and display mechanism for graphics. GIF is lossless and, therefore, good for reduction and enlargement. It uses LZW for compression and is the best format for line art, logos, and other graphics that have few colors, because edge sharpness can be preserved. If speed – not file size – is important, uncompressed bitmap formats are better than GIF. GIF is limited to 256 colors but is a great choice for simpler images that require enlargement. GIF is increasingly replaced by PNG.
Portable Network Graphics (PNG)	The ISO-standard PNG file format is now the de facto standard for many scanner manufacturers. Developed as a solution to a licensing scheme around the GIF file format, PNG supports more colors than GIF and provides lossless compression. PNG is a good choice for images with sharp edges, such as line art and logos, and PNG can handle gradient-rich images as well as or better than JPEG, although the PNG file sizes are larger than JPEG. PNG handles transparency better than other file formats, enabling you to place a PNG image over just about any background without loss of quality.

Scanning process

When you scan a document or photograph, after an original is laid on the glass or fed into a multifunction device, the scanner performs the process described below:

1. The document is illuminated by a lamp.
2. The light reflected by the document is acquired by the image sensor.
3. The light (analog signal) is converted to digital signals by the *analog-to-digital converter (ADC)*.
4. The digital signals are processed and presented to the application that initiated the scan or the application that's associated with the scanner and file type.

Do it!

B-1: Examining the scan process

Be sure to have working and nonworking scanners ready before the start of this activity. The working scanner should be connected to your computer and ready to scan.

Select various scan settings for each document or picture. Be sure to have documents with anti-counterfeiting features.

As you scan several documents and pictures, walk students through the steps in the scan process.

Here's how	Here's why
1 Observe the scanners at your instructor's work station	Be sure to follow standard ESD and electrical safety procedures.
2 Work with your instructor and the other students to identify as many of the scanner components as you can	Refer to the book if necessary.
3 Watch as your instructor scans several documents and pictures	
4 Work with your instructor to identify the various steps and components as each page is scanning	
5 Scan several documents and pictures using different settings and file formats	To examine the impact different settings and file formats have on the scan process.

Unit summary: Printing and scanning

Topic A In this topic, you learned to identify printer components and the steps in both the inkjet and EP print process. You learned to identify laser printer components, such as the **developer** unit, the **fuser** unit, and the **power supply**, and inkjet printer components, such as the **print heads** and the **carriage**.

Topic B In this topic, you learned about scanners and the scanning process. You learned about the **TWAIN** standard and about file formats, such as **PDF, JPG, TIF,** and **GIF.** You also learned about scanner components, such as the **CCD, CIS,** and the **CMOS.** Finally, you learned about the scan process and how it produces image files.

Review questions

1 Which of the following Windows components renders graphics for output on a printer or monitor?

   A EMF

   B GDI

   C API

   D Win32

2 Which of the following Windows components provides layout and instructions for each print job?

   A Spooler

   B API

   C Win32

   D HVPS

3 Which of the following are printer control languages? (Choose all that apply.)

   A PostScript

   B Win32

   C API

   D PCL

4 Windows Vista introduced a new print specification called _____.

   XML Paper Specification (XPS)

5 True or false? Monochrome printers print in both black-and-white and color.

   False

6 What are the colors used in RGB?

   Red, green, and blue.

7 What are the colors used in CMYK?

   Cyan, magenta, yellow, and black.

8 _____ color is the method of creating color using pigment or paint.

Subtractive

9 _____ color is the method of creating color using colored lights.

Additive

10 Which of the following color combinations is most often used in color printing?

   A RGB

   B RBYK

   C CYK

   D CMYK

11 _____ is the term used to describe the entire range of colors a printing device can produce.

Color gamut

12 The resolution of text and graphics is measured in _____ per inch.

dots

13 _____ is the onboard software that controls the printer's functions.

Firmware

14 _____ is a property of liquids that describes their ability to flow.

Viscosity

15 Which of the following are the two methods used to apply ink to paper in an inkjet printer? (Choose all that apply.)

   A Piezomagnetic

   B Thermal bubble

   C Piezoelectric

   D Thermal magnetic

16 EP printers use which two technologies to write images onto a photoconductive drum?

Laser and LED

17 In an EP printer, which component charges the drum?

Primary corona or charge roller

18 What are the two types of toner?

Mono-component and dual-component

19 The _____ blade ensures that only a thin layer of toner is removed from the toner trough by the magnetic roller.

doctor, skimming, or metering

20 The paper is given a positive charge by which of the following components?

   A Primary corona

   B Pawls

   C Transfer corona

   D Fuser

21 A thermistor monitors temperature in which of the following EP printer assemblies?

   A Primary corona

   B Transfer corona

   C Fuser

   D Toner cartridge

22 What's the importance of heat in the EP print process?

   The heat melts the toner and fuses it to the paper.

23 Which of the following components pushes paper into the printer at the start of the paper path?

   A Heated roller

   B Pickup roller

   C Separation pad

   D Transfer corona

24 What's the function of the registration assembly?

   The registration assembly keeps the paper flat and ensures that it's in the proper position inside the printer.

25 True or false? A duplex unit enables the printer to print two pages simultaneously.

   False

26 Which of the following components is used to feed multi-page documents into a scanner or fax machine?

   A RGB

   B MSD

   C API

   D ADF

27 There are _____ sheets in a ream of paper.

   500

28 Which of the following paper weights is commonly used for everyday printing?

　A 10

　B 20

　C 65

　D 100

29 Which of the following is a brightness rating of typical printer paper?

　A 20

　B 68

　C 92

　D 100

30 Inkjet paper typically has a coating of which material?

　A Clay

　B Plastic

　C Wax

　D Silicon

31 Which of the following are common scanner image sensors? (Choose all that apply.)

　A CDD

　B CCD

　C CIS

　D CSI

32 True or false? TWAIN is a standard that defines communication standards between a scanner and a computer.

　True

33 Which of the following is Microsoft's driver model for image-capture devices?

　A SANE

　B ISIS

　C WIA

　D Win32

34 Which of the following file formats include compression as part of their specification? (Choose all that apply.)

   A TIF

   B PDF

   C JPG

   D PNG

Independent practice activity

In this activity, you'll identify printer and scanner components and examine the print and scan processes. (Note: Be sure the printers and scanners you use are NOT connected to a power supply. Be sure to follow proper electrical safety and ESD procedures.)

1 Use the printer provided to you to identify the printer components you learned about in this unit. Make notes detailing the name and location of each component you're able to identify. If necessary, make a quick sketch of the component and its location in the printer. You might not be able to find every component listed in this unit.

2 Use the scanner provided to you to identify the scanner components you learned about in this unit. Make note detailing the name and location of each component you're able to identify. You might not be able to find every component listed in this unit.

Unit 3
Connectivity

Unit time: 150 minutes

Complete this unit, and you'll know how to:

A Connect to and use local printers and scanners.

B Connect to and use network printers and identify network scanning requirements.

Topic A: Local printing and scanning

This topic covers the following CompTIA PDI+ exam objectives.

#	Objective

5.4	**Identify the basic purpose and use of printer drivers**
	• Install, remove and update drivers (using Windows 2000 and XP)
	• Verify driver versions
	• Follow manufacturer documentation when installing USB devices (software vs. hardware install)
	• Basic features and settings of printer drivers
	   • Duplex printing, tray settings, media settings, paper sizes, finishing, quantity, scaling
	• Printer control languages
	   • PCL, Postscript, GDI, PJL
	   • Demonstrate awareness of vendor specific drivers and languages
	• Spooling
	   • Operation and configuration
	• Differentiate between shared printing and direct printing
	• Demonstrate awareness of the effect of application settings on driver settings

5.5	**Identify common device ports**
	• Types of physical ports
	   • LPT, USB, Serial, Firewire, Parallel, miniparallel, SCSI
	• Types of memory card slots
	   • SD Slot, Compact Flash
	• Assignment of printer driver to ports

Local printing versus network shared printing

In this unit we're going to cover both *local printing*, which is printing directly to a printer connected the computer you're working on, and *network printing*, which is printing to a shared printer connected to a print server on the network or connected directly to the network by an onboard network adapter.

Ports and cables

Every computer has special sockets called *ports*. Cables from external devices and sometimes the devices themselves are connected to a computer using these ports. Common ports include serial, parallel, USB, and IEEE 1394.

Serial ports

Serial ports are the connectors into which you plug devices that use serial transmission to communicate with your PC. Although many types of devices and ports use serial transmission, when most people speak of serial ports, they mean the communications-oriented (COM) ports to which you connect devices, such as modems.

You can use your system's BIOS setup utility or Windows Device Manager to configure the resources used by these ports. Plug and Play (PnP) should detect these settings and configure Windows accordingly. You can use Windows Device Manager to view the status of any connected device.

Serial connectors are typically either 9-pin or 25-pin connectors. Few modern devices use the 25-pin connector, instead favoring the smaller 9-pin variety. Connectors come in two types, called *genders*. Male connectors have pins, and female connectors have sockets, as shown in Exhibit 3-1.

Exhibit 3-1: Male and female connectors (left to right)

PCs typically have the male connector, while devices, such as printers and multifunction devices, usually have the female connector. Thus, to connect a serial device, you need a cable with a male connector on one end and a female connector on the other end.

By convention, the serial ports on modern PCs are teal-colored or surrounded by a teal label. This color helps you differentiate the serial port from the other connectors on your PC. Sometimes serial ports are labeled with "COM" or with a series of ones and zeros to suggest the one-by-one transmission of the serial transmission of the data bits.

In male-to-female cables, the pins at one end of the cable are connected to sockets at the other end. In male-to-male cables, pins connect to pins, and in female-to-female cables, sockets connect to sockets.

Serial cables come in two forms: straight-through and null modem. You use *straight-through cables* to connect your PC to serial devices. You use a *null modem cable* to connect two PCs, as if each were connected to a modem.

In a straight-through cable, the corresponding pins and sockets at each end of the cable are connected. In other words, pin 1 is connected to socket 1, pin 2 to socket 2, and so forth.

In a null modem cable, pins at one end of the cable are connected to specific pins at the other end to simulate the presence of a modem between two devices. A pin at one end of the cable might be connected to two or more pins at the other.

Do it!

You need to supply students with a serial cable.

A-1: Connecting a serial cable

Here's how	Here's why
1 Locate the serial port on your PC and describe how you know that it's the serial port	Serial ports on a PC are 9-pin male connectors, usually teal or surrounded by a teal label. Some serial ports are labeled as COM ports or have 01010-type labels that indicate a serial transmission of bits.
2 On the cable supplied by your instructor, determine which end connects to your PC and which end connects to an external serial device	
3 Attach the serial cable to your computer	

Parallel ports

Explanation

Parallel ports are the connectors into which you plug devices that use parallel transmission to communicate with your PC. Most often, when people speak of parallel ports, they're referring to the LPT ports used for printers. LPT stands for line printer, reflecting the use of this sort of port with early-model PCs. SCSI is an example of another technology that uses parallel transmission.

The basic PC hardware supports two LPT ports: LPT1 and LPT2. You can add additional LPT ports through expansion adapters. Many modern printers don't use the LPT port at all, instead favoring the newer and more capable USB port. *Normal* or *default* printer ports are LPT ports with a one-way communications port: the PC sends data to the printer, but the printer never sends data to the PC. Few modern printers support this old unidirectional parallel-port mode.

Various techniques have been used to enable two-way communications, among them *standard parallel port (SPP), enhanced parallel port (EPP),* and *extended capabilities port (ECP).* Modern PCs support each of these modes. You can use the BIOS setup utility to enable or disable specific modes.

The Centronics operational mode was originally conceived by the Centronics Corporation. However, Epson Corp. developed the actual mode and connector style used with PCs and printers.

With any of the bidirectional port technologies, the PC and printer must communicate their status to each other. With SPP, the method they use is called *compatibility* or *Centronics mode.* In this method, the PC puts data onto the appropriate wires of the parallel port and then checks other wires for the printer's state, indicated by a positive or negative voltage on various wires in the parallel port. If the printer is busy, the PC waits and then tries again.

EPP and ECC enable the PC to check the printer's status before sending data. That alone saves wasted time if the printer is busy. Additionally, these ports use DMA and enhanced handshaking protocols to speed data transfer across the parallel port.

Typically, parallel ports are 25-pin ports. The PC normally uses a female D-connector, matching that used by a 25-pin serial port, though opposite in gender on the PC and devices.

Connectivity **3-5**

By convention, the parallel ports on modern PCs are magenta-colored or are surrounded by a magenta label. This color helps you differentiate the parallel port from the other connectors on your PC. Sometimes parallel ports are labeled with a printer symbol.

Printers normally feature a 36-pin Centronics connector, officially called the Centronics-36 connector. The female connector is mounted on the printer. The mini-parallel, or mini-Centronics, connector is a smaller version of the Centronics connector, but it still has 36-pins. The mini-parallel connector is found on the printer end of the cable; however, it isn't a widely used standard.

Older SCSI devices used a 50-pin Centronics connector. Typical parallel printer cables feature a male DB-25 connector on the end that you connect to the PC and a male Centronics-36 connector on the printer end.

Do it!

You need to supply students with a parallel cable.

A-2: Connecting a parallel cable

Here's how	Here's why
1 Locate the parallel port on your PC and describe how you know that it's the parallel port	Parallel ports on a PC are 25-pin female connectors, usually pink or bright magenta, or surrounded by a pink or bright magenta label. Some parallel ports are labeled as LPT ports or with small printer icons.
2 On the cable supplied by your instructor, determine which end connects to your PC and which to the printer	
3 Attach the parallel cable to your computer	

Universal Serial Bus (USB)

Explanation

The *Universal Serial Bus (USB)* is a standardized peripheral specification developed by Compaq, Digital Electronics Corp., IBM, Intel, Microsoft, NEC, and Northern Telecom. USB defines an architecture for buses, similar in concept to the PCI or ISA buses, to which you can connect one or more expansion devices. USB offers these features:

- Hot-swapping and self-configuration
- Multiple device support
- High-speed data transfer

The USB specification is an active and growing standard. Currently there are two popular versions: USB 1.1 and USB 2.0.

Version	Transfer rates	Notes
USB 1.1	12 Mbps	Generally called just USB. Still sometimes used by devices, such as keyboards and mice that don't require the high-speed data transfers or other functions provided by the USB 2.0 specification.
USB 2.0	Low-speed: 1.5 Mbps Full-speed: 12 Mbps High-speed: 480 Mbps	Backward-compatible with USB 1.1, in that you can connect USB 1.1 devices to this bus, but they'll operate at USB 1.1 speeds and the entire bus is slowed to USB 1.1 speeds. Most USB 2.0 devices also work on a USB 1.1 bus, but at USB 1.1 speeds (USB 2.0's full-speed mode).

Exhibit 3-2: The USB port symbol

You can determine which USB version a device supports by examining the USB logo on the device or its connector. USB connectors are typically identified by the symbol shown in Exhibit 3-2. Devices that comply with the USB 2.0 specification often display the label shown in Exhibit 3-3.

Exhibit 3-3: The USB 2.0 label

On Windows computers, you can use Device Manager to determine which type of USB is available in your system. USB 2.0 hosts, which Windows calls hubs, include "Enhanced" in their names. Hubs without that word in the name are USB 1.1 hubs. Modern computer systems often include hubs of both types.

USB ports and connectors come in two shapes, generally called Type A and Type B. Both types use four pins or conductors. Type A ports and connectors are wide and flat and are used at the PC end of a USB-to-device connection. If the device uses a removable cable rather than a permanently connected one, it uses the Type B connector. These two types of ports and connectors are shown in Exhibit 3-4 and Exhibit 3-5.

Exhibit 3-4: USB ports: Type A (left) and Type B (right)

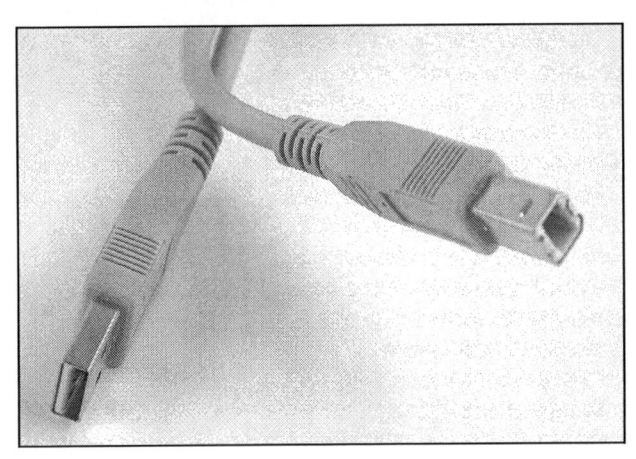

Exhibit 3-5: USB connectors: Type A (left) and Type B (right)

The USB host provides the USB bus with 5-volt power at up to 6 amps. Some devices can use this as their sole source of power, although most peripheral devices require too much power to rely solely on the USB bus for power. Devices, such as external printers, must be plugged into an electrical outlet. However, low-power devices, such as some scanners, can rely solely on the USB bus for power. You can run into problems if you connect too many unpowered devices to the bus, and in some situations, you need to place a powered USB hub between the computer and the peripherals.

Do it!

A-3: Connecting a USB cable

Here's how	Here's why
1 Locate one or more USB ports on your PC	Ports are often included on both the front and back of the unit.
2 Determine whether your PC's USB ports are USB 1.1 or USB 2.0 ports, and describe how you were able to determine this information	The labels accompanying the ports might indicate the USB version, or you might have to use Windows Device Manager to determine the answer.
3 Examine the USB cable supplied by your instructor to locate the Type A and Type B connectors	
4 Connect the USB cable to your computer	

Supply students with a mix of USB 1.1 and 2.0 Type A and Type B cables.

IEEE 1394

Explanation

Institute of Electrical and Electronics Engineers (IEEE) 1394, also known as *FireWire* and *i.Link*, is a high-speed peripheral interconnection bus. IEEE 1394 offers these features:

- Hot-swapping and self-configuration
- Multiple device support: You can connect a maximum of 63 devices to the IEEE 1394 bus.
- High-speed data transfer: IEEE 1394 supports transfer rates of 800 Mbps and beyond.
- Asynchronous and isochronous transfer modes: IEEE 1394 supports devices that require time-critical transfers on the bus.

The IEEE 1394 specification has undergone some revisions since its original release. Some people now refer to the original IEEE 1394 specification as *FireWire 400*. IEEE 1394b is the next revision and is sometimes called *FireWire 800*.

- FireWire 400 supports data transfers of up to 400 Mbps with cable lengths of up to 4.5 meters.
- FireWire 800 supports transfers at up to 800 Mbps with cable lengths of up to 4.5 meters.

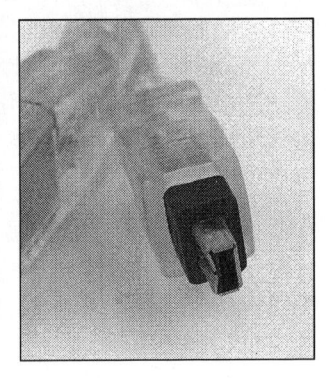

Exhibit 3-6: A 4-pin FireWire 400 port and connector

FireWire 400 devices use either a 4- or 6-pin connector. The 4-pin connector doesn't supply power to the device. The two additional pins in a 6-pin connector provide voltage and ground, thereby delivering power to a connected device. Examples of these connectors are shown in Exhibit 3-6 and Exhibit 3-7.

Exhibit 3-7: A 6-pin FireWire 400 port and connector

FireWire 800 devices use a 9-pin connector at both ends of the cable. With the appropriate adapter cables, you can connect FireWire 400 devices into FireWire 800 ports and vice versa. FireWire 800 devices operate at full speed only when you connect them to a FireWire 800 port.

The IEEE specification calls for up to 1.5 amps at 30 V for a total of 45 watts of power provided on the IEEE 1394 bus. This is considerably higher than USB, so you should have fewer problems connecting un-powered IEEE 1394 devices to the bus.

Do it!

A-4: Connecting an IEEE 1394 cable

Supply students with a mix of IEEE 1394 and 1394b cables.

Here's how	Here's why
1 Locate one or more IEEE 1394 ports on your PC	Many PCs don't include these ports on the motherboard. They're added, instead, through expansion cards.
2 Do the IEEE 1394 ports on your PC support FireWire 400 or FireWire 800, and how can you tell?	You can tell by examining the connector. FireWire 800 uses a 9-pin connector, whereas FireWire 400 uses a 6-pin connector at the PC.
3 Examine the IEEE 1394 cable supplied by your instructor and determine the IEEE 1394 specification it supports	
4 Connect the IEEE 1394 cable to your computer	

Printer drivers

Printer drivers are small software applications that enable the computer and applications to communicate with the printer. The print drivers work with the GDI to render the print job in a format the printer understands.

Driver settings

You can use printer drivers, printer software, and Windows print properties for a selected printer to configure the following settings (not all settings are available for all printers):

- *Duplex printing*: Use this setting to configure double-sided printing.
- *Tray settings*: Select the tray to pull paper for a specific print job. Using these settings you can select the tray or drawer into which you've loaded special paper, such as colored paper or paper with a business letterhead.
- *Media settings*: Select paper size, such as letter or legal (or any size your printer supports) and specify whether the page is printed in *portrait* (top-to-bottom) or *landscape* (side-to-side) orientation.
- *Scaling*: Select whether to print the document or photo at the same size or larger or smaller than the original file.
- *Color and print quality*: You can choose to print in color, if you have a color printer, or in grayscale or monochrome. You can choose to make the printed page lighter or darker than the default, and you can select the print resolution.
- *Quantity*: The number of copies you want to print.
- *Finishing*: You can choose to have the printed pages collated, stapled, hole-punched, or more, depending on whether your printer has a finisher that supports these functions.

Applications, such as Word or Photoshop, have a set of properties that you can configure for a job you're printing from the application. Generally, applications work with the printer driver for the selected printer to format the job correctly. Some application settings might not be available if your printer doesn't support them. Unavailable options are grayed out in the application's Print dialog box.

Print control languages

There are several industry-standard printer languages, known as *printer control languages* or *page description languages*. You can use them for advanced desktop publishing jobs that contain special fonts or graphics that might otherwise degrade in the translation into a generic print job.

- PostScript, created by Adobe Systems
- Printer Command Language (PCL) and Printer Job Language (PJL), both created by HP

If you have a printer that recognizes one of these languages, you can program print jobs that take advantage of the finer control you can get by directly creating print jobs using a specific language. However, most day-to-day jobs don't require any special programming.

Inkjet printer installation

Most inkjet printers today connect via USB, so when you connect the printer, Windows automatically detects it and attempts to install the driver for you. Exhibit 3-8 shows the bubble alerting you that new hardware was found on your computer.

Exhibit 3-8: New hardware bubble

Your printer probably shipped with a CD-ROM containing drivers and additional software to enhance the printing quality. You should follow the manufacturer's recommendation for installing the printer: some tell you simply to connect the printer and let Windows install the printer drivers, while others direct you to install software and drivers first before connecting the printer to the computer.

One useful utility that's usually installed with a printer is a monitor for the ink levels in the cartridges. This helps you know when ink supplies are getting low and need to be replaced. Exhibit 3-9 shows the utility displayed during a print job. Notice that it includes information about the printer's status and about the print cartridges ink levels.

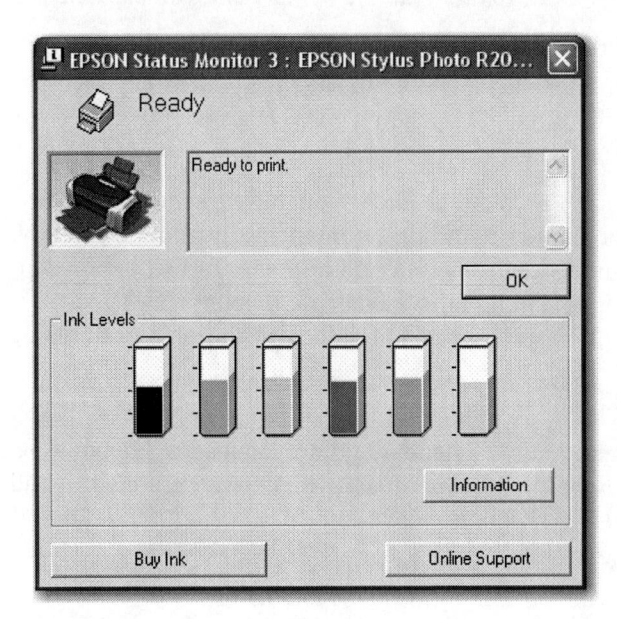

Exhibit 3-9: Ink level utility

Printer interfaces

Most inkjet printers today are connected by USB interfaces. In supporting inkjet printers, you might encounter some that still use the parallel port interface, although it's unlikely that you will. Even less likely, you might encounter some with SCSI or serial interfaces. Exhibit 3-10 shows the communications interfaces on an inkjet printer. In this case, this printer has a parallel and a USB port.

Exhibit 3-10: Communications interfaces on an inkjet printer

Be sure to specify the appropriate interface in Windows according to the connection type of the printer:

- If the connection type is SCSI, be sure to assign a unique device ID.
- If the connection type is parallel, be sure to specify the correct LPT port.
- If the connection type is serial, verify that you've specified the correct COM port.

Exhibit 3-11 shows Device Manager information for a printer connected to a computer.

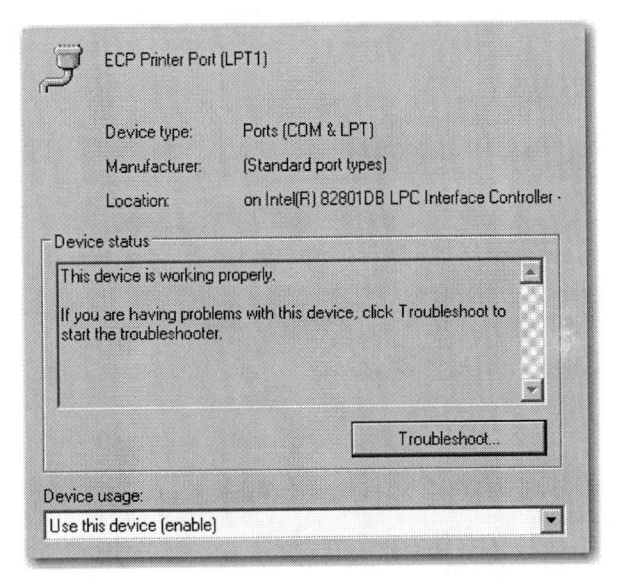

Exhibit 3-11: Port identified for the printer

Removable storage

Some printers also allow you to print directly from a removable storage card, such as a *Secure Digital (SD)* card, as shown in Exhibit 3-12, or a *Compact Flash* card. These cards provide nonvolatile storage that you can use in many multimedia devices, including cameras and some smart phones.

Exhibit 3-12: SD card

You can insert these cards directly into a slot on the printer, such as the ones shown in Exhibit 3-13, and access their contents, including documents and photos. Some printers have a small screen on which you can view thumbnails of the files stored on the card so you can choose which to print. If you can't insert these cards into a printer, you can often insert them into a computer, especially newer multimedia and notebook computers, and external card readers. You can then print the files from the computer, just as you would with a file on the hard disk.

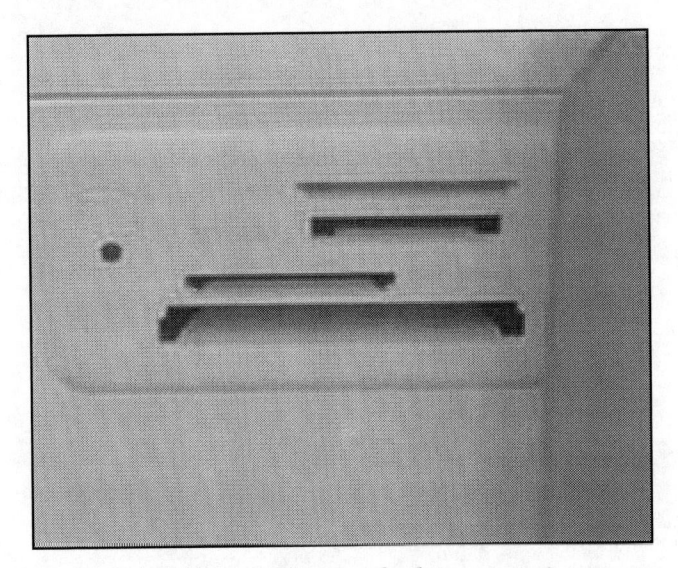

Exhibit 3-13: SD and other cards slots on a printer

Installing an inkjet printer

To install an inkjet printer in Windows 2000, Windows XP, or Windows Vista:

1 Connect the printer to a computer, using the correct interface.
2 Plug the printer in to a nearby outlet.
3 Power it up. Windows is likely to recognize the new device and automatically install the required drivers.
4 If the drivers aren't installed automatically, you can install them manually, using the materials that shipped with the printer or one of the hardware wizards in any of the versions of Windows.

Alternately, you can use an installation program that comes from the manufacturer. Sometimes you just need to run an executable file before you connect the printer to the computer so the driver is on the hard disk and available to Windows for PnP installation.

USB printers can be hot-plugged (connected while the computer is powered up), but if the printer connection is SCSI or parallel, the PC has to be powered down before the printer is connected.

To configure print settings:

1 In the Printers window (Windows 2000 and Windows Vista) or the Printers and Faxes window (Windows XP), right-click the printer and choose Properties.
2 Use the settings on the tabs to configure printer options.

To verify the version of a printer driver in Windows 2000, Windows XP, and Windows Vista:

1 In Device Manager, right-click the printer and choose Properties.
2 On the Driver tab, view the name, date, version, and signature information for the current driver.

To update a device driver:

1 In Windows XP and Windows Vista, in Device Manager, right-click the printer and choose Update Driver. (In Windows 2000, in Device Manager, right-click the printer and choose Properties. On the Driver tab, click Update Driver.)
2 Complete the wizard to install the new driver.

To remove a printer (and leave the printer driver files intact), right-click on the printer icon, choose Delete, and confirm the deletion. To delete the driver files:

1 Right-click in a blank area of the Printers and Faxes window (in Windows XP) or the Printers window (in Windows 2000 and Windows Vista), and choose Server Properties.
2 On the Drivers tab, select the driver you want to delete and click Remove.
3 Confirm the deletion.

To print a test page:

1 In the Printers window of Windows 2000 or Windows Vista or in the Printers and Faxes window of Windows XP, right-click the printer and choose Properties.
2 On the General tab, click Print Test Page.

CompTIA PDI+ Certification

Do it!

A-5: Installing an inkjet printer

Have students work in groups, if necessary, or have them work individually and pass around the printer. You could also all work together with one printer on a single computer.

Here's how	Here's why
1 If necessary, turn on your computer	You'll install an inkjet printer on your computer.
Log on to Windows XP as **PDIADMIN##** with a password of **Pa$$321**	(Where ## is your unique student number.)
2 Connect the power cord to the printer, but don't turn the printer on yet	
3 Connect the interface cable to the printer	The interface cable, varies based on the connection type the printer uses. Most current inkjet printers are USB printers, but some also have parallel or serial ports, and some have SCSI ports.
4 Plug the power cord into an electrical outlet	If possible, plug it into a surge protector strip.
5 Connect the interface cable to the computer	The port varies based on the connection type the printer is using.
6 Insert paper in the printer	If none is loaded.
Install print cartridges	If they aren't already installed. Refer to the printer's documentation for the cartridge installation procedure.
Turn on the printer	The Found New Hardware wizard displays.
7 Select **Yes, this time only**	You could select the other options, but for classroom purposes, we'll choose this option.
Click **Next**	
8 Click **Next**	To install the software automatically, the default selection.
9 Click **Back**	If the software wasn't found.
10 Select **Install from a list or specific location**	
Click **Next**	

Connectivity **3–17**

11	Select the appropriate option	If you have the drivers on CD or floppy disk or have downloaded them, select Search for the best driver in these locations, then check the appropriate option. If the driver is provided by the operating system, you can choose "Don't search. I will choose the driver to install."
	Click **Next**	Follow the prompts to finish installing the drivers.
	If appropriate, cancel the wizard, then install the software from the appropriate location	Some printers require that you install software from the manufacturer's CD or from a download rather than installing the driver through the Add Hardware wizard.
12	Click **Start**, **Printers and Faxes**	Your newly installed printer should be listed.
13	Right-click the printer	
	Choose **Properties**	
	Click **Print Test Page**	
	Click **OK**	Verify that the test page printed correctly.
14	If possible, insert an SD card or other media card and select a photo or file to print	
	Print the file	
15	Print several pages using various printer features	
16	Close all open windows and dialog boxes	

Provide students with a media card pre-loaded with files.

Laser printer installation

Explanation

When a printer is shipped from the factory, the toner cartridge is removed to prevent spills and damage to the printer from internal spillage. Therefore, the first step to installing a laser printer is to install the toner cartridge. Check the documentation with the toner cartridge for installation procedures. It usually begins with gently rocking the cartridge from side to side. This distributes the toner, as it likely settled during shipment.

On some printers, the drum and various other components are outside the cartridge. If this is the case, refer to the documentation for how and where to install these components.

Laser printers usually come with chunks of Styrofoam inserted where the toner cartridge will be installed. Other components might be secured with sticky tape, so that they don't move during shipment. Be sure to remove all of the packing materials and tape before trying to use the printer.

Interfaces

Laser printers are used in a wide variety of situations. These printers have the most widely varied connection types of any printers. Most laser printers have two or more connection interfaces. These include:

- Parallel
- SCSI
- USB
- Serial
- IEEE 1394/FireWire
- Wired or wireless Ethernet network connections

Examples of the communications interfaces on a laser printer are shown in Exhibit 3-14.

Exhibit 3-14: Communications interfaces on a laser printer

Connectivity **3-19**

Installing a laser printer

To install a laser printer on a Windows 2000, Windows XP, or Windows Vista computer:

1. Connect the printer to the computer using the correct interface.
2. Plug it in.
3. Power it up. Windows might recognize that you've connected a new device and install drivers for it automatically.
4. If drivers aren't installed automatically, you can do it manually, using the materials that shipped with the printer or one of the hardware wizards in any of the versions of Windows.

Alternately, you can use the installation program provided by the manufacturer. As with inkjet printers, sometimes you just need to run an executable file before you connect the printer to the computer.

USB printers can be hot plugged, but if they are SCSI or parallel, the PC has to be powered down before the printer is connected. Some LP manufacturers recommend plugging their devices directly into a wall outlet that supports a ground connector.

To configure print settings, view driver version, and remove or update the driver, you can use the same steps you'd use for an inkjet printer and your specific operating system.

Do it!

Have students work in groups, if necessary, or have them work individually and pass around the printer, if possible. You could also all work together with one printer on a single computer.

Some laser printers need to be configured to specify the port, the printer language, and other settings prior to installation. If the printer the students are installing needs such settings configured, guide students through the process or provide them with the documentation to do it themselves.

A-6: Installing a laser printer

Here's how	Here's why
1 Connect the power cord to the printer	You're going to install a laser printer on your computer.
2 Connect the interface cable to the printer	The interface cable varies, based on the connection type the printer uses.
3 Plug the power cord into an electrical outlet	If possible, on a surge protector strip.
4 Connect the interface cable to the computer	
5 If necessary, insert paper into the printer	(Consult the printer documentation or ask your instructor for help.)
Install the toner cartridge	If it isn't already installed. Refer to the printer documentation for the toner cartridge installation procedure. Also, if any other components need to be installed prior to printing, install those components as well.
Turn on the printer	The Found New Hardware wizard displays.
6 Select **Yes, this time only**	You could select the other options, but for classroom purposes, we'll choose this option.
Click **Next**	

7	Click **Next**	To install the software automatically, the default selection.
8	Click **Back**	If the software isn't found.
9	Select **Install from a list or specific location** Click **Next**	
10	Select the appropriate option	If you have the drivers on CD or floppy disk or have downloaded them, select Search for the best driver in these locations, then check the appropriate option. If the driver is provided by the operating system, you can choose "Don't search. I will choose the driver to install."
	Click **Next**	Follow the prompts to finish installing the drivers.
	If appropriate, cancel the wizard, then install the software from the appropriate location	
11	Click **Start**, **Printers and Faxes**	Your newly installed printer should be listed.
12	Right-click the printer Choose **Properties** Click **Print Test Page** Click **OK**	Verify that the test page prints successfully.
13	Print several pages using different features of the printer, and then close all open windows and dialog boxes	To test various settings, including tray settings, duplexing, and finishing.

Scanner installation

Scanners used to be either slow parallel port devices or SCSI devices that were temperamental and not easily configured. Current offerings are mostly USB or IEEE 1394 devices that are plug-and-play compatible.

After connecting the scanner to your PC, if necessary, plug the scanner into a power outlet (an adaptor is provided). Remember that some scanners are powered through their USB connection and don't require external power. You're likely to be prompted to install the appropriate drivers for your scanner. Alternatively, your scanner might require you to install the software it shipped with before connecting it to your computer. Always check the scanner's documentation to determine the proper connection procedure.

USB scanners can be hot plugged, but if they're SCSI or parallel, the PC has to be powered down before the scanner is connected.

To update a device driver:

1 In Windows XP and Windows Vista, in Device Manager, right-click the scanner and choose Update Driver. (In Windows 2000, in Device Manager, right-click the scanner and choose Properties. On the Driver tab, click Update Driver.)
2 Complete the wizard to install the new driver.

You can also use the manufacturer's installation program to install a new driver. After attaching the scanner, scan a test page to ensure that the scanner is working properly.

Do it!

A-7: Installing a scanner

Here's how	Here's why
1 Determine the connection type for the scanner	You're going to connect a scanner to your computer.
2 Locate a cable that's compatible with the scanner connection	It's likely a USB, SCSI, IEEE 1394, or parallel port connection.
3 Connect the scanner to the computer	Using the appropriate cable.
4 If necessary, connect the scanner to the power outlet	
5 Install the software to create scanned images	If the scanner also includes OCR software, you can install that as well.
6 Scan a picture	To test the scanner. You can use a page from this course, if you don't have another picture to scan.

Have various students scan the same picture at different resolutions or using various file formats, so that they can compare the results.

Topic B: Network printing and scanning

This topic covers the following CompTIA PDI+ exam objectives.

#	Objective

5.1	**Identify and describe basic network and communications technologies**
	• Protocols
	   • TCP/IP
	• Communication settings
	   • 10/100/1000 Mbps
	   • Dialog modes (ie: simplex, half/full duplex, auto negotiation)
	• Physical connections
	   • Port types (ie: RJ-45)
	   • Cable types (ie: UTP, STP, CAT-5 crossover/standard cable)
	   • Network interface card
	• Wireless connectivity
	   • 802.11x, SSID, WEP-WPA encryption, infrastructure vs. adhoc
	   • Bluetooth, infrared
	• Fax / modem
	   • Port types (ie: RJ-11)
	   • Analog phone line
	   • Transmission speeds (ie: baud rates)

5.2	**Describe and demonstrate the use of the TCP/IP protocol and related tools**
	• Static addressing
	   • IP address, Subnet mask, Default gateway, DNS
	• Dynamic addressing
	   • DHCP
	   • APIPA
	• Validate network connectivity using tools and utilities
	   • PING, IPCONFIG, TELNET, NSLOOKUP, web browser, configuration page, cross-over cable
	   • Link lights (LEDs), Activity lights

#	Objective
5.3	Identify the basics of network scanning technologies
	• Requirements to utilize Scan to Email functionality
	• SMTP, authentication, POP3, LDAP, file size limitation
	• Requirements to utilize Scan to Folder functionality
	• Shared folder on network, permission levels, SMB, UNC path
	• Requirements to utilize Scan to File functionality
	• Application based, drivers, TWAIN, ISIS
	• Requirements to utilize Scan to FTP functionality
	• FTP server, permissions
5.5	**Identify common device ports**
	• Type of network ports
	• LPR, RAW, port 9100, SMB – Simple TCP/IP, External print server port

Wired networks

To form a network, computers need a pathway to connect to each other. A network can be a physical connection of one type of wire or cabling or another. It can also be a connection through radio waves, infrared, or other wireless connection methods. In this section we'll cover networks that require wires and cabling.

Network wiring

Until recently, most networks have used *unshielded twisted pair (UTP)* or *shielded twisted pair (STP)* cabling to connect computers or other devices in the network. Both are composed of four pairs of wires. The wires in each pair are twisted around each other, and the pairs are twisted together and bundled within a covering.

UTP cable comes in categories. Each category has a specific use, number of *twists per foot (TPF)*, and a speed rating. The more twists, the less crosstalk and electrical magnetic interference (EMI) that affects the data on the cable.

- *Cat3* cable used to be dominant, however it operates at up to only 10 Mbps with about two or three twists per foot.
- *Cat5* cable is the current standard. It operates at up to 100 Mbps. *Cat5e* operates at up to 1 Gbps. These cables have a range of 20 twists per foot.
- *Cat6* cables use higher quality materials for data conduction and have the potential to operate at up to 2.5 Gbps.

RJ-45 connectors on UTP cables look a lot like the regular RJ-11 snap-in telephone connectors, except they're a little larger. The RJ-45 connects eight wires, as opposed to six in the RJ-11. The jacks, with which the two types of connectors mate, have corresponding conductor counts and different sizes. An RJ-45 connector won't fit into an RJ-11 jack. Examples of RJ-45 and RJ-11 cables are shown in Exhibit 3-15.

Exhibit 3-15: RJ-45 connector at left and RJ-11 at right

In addition to UTP and STP cable, *fiber optic cables*, which carry data as light through strands of glass finer than a human hair, are the fastest and the most expensive transmission medium yet devised. Fiber optic cabling is used as the *backbone* for network (a backbone is the main line running through a building from which network traffic devices and twisted-pair cabling runs are connected). Fiber optic cable is also used for long distance lines run by telephone and cable companies to deliver information around the world.

Ethernet networks

Ethernet is the most common form of network in use today, because it strikes a good balance of ease of setup and use, speed, and cost. Three versions of Ethernet architecture are available now. Each version is distinguished primarily by the speed at which it operates. Each version can be set up using various types of wire or cable, but the different speeds of the versions and the various conditions in which they operate might dictate what type of connecting wires is used. Computers and other devices (through their *network interface cards*, or *NICs*) and the network use a process of *auto-negotiation* to determine which speed they use to communicate.

- *10-Mbps Ethernet* operates at a speed of 10 megabits per second (Mbps) of data. The first Ethernet version was developed by the Xerox Corporation in the 1970s. It later became known as Ethernet IEEE 802.3. There are several variations of the 10-Mbps Ethernet, distinguished by the type of cable and connectors used.
- *100-Mbps Ethernet* (also called *Fast Ethernet*) operates at a speed of 100 Mbps. It can also handle data at 10 Mbps, and this feature allows devices running at the slower speed to operate on the same network along with those operating at 100 Mbps. As with 10-Mbps Ethernet, there are variations of 100-Mbps Ethernet distinguished by the cable used to create them. 100BaseTX, for example, uses two pairs of wire in a CAT5 twisted-pair cable that contains eight wires, while 100BaseFX uses fiber optic cable.
- *1000-Mbps Ethernet* (also called *Gigabit Ethernet*) operates at a speed of 1000 Mbps (1 gigabit per second). It's the newest version of Ethernet and is intended for large, high-speed LANs and heavy-traffic server connections. Few, if any, home networks require Gigabit Ethernet.

Most current Ethernet installations use shielded twisted-pair (STP) cable, unshielded twisted-pair (UTP) cable, or fiber optic cable. Older Ethernet installations used either 50-ohm RG58/U coaxial cable, also known as thin Ethernet, or 50-ohm RG8/U coaxial, known as thick Ethernet, but these are both obsolete now.

Other types of wired connections

There are a couple other methods for created wired connections between computers:

- *RS-232*, now known as EIA232 after the Electronic Industries Association that developed it, is an interface standard for data communications equipment. RS-232 enables and ensures reliable communication among various manufacturers' equipment. Most RS-232 standards are employed in 25-pin or 9-pin *null-modem cables* that you can use to connect two computers together. There were also a few printers that used RS-232 interfaces to connect to PCs. The RS-232D standard uses RJ-45 connectors.

- *Crossover cables* (or null modem cables) are Ethernet cables with RJ-45 connectors that you can use to create a network between two computers. Normally you need to connect the computers to a hub or router using Cat-5 cable, but with a crossover cable, you can connect the computers directly. Crossover cables offer a quick and easy way to transfer data between two computers. You could also a null modem/crossover cable to connect to a printer, if the printer has a network card.

Network cards and modems

The connection from the communications medium (network cable or telephone line) to a computer, printer, or multifunction device is established with a network adapter or *network interface card (NIC)* for networks, both wired and wireless, and a modem for telephone lines.

Network interface cards

The function of the NIC is to manage communication between the network and the computer or device. Network cards are responsible for both sending and receiving data:

- *Full-duplex* devices can send and receive data at the same time.
- *Half-duplex* devices can't send and receive data simultaneously; they can perform only one function at a time, which means that they're much slower than full-duplex devices.
- *Simplex* devices can communicate in only one direction, so in effect, they broadcast rather than communicate and can be used to stream content to multiple locations. Television and radio broadcasting devices are good examples of simplex devices.

The process of auto-negotiation between the NIC and the network begins with the determination of whether the data exchange is by full or half-duplex. Exhibit 3-16 shows an example of a NIC for wired network; a NIC for a wireless network appears similar, although some have small, but visible antennae attached to them.

Exhibit 3-16: Examples of NIC for a wired network

NICs have identifying addresses coded into them by the manufacturers. These addresses, used by the network to identify the device using the card, are called *media access control (MAC)* addresses, physical or adapter addresses, or Ethernet addresses. No two NICs ever have the same MAC address.

Most NICs have LEDs or similar lights that you can use to verify network activity. If the link lights are off or inactive (not blinking), the NIC is probably not communicating on the network.

Modems

Modems are devices that enable you to connect your computer to another computer through a phone line. Modems are also found on multifunction devices that have a fax component. The modem in the sending device must convert the digital signals within the device to analog signals that can be carried by regular analog phone lines. The receiving modem must convert analog signals to computer-readable, i.e., digital signals.

Modems convert a digital signal into an analog one through a process called *modulation*. The digital signal is layered over a standard analog wave to produce a composite analog wave. To convert the composite signal back to digital, the receiving modem demodulates it. *Demodulation* is the process by which the modem electronically subtracts the carrier analog wave, revealing the digital signal the wave is carrying. (A modem gets its name from this process. It *mod*ulates and *dem*odulates; hence a "modem.")

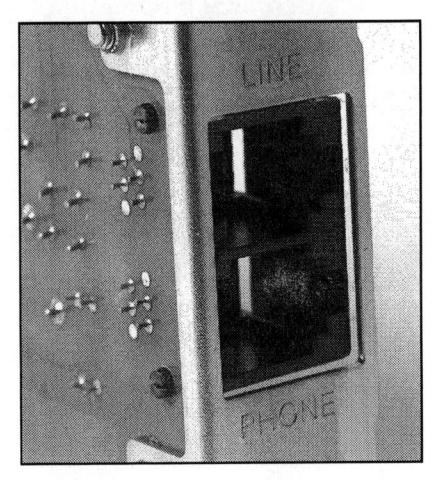

Exhibit 3-17: Modem jacks showing the line and phone connection points

A modem can be an external component that you connect to your PC through a serial port. (In fact, that was the original purpose of serial ports on PCs.) Internal modems are also common, especially in multifunction devices and laptop computers. These modems can be built into the device's logic board or motherboard, implemented on an adapter card that you insert into your device. Exhibit 3-17 shows a modem jack on a device.

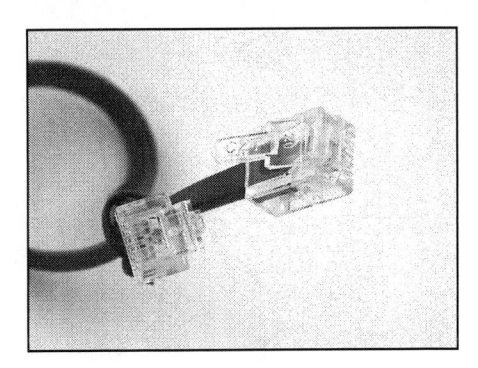

Exhibit 3-18: RJ-11 connectors

Modems use phone lines to communicate with other computers and multifunction devices and fax machines. You connect your modem to a phone line using a standard phone cord. Such cords feature *RJ-11* connectors, as shown in Exhibit 3-18, which are square connectors featuring six pins. (The "RJ" in the jack's designation simply means registered jack, and the number refers to the specific wiring pattern used for the jacks and connectors.) Modems typically feature two RJ-11 jacks. You use one to connect the modem to the phone line. You can use the other for connecting a telephone. The phone signals pass from the wall jack, through your modem, and to the phone.

A modem's data transmission speeds are measured in bits per second. However, you might also encounter the term, baud, which is used to represent modem speed. *Baud* is a measure of signal changes per second. Since modem signals are analog, the baud rate is comparable to the frequency of an analog wave. The International Telecommunications Union (ITU) defines standards for modems and modem connections. Such standards are given "V dot" names, such as V.32 or V.90. Revisions to existing standards are noted with the French terms bis for second revision or terbo for third revision.

Standard	Maximum speed	Additional information
V.32	4,800 bps (async) 9,600 bps (sync)	
V.32 bis	14,400 bps	
V.32 terbo	19,200 bps	Not an actual ITU standard, though modems were widely marketed with "V dot" names as if they'd been a standard.
V.34	28,800 bps	
V.34 bis	33,600 bps	
V.90	56,000 bps download and 33,600 bps upload	This ITU standard encompassed the two proprietary 56K modem technologies: 3COM's 56K Flex and US Robotics 56K X2. In the US and Canada, download speeds are limited to 53,000 bps due to telephone system design limits.
V.92	56,000 bps download and 48,800 bps upload	Provides reduced connection times by using previously negotiated connection settings. It also provides data call waiting in which the data session can be put on hold while you take a voice call. In the US and Canada, download speeds are limited to 53,000 bps due to telephone system design limitations.

V.42 and V.42bis standards are sometimes confused as modem standards. Actually, they're ITU standards for error detection and compression, respectively.

Do it!

B-1: Connecting to the network

Here's how	Here's why
1 Shut down your computer and unplug it from the power supply	
2 Examine the back of the computer to locate network cable and network card	
3 Remove the cable from the network card	Pinch the small clasp.
What kind of connector is it? What type of cable? What type of network are you connected to?	*It's likely an RJ-45 connector on a Cat-5 cable, connecting your computer to an Ethernet network.*
Can you see a modem port? Can you fit the network cable into the modem port?	*If you have a modem port, the network cable connector will not fit because it's an RJ-45 connector, not an RJ-11.*
4 Reconnect the cable and the power cord and turn on your computer	
Verify that the LED on the network card is lit	A lit or blinking LED indicates an active network card.
Log on to your computer as **PSIADMIN##** with a password of **Pa$$321**	(Where ## is your unique student number.)

If necessary, help students find the network cable and explain what type of network you're using in the classroom.

Connectivity **3–29**

5 Click **Start**, and choose **My Computer**	
6 In the task pane on the left, click **My Network Places**	You're going to browse the network
What do you see in this window?	*If there are any shared folders on the network, you'll likely see them in this window.*
7 In the task pane, under Network Tasks, click **View workgroup computers**	
What do you see in the window?	*You can see all the computers on the network that are in the same workgroup.*
8 Close all open windows	
9 Click **Start**, and right-click My Computer and choose **Manage**	To open Computer Management. You're going to display Device Manager.
10 In the tree pane, select **Device Manager**	

Double-click **Modems**	
	Modems
	  Conexant D480 MDC V.9x Modem
	  Standard Modem
	
	To expand the category and view the installed devices.

Do you have any modems installed? If so, what type of modem is it, and at what speed does it operate?	*Answers will vary.*
11 Double-click **Network Adapters**	
How many network adapters do you have installed?	*Answers will vary, but you should have at least an adapter for the wired network. You might also see a wireless adapter.*
12 Right-click the network adapter for the wired network and choose **Properties**	To open its Properties dialog box.
On the Advanced tab, observe the link speed and duplex settings	You can configure the network speed and duplex settings here. Most adapters are configured to automatically detect network settings.
13 Click **Cancel** to close the Properties dialog box, and close all open windows	

It might take a few minutes for students' computers to appear in the window. Have students press F5 to refresh the view.

Network protocols

Network *protocols* are the languages that computers, servers, and network devices use to communicate with each other. Protocols send data across the network in units called *packets*. The following table lists some common network protocols that you can use in Windows networks.

Protocol	Description
Transmission Control Protocol/Internet Protocol (TCP/IP)	The predominant Windows network protocol. It's supported by all versions of Windows and most other non-Microsoft operating systems. TCP/IP is also the protocol of the Internet.
Internetwork Packet Exchange/Sequenced Packet Exchange (IPX/SPX)	A proprietary protocol that was the native protocol in early versions of Novell NetWare. Later versions of NetWare supported TCP/IP as the native protocol. Windows computers can connect to IPX/SPX networks and NetWare servers by using Microsoft's version of IPX/SPX, called NWLink. To share files and printers on a NetWare server, you must install the Microsoft Client for NetWare. You may still find some NetWare networks and print servers around.
AppleTalk	A network protocol supported by Apple Macintosh computers. Windows 2000 supports AppleTalk. Mac OS X (10.2 and later) supports TCP/IP and can connect to Windows networks without requiring AppleTalk support.

TCP/IP configuration

Explanation   TCP/IP is the network communication protocol used in just about every organization, so it's important to know how to configure TCP/IP on computers, printers, and multifunction devices. Basic TCP/IP configuration consists of the IP address and subnet mask, which are shown in the example in Exhibit 3-19.

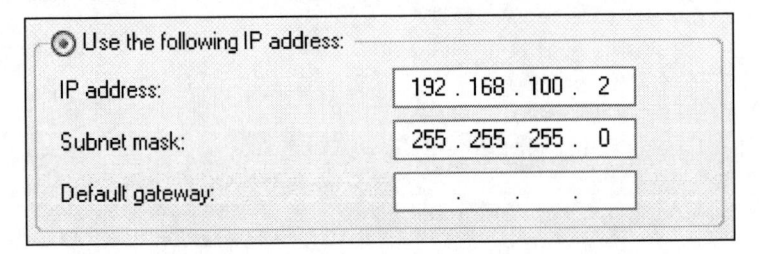

Exhibit 3-19: IP address and subnet mask

IP addresses

All devices, including computers, printers, and multifunction devices on a TCP/IP network, are assigned a unique numerical address called an IP address. An IP address is like a house number or a cell phone number; it's used to provide a unique identification that distinguishes the device it's assigned to from all other devices. Without an IP address, a device can't communicate on a network using TCP/IP.

IP addresses consist of four one-, two-, or three-digit numbers separated by periods, like this: 192.168.115.231. You must have all four parts of the number for the IP address to be complete. Part of the IP address defines the network address, also known as the *subnet*; the other part of the IP address defines the computer address.

Taken together, the two parts uniquely identify a device, much as an area code and phone number identify a specific phone. In the example 192.168.115.231, the network portion of the address (the area code) is 192.168.115, and the computer or device address (the phone number) is 231.

IP addresses can be assigned manually (a *static IP address*), or they can be assigned automatically by a server running *Dynamic Host Configuration Protocol (DHCP)*. Printers can use DHCP to receive an IP address, but you can use the configuration software that shipped with the printer or the printer's control panel to configure a static IP address.

When you use DHCP, you tell the computer or device to ask the DHCP server for an address. The DHCP server sends the address to the computer or device and keeps track of all addresses it has assigned to all devices on the network, so there are no conflicts. The computer or device then uses that address as its IP address. The IP address is assigned or leased to the computer or device for a specified duration—anywhere from a few hours to a few days, depending on how the DHCP server is configured by the network administrator. If you need to update IP addressing information, you can remove the DHCP address that's been assigned to the device and then manually send a request to the DHCP server for another IP address. This procedure is called *release and renew*.

Windows 2000 Professional, Windows XP, and Windows Vista computers can assign themselves IP addresses by using *Automatic Private IP Addressing (APIPA)*. They assign themselves IP addresses in the range of 169.254.0.0 to 169.254.255.255, if they haven't been assigned an IP address manually and if there's no DHCP server on the network. APIPA is a great feature for a small network because the computers just assign themselves IP addresses so they can communicate. You don't have to worry about doing it manually or setting up a DHCP server. However, APIPA addresses can't be used to access the Internet.

Subnet masks

The *subnet mask* is a number that looks something like an IP address. Its function is to separate the IP address into the network address and the computer address so that routers and other network devices know where to send data packets. A subnet mask often looks like this: 255.255.255.0. This example would be the default subnet mask for the IP address example in the preceding section; this subnet mask would tell other computers, devices, and routers that 192.168.115 is the network address and 231 is the computer or device address.

Subnet masks can get very complicated, but as a technician, you don't have to worry about figuring them out. You just need to assign the appropriate subnet masks, which the network administrator or engineer provides, and you need to verify that a computer or printer has been assigned the correct subnet mask, if you're troubleshooting networking errors.

Additional TCP/IP properties

The following table lists some of the other TCP/IP properties you can configure. Keep in mind that these properties can also be assigned by using a DHCP server—a method that provides greater ease and flexibility when managing a large network.

Property	Description
Default gateway (gateway)	This is the IP address of the server on the subnet that forwards packets to other subnets. You need to configure a default gateway, if the computer or device needs to communicate with other subnets or with the Internet. This is for communication over a network only; communication through a modem doesn't require this property.
DNS server address	This is the IP address of the DNS server. The DNS server helps the client computer find other computers on the internal network or on the Internet. The DNS server might be on the LAN, or it might be maintained by the Internet service provider (ISP). There can be multiple DNS server addresses.

IP address assignments

To assign an IP address or configure a computer to use DHCP:

1. In Windows 2000 Professional or Windows XP Professional, open Network and Internet Connections. In Windows Vista, open the Network and Sharing Center, and in the tasks pane, click "Manage network connections."
2. Right-click Local Area Connection and choose Properties.
3. Double-click Internet Protocol (TCP/IP). (In Windows Vista, it's Internet Protocol Version 4.)
4. Choose to use DHCP or assign an IP address manually. Configure additional TCP/IP properties, as necessary, if configuring a static IP address.

Do it!

B-2: Viewing network protocol settings

Here's how	Here's why
1 Click **Start** and choose **Control Panel**	You're going to see which protocol you have installed.
2 Click **Network and Internet Connections** Click **Network Connections**	
3 Right-click **Local Area Connection** and choose **Properties**	This connection uses the following items: ☑ Client for Microsoft Networks ☑ File and Printer Sharing for Microsoft Networks ☑ QoS Packet Scheduler ☑ Internet Protocol (TCP/IP) TCP/IP is the only protocol installed on the computer for network communication, unless you also have a wireless networking card; then the AEGIS Protocol (IEEE 802.1x) is also installed.
4 Double-click **Internet Protocol**	To open the Properties dialog box.
Are you using a static IP address or DHCP? Are you using APIPA? How can you tell?	*Answers will vary. If you're using DHCP, there's no IP addressing information visible in this dialog box, and the option to obtain an IP address is automatically selected.*
5 Close all open dialog boxes and windows	

Wireless networks

Explanation

Wireless LAN (WLAN) technology uses radio waves or infrared light instead of cables or wires to connect computers or other devices. Connections are made using a wireless NIC that includes an antenna to send and receive signals. WLANs are popular in places where networking cables are difficult to install, such as outdoors or in historic buildings that have wiring restrictions, or where there are many mobile users, such as on a college campus.

All wireless devices that communicate with each other must have the same *Service Set Identifier (SSID)*, which is the unique name of the wireless network they're using. Devices using different SSIDs can't communicate.

Wireless devices can communicate directly (for example, a handheld device communicating with a computer via an infrared connection), in what's called *ad-hoc mode*. Or they can connect to a LAN by way of a *wireless access point (WAP)*. Access points are placed so that nodes can access at least one access point from anywhere within the coverage area. When devices use an access point, they communicate through the access point instead of communicating directly. This is known as *infrastructure mode*. Exhibit 3-20 shows an example of a wired network with wireless segments.

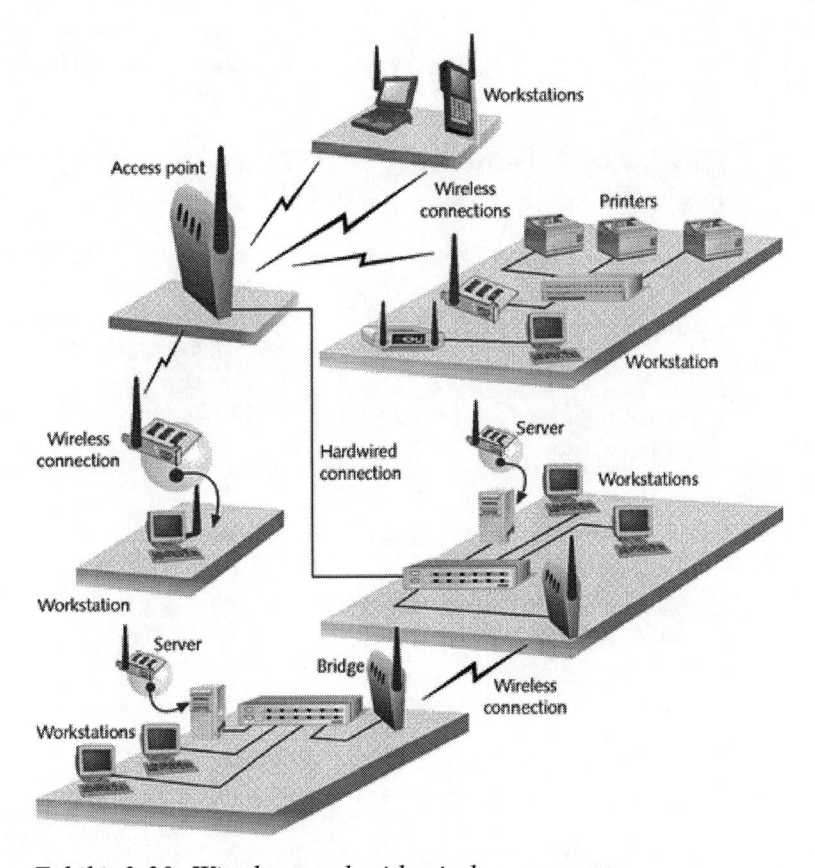

Exhibit 3-20: Wired network with wireless segments

The benefits of WLAN technology are many. The most obvious benefit is the increased flexibility and mobility that's created when using WLANs. Employees can move freely around the organization without disconnection from the network.

Although WLANs have some obvious advantages in places where running cables would be difficult or expensive, WLANs tend to be slower than wired networks, especially when they're busy. Another problem with WLANs is security. Companies are often reluctant to use them, because it's possible for an unauthorized person with a receiving device to intercept wireless LAN transmissions. Security on a WLAN is accomplished by filtering the MAC addresses of wireless NICs that are allowed to use the access point and by encrypting data sent over the wireless LAN.

Wi-Fi

The first IEEE standard that outlined wireless LAN specifications was IEEE 802.11, published in 1990. Most current WLAN devices operate under the 1999 IEEE 802.11b standard or 802.11g standard. These standards are also called *Wi-Fi (Wireless Fidelity)*. Apple calls this standard *AirPort*.

- 802.11b uses a frequency range of 2.4 GHz in the radio band and has a distance range of about 100 meters. Up to 11 Mbps of data can be sent over distances ranging up to several hundred feet. The range of any specific transmitter depends on what type of obstructions its signal encounters and whether there's a clear line of sight between transmitter and receiver. 802.11b is a popular and inexpensive network solution for home and office. 802.11b is the wireless extension of the Ethernet protocol to wireless communication. It can handle many kinds of data. It's primarily used for TCP/IP, but it can also handle other forms of networking traffic, such as AppleTalk or PC file-sharing standards.

- 802.11a works in the 5.0-GHz frequency range and isn't compatible with 802.11b. It allows for a shorter range between a wireless device and an access point (50 meters compared with 100 meters for 802.11b) but is much faster than 802.11b and doesn't encounter interference from cordless phones, microwave ovens, and Bluetooth devices, as does 802.11b.

- 802.11g is another IEEE wireless standard that uses the 2.4-GHz band and has become widely available. It's backward compatible with 802.11b but has higher throughput at 54 Mbps. (Apple Computer, Inc. calls 802.11g *AirPort Extreme*.)

Wireless security comes in two major varieties today:

- Wired Equivalent Privacy (WEP)
- Wi-Fi Protected Access (WPA)

Both include methods for encrypting wireless traffic between wireless clients and access points (APs). WEP has been included in 802.11–based products for some time and uses a strategy for restricting network access and encrypting network traffic based upon a shared key.

Bluetooth

Another popular wireless technology is called *Bluetooth*. Bluetooth is a standard for short-range wireless communication and data synchronization between devices. This standard was developed by a group of electronics manufacturers, including Ericsson, IBM, Intel, Nokia, and Toshiba, and it's overseen by the Bluetooth Special Interest Group. The transmitters and receivers are application-specific integrated circuits (ASICs) and can transmit data at rates as high as 721 Kbps with up to three voice channels also available. Bluetooth, which has a range of only 10 meters, also works in the 2.4-GHz frequency range, is easy to configure, and is considered a viable option for short-range connections, such as connecting a PDA to a cell phone, so that the PDA can connect to a remote network.

Bluetooth technology allows wireless connections between computers, printers, fax machines, and other peripherals, but it doesn't have the range to serve as a wireless connection between an access point and laptops dispersed throughout a home and yard. Some vendors have developed Bluetooth devices with higher transmitting power, which increases the range of the technology up to 100 meters, but these higher-power devices haven't yet gained wide acceptance.

WiMAX

WiMAX, which stands for Worldwide Interoperability of Microwave Access, provides wireless DSL and T1-level service. It's an emerging technology standard that services Wide Area and Metropolitan Area Networks, allowing wireless users with 802.16e devices to roam between current wireless hot spots. As a comparison, WiMAX wireless coverage is measured in square miles, while Wi-Fi is measured in square yards. WiMAX doesn't rely on line-of-sight for connection. WiMAX technology can be deployed in areas where physical limitations, such as no existing DSL or T1 cabling, prevent broadband access.

Exhibit 3-21: An IrDA infrared port on a laptop

Infrared

Laptops and portable devices, such as PDAs, with infrared ports, such as the example in Exhibit 3-21, can often use IrDA-standard infrared communication, which offers a wireless serial connection at 1.5 Mbps with a maximum range of 20 feet. The main weakness of infrared as a communication medium is the line-of-sight requirement: the path between the ports of the communicating devices must remain unobstructed. Accidental movement of the devices can spoil the line of sight and cause connection to be lost. This limitation makes infrared undesirable as a medium for exchanging data heavy files or performing real time communication.

Do it!

B-3: Using wireless communication technologies

Here's how	Here's why
1 In wireless communications, what replaces the wire?	Wireless LAN (WLAN) technology uses radio waves or infrared light instead of cables or wires to connect computers or other devices.
2 List the major wireless protocols.	Wi-Fi (802.11b), Bluetooth, 802.11a, 802.11g, and WiMAX.
3 Does your PC have a wireless card? (Hint: Check Device Manager again.)	Answers will vary.
4 Does your PC have an infrared wireless port?	Answers will vary. Desktop PCs typically don't have such ports, though laptops typically do.
5 How far could you move from the PC before you lose the infrared connection?	Exact distances vary based on the devices you're using. But in general, infrared wireless is limited to 10–20 feet.
6 Examine the Bluetooth wireless device provided by your instructor	Your cellular telephone or PDA might support Bluetooth. You could examine it instead.
7 Do the Bluetooth devices have a visible, obvious antenna or more than one antenna?	Answers will vary.
8 What's the range of the original Bluetooth technology?	10 meters.
9 Can you connect to other Bluetooth devices in the classroom?	Answers will vary.

Have at least one Bluetooth device for students to examine alone, in pairs, or in groups.

Shared printers

Explanation

Many offices have multiple computers but only one printer. Even offices that have multiple printers often don't have printers for every computer, so users must share printers with other users on a network. In large organizations, network printers are shared by administrators with large numbers of users, or print servers are used to make one or more printers available to the organization. Some large network printers also offer access to shared network files, which users can print right from the printer's onboard control panel. In a smaller office or workgroup environment, users can share a local printer on a Windows XP or Windows Vista computer with other users in the office.

Not every user can connect to every network printer. Typically, different users have rights to specific printers, and even then, users sometimes can't do anything but print documents. They have no permissions to manage the printers at all. Usually support technicians have a higher level of permissions that allow them to start, stop, and cancel print jobs, and connect to the printer to modify some of its settings.

To connect to a shared printer using Windows 2000, Windows XP, or Windows Vista, you usually need just the printer's name. (Sometimes you also need a username and password to make the connection.) When you know the printer's name, you can browse the network for it and connect to it. Any necessary drivers must be installed on your computer.

- On Windows 2000 and Windows XP, to connect to a shared printer, browse to the computer with the shared printer or the shared network printer through Network Neighborhood or My Network Places. Then drag the shared printer to your desktop or right-click the printer and choose Connect.
- On Windows Vista computers:
  1. Open the Network folder.
  2. Browse to the computer with the shared printer, or browse to find the shared network printer.
  3. Right-click the printer and choose Connect.
  4. If prompted, acknowledge the security risk of installing the driver.

To remove a printer (and leave the printer driver files intact), right-click on the shared-printer icon, choose Delete, and confirm the deletion. To delete the driver files:

1. Right-click in the Printers and Faxes window or the Printers window, and choose Server Properties.
2. On the Drivers tab, select the driver you want to delete and click Remove.
3. Confirm the deletion.

To print a test page:

1. In the Printers window or the Printers and Faxes window, right-click the printer and choose Properties.
2. On the General tab, click Print Test Page.

Network printer ports

As you saw earlier in this unit, when you print to a local printer, you connect the printer to a physical port on the computer, such as USB or parallel. But when you print to a network printer, it doesn't connect to a physical port. However, by using the LPR and RAW protocols (described below), your operating system can create a virtual port through Server Message Block (SMB) and the TCP/IP control and transport protocols operating between the computer and network printer or external print server port.

Connectivity **3-39**

- *Line Printer Remote (LPR)* is a protocol that provides network printing over TCP/IP. In Windows 2000 and later, Standard Port Monitor (SPM) uses LPR to provide printer services but offers more reliable network print services than LPR alone.
- The *RAW* printing protocol is the default protocol for many network print devices. It enables communication with the print device by accessing port 9100 on the device. SPM also uses RAW as a print protocol.

Do it!

B-4: Connecting to a shared printer

Share a working printer on your computer either before the activity begins or as part of this first step. Invite students to join you at your computer and watch as you share the printer.

Write the name on a whiteboard, chalkboard, or flipchart.

Here's how	Here's why
1 If necessary, wait until your instructor shares a printer on his or her computer Obtain the name of your instructor's computer and the shared printer	
2 Open My Network Places	
3 Browse to find the shared printer	
4 Right-click and choose **Connect**	
5 Enter a name and password, if necessary	
6 Observe the printer in the Printers and Faxes window	Xerox on printsrv 0 Ready The network printer icon looks a little different from a local printer's icon.
7 Right-click the icon and choose **Properties** On the Ports tab, identify the type of port What type of port is being used? Is it a TCP/IP port using RAW or LPR?	*Answers will vary.*
8 Close the printer's Properties dialog box	
9 Print a test page on the network printer	
10 Close any open windows	

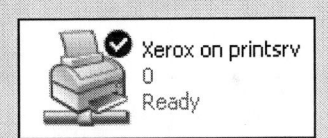

Testing TCP/IP connectivity

Explanation

Two of the most common complaints you hear from users are that they can't get to something on the network, such as a printer, or "the Internet is down." When you hear a complaint that users can't connect to a network printer or a print server, your first step should be to check the user's network connection and TCP/IP settings. You should also verify the networking settings on the print server or network printer, a task you might have to escalate to the network administrator.

TCP/IP utilities

TCP/IP includes a group of utility tools, some of which can be used to troubleshoot problems with TCP/IP connectivity. The following table describes some common utilities.

Utility	Purpose
Ipconfig (ipconfig.exe)	Displays the IP address of the host and other configuration information. Some parameters are: `ipconfig /all`—Displays all information about the connection. `ipconfig /release`—Releases the current IP address. `ipconfig /renew`—Requests a new IP address. `ipconfig /?`—Displays information about ipconfig.
FTP (ftp.exe)	Transfers files over a network. The File Transfer Protocol enables you to transfer files among various types of computers and devices with the same or different operating systems.
Nslookup (nslookup.exe)	Reports the IP address of an entered host name or the host name of an entered IP address.
Ping (ping.exe)	Verifies a connection to a network between two hosts.
Telnet (telnet.exe)	Allows you to communicate with another computer on the network remotely, entering commands on the local computer that control the remote computer.
Trace Route (tracert.exe)	Traces and displays the route taken from the host to a remote destination; tracert is one example of a trace-routing utility.

Most of these commands are entered from a command prompt. To open a Command Prompt window in Windows 2000, Windows XP, and Windows Vista, click Start and choose All Programs, Accessories, Command Prompt. You can also open the Command Prompt window by typing `cmd` in the Run dialog box and then clicking OK. From the Command Prompt, you can enter a Windows or DOS command, including any of those in the previous table. You can view the results of the command in the window.

If you need to test connectivity for a network printer, you can usually access its configuration page using a Web browser or using the printer configuration software that shipped with the printer. You can also use a crossover cable to connect to a network printer. This method provides a direct connection to the printer and can help you determine if the connectivity problems are with the printer itself or with a component on the network. (Network issues should be escalated to the network administrator.)

You can also view the LED indicators or activity lights on a printer or the printer's on-board NIC to verify that the printer is working. Normally, these lights display various colors or flash if the printer has encountered a problem with the network.

Ipconfig

When a user complains of network problems, you should first check the TCP/IP settings on the user's computer. When using any version of Windows, use ipconfig, as shown in Exhibit 3-22, to display the current configuration of the TCP/IP, including IP address, subnet mask, and default gateway. Several switches can be added to the ipconfig command line to display additional information, including `ipconfig /all`.

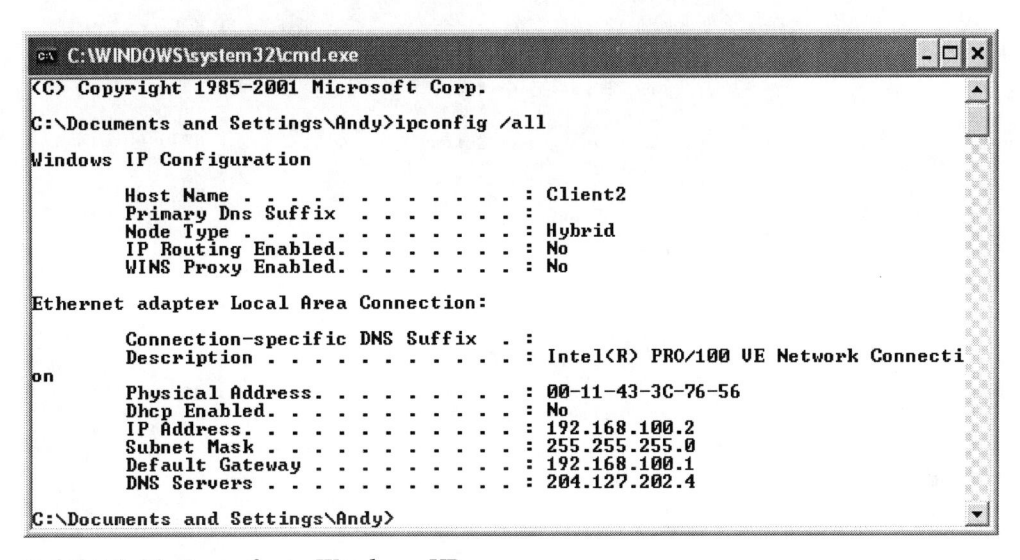

```
C:\WINDOWS\system32\cmd.exe

(C) Copyright 1985-2001 Microsoft Corp.

C:\Documents and Settings\Andy>ipconfig /all

Windows IP Configuration

        Host Name . . . . . . . . . . . . : Client2
        Primary Dns Suffix  . . . . . . . :
        Node Type . . . . . . . . . . . . : Hybrid
        IP Routing Enabled. . . . . . . . : No
        WINS Proxy Enabled. . . . . . . . : No

Ethernet adapter Local Area Connection:

        Connection-specific DNS Suffix  . :
        Description . . . . . . . . . . . : Intel(R) PRO/100 VE Network Connection
        Physical Address. . . . . . . . . : 00-11-43-3C-76-56
        Dhcp Enabled. . . . . . . . . . . : No
        IP Address. . . . . . . . . . . . : 192.168.100.2
        Subnet Mask . . . . . . . . . . . : 255.255.255.0
        Default Gateway . . . . . . . . . : 192.168.100.1
        DNS Servers . . . . . . . . . . . : 204.127.202.4

C:\Documents and Settings\Andy>
```

Exhibit 3-22: Ipconfig in Windows XP

Do it!

B-5: Using ipconfig to display TCP/IP settings

Here's how	Here's why
1 Click **Start**, choose **Run**, and enter `cmd`	To open a Command Prompt window. You're going to use Ipconfig to view your IP address settings.
2 At the command prompt, enter `ipconfig`	To view your current IP address, subnet mask, and default gateway, as shown here.

```
Connection-specific DNS Suffix  . :
IP Address. . . . . . . . . . . . : 192.168.100.185
Subnet Mask . . . . . . . . . . . : 255.255.255.0
Default Gateway . . . . . . . . . : 192.168.100.1
```

This is a quick way to find a computer's basic IP address information.

3 At the command prompt, enter `ipconfig /all`	To view extended IP addressing information, as shown here.

```
Windows IP Configuration

        Host Name . . . . . . . . . . . . : osclient01
        Primary Dns Suffix  . . . . . . . : APlusOS.class
        Node Type . . . . . . . . . . . . : Unknown
        IP Routing Enabled. . . . . . . . : No
        WINS Proxy Enabled. . . . . . . . : No
        DNS Suffix Search List. . . . . . : APlusOS.class

Ethernet adapter Local Area Connection:

        Connection-specific DNS Suffix  . :
        Description . . . . . . . . . . . : Intel(R) PRO/100 VE Network Connecti
on
        Physical Address. . . . . . . . . : 00-11-11-8B-0B-91
        Dhcp Enabled. . . . . . . . . . . : No
        IP Address. . . . . . . . . . . . : 192.168.100.185
        Subnet Mask . . . . . . . . . . . : 255.255.255.0
        Default Gateway . . . . . . . . . : 192.168.100.1
        DNS Servers . . . . . . . . . . . : 192.168.100.254
```

It can be easier to view this information at the Command Prompt than to click through a few dialog boxes to find the same information in the Windows GUI.

Ping and basic TCP/IP connectivity

While you're in the MS-DOS prompt or Command Prompt window, there's another tool you can use to verify basic TCP/IP connectivity. *Ping (Packet Internet Groper)* is a simple program that allows one computer to send a test packet to another computer or device, such as a printer or multifunction device, and then receive a reply. You use ping to discover if another network device is available for communication on a TCP/IP network. You need to know the NetBIOS name, DNS name, or IP address of the other computer—perhaps a router or server that you know is operational. At the MS-DOS or command prompt, enter `ping computer` or `ping ipaddress`. A successful result looks similar to the one shown in Exhibit 3-23.

The name comes from submarine sonar, which broadcasts a signal, called a ping, that hits surrounding objects and makes a sound revealing the object's size and position.

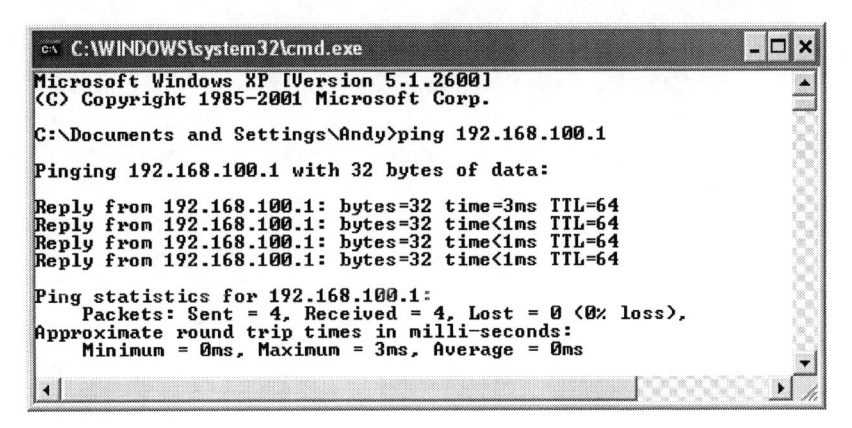

```
C:\WINDOWS\system32\cmd.exe

Microsoft Windows XP [Version 5.1.2600]
(C) Copyright 1985-2001 Microsoft Corp.

C:\Documents and Settings\Andy>ping 192.168.100.1

Pinging 192.168.100.1 with 32 bytes of data:

Reply from 192.168.100.1: bytes=32 time=3ms TTL=64
Reply from 192.168.100.1: bytes=32 time<1ms TTL=64
Reply from 192.168.100.1: bytes=32 time<1ms TTL=64
Reply from 192.168.100.1: bytes=32 time<1ms TTL=64

Ping statistics for 192.168.100.1:
    Packets: Sent = 4, Received = 4, Lost = 0 (0% loss),
Approximate round trip times in milli-seconds:
    Minimum = 0ms, Maximum = 3ms, Average = 0ms
```

Exhibit 3-23: Successful Ping results

Do it!

B-6: Testing TCP/IP connectivity

Explain to students that, with a TCP/IP connectivity problem, they can use ping to test connectivity from their computer out, verifying successful communication closest to them first.

Here's how	Here's why
1 At the command prompt, type **ping 127.0.0.1** and press ENTER	This is the loopback address and verifies that TCP/IP is working on this computer. Pinging the loopback address tests a computer's own basic network setup. You should receive four successful responses.
2 Type **ipconfig /all** and press ENTER	Record your IP address and your default gateway address. IP address: Default gateway address:
3 Ping your IP address	This verifies TCP/IP communication can be sent out on to the network cable from your NIC card and back in again. You should receive four successful responses.
4 Ping your instructor's computer	
5 Ping the IP address of your classroom's gateway	This verifies that you can reach the gateway that connects you to other subnets. You should receive four successful responses.

Nslookup

You can use the command-line tool nslookup to verify name resolution (DNS) settings. At an MS-DOS prompt or a command prompt, enter `nslookup servername` to verify name resolution settings. Entering just `nslookup` returns the name of the DNS server you're configured to use. Any unusual results should be reported to the network administrator.

Do it!

B-7: Using nslookup to verify settings

Here's how	Here's why
1 At the command prompt, enter `nslookup`	To test your DNS configuration. Depending on your configuration, you might see a DNS server name and IP address returned, or you might see just an IP address and an error message telling you that nslookup can't find the server name. This is a DNS server configuration issue.
2 Enter `nslookup` followed by a Web address	Try www.yahoo.com. You should see DNS addressing information for that domain.
3 Enter `exit`	To exit nslookup.
4 Close all open windows	

Network scanning

Explanation

Some scanners and multifunction units enable you to send an image file from the scanner through e-mail or to a folder on a network or an FTP server. There are different requirements for each option, and while not all scanners or multifunction devices have these capabilities, those that do generally have the same requirements.

Functionality	Requirements
Scan-to-file	• An application, either an application that ships with the scanner or a third-party application.
	• Drivers for the scanner. Most scanner drivers are TWAIN-compliant, and can be used with any TWAIN-compliant application or utility. ISIS drivers also enable communication between the scanner and application.
Scan-to-folder	• A shared network folder, which can be on a file server or even another workstation.
	• Permissions to write files to the shared folder. There's a broad range of share permissions and NTFS permissions that control who can access shared folders, not just on Windows computers, but also on Linux, Unix, Mac, and NetWare computers. Some permissions allow users only to read files, while some permissions allow users both to read and to modify files and folders within a shared folder. Other permissions deny access completely.
	• Server Message Block (SMB) protocol, to enable transfer of files across the network. SMB is implemented in Windows networking and can be used to access Windows and non-Windows computers and devices.
	• *Universal Naming Convention (UNC)* file path to the shared folder. The normal format is usually: \\servername\sharename.
Scan-to-e-mail	• An e-mail application configured with a *Simple Mail Transfer Protocol (SMTP)* server address and a *Post Office Protocol 3 (POP3)* server address. SMTP servers handle outgoing mail; POP3 servers handle incoming mail. The same server can handle both functions. Some e-mail servers limit file sizes to conserve network bandwidth and server hard-disk space. Be sure the size of the image file doesn't exceed mandatory limits.
	• Permissions to access the e-mail servers. Some e-mail servers require user authentication through username and password. Authentication is provided by a directory server, such as a Windows Active Directory domain controller, through the *Lightweight Directory Access protocol (LDAP)*.
Scan-to-FTP	• An FTP server and the file path to the FTP server. FTP file paths are in the format: ftp://server.domain/folder.
	• Permissions to access the FTP server.

Do it!

B-8: Identifying network scanning basics

Here's how	Here's why
1 Identify the primary requirements for the scan-to-e-mail functionality.	*An e-mail application configured with POP3 and SMTP server addresses; authentication to a directory service over LDAP for e-mail server access.*
2 List the requirements for using the scan-to-folder functionality.	*Shared folder, adequate permissions, SMB or other file-sharing protocol, and a UNC to the shared folder.*
3 What are two types of drivers that enable application and scanner communication?	*TWAIN and ISIS*
4 What is an FTP server?	*A server to which you can upload or download files using the FTP protocol.*

Unit summary: Connectivity

Topic A In this activity, you learned about printing and scanning on the local computer. You identified ports, such as **serial**, **parallel**, **USB**, and **IEEE 1394** ports, and you learned to connect printers and scanners to a computer. You also learned to test **TCP/IP** connectivity using tools such as **PING** and **IPCONFIG**.

Topic B In this topic, you learned **networking** basics, including **protocols**, **cables**, **connectors**, and the basics of **Ethernet** and **wireless** networks. You also connected to a shared printer on the network, and you identified the requirements for using a scanner to scan documents and e-mail them or store them in shared folders on the network and **FTP** servers.

Review questions

1 True or false? Serial transmission provides two-way communication between a printer and the computer.

   True

2 You can use a _____ modem cable to connect two computers directly.

   null

3 LPT ports use _____ transmission.

   parallel

4 Typically, parallel ports have _____ pins.

   25

5 What are the two versions of USB currently in use?

   USB 1.1 and USB 2.0

6 True or false? USB ports can power some peripheral devices, including scanners.

   True

7 What are the two versions of the IEEE 1394 standard currently in use?

   FireWire 400 and FireWire 800

8 True or false? IEEE 1394 connections can provide power to connected devices.

   True

9 Which of the following printer control languages were developed by HP? (Choose all that apply.)

   A PostScript

   B PLC

   c PCL

   D PJL

10 Which of the following connections enable hot-plugging? (Choose all that apply.)

    A Serial

    B Parallel

    C USB

    D IEEE 1394

11 Which of the following UTP cables is the current standard?

    A Cat3

    B Cat4

    C Cat5

    D Cat5

12 Which of the following connectors is used on an UTP cable in an Ethernet network?

    A RJ-11

    B RJ-40

    C RJ-45

    D RJ-65

13 Which of the following connectors is used on a telephone cable?

    A RJ-11

    B RJ-40

    C RJ-45

    D RJ-65

14 _____ is currently the fastest Ethernet network architecture available today.

1000-Mbps Ethernet (Gigabit)

15 _____ cables are Ethernet cables that you can use to create a network between two computers.

Crossover

16 Which of the following is the built-in address that uniquely identifies each network card?

    A NIC

    B MAC

    C PCL

    D COM

17 _____ is a measure of signal changes that's used to represent modem speed.

Baud

18 Which of the following is the predominant wired network protocol?

    A IPX/SPX

    B WiMAX

    C Ethernet

    D TCP/IP

19 _____ is used to assign IP addressing information automatically to computers and other network devices.

DHCP

20 At a minimum, to communicate on a local area network segment, a computer needs which of the following? (Choose all that apply.)

    A IP address

    B DNS server address

    C subnet mask

    D default gateway

21 The _____ standard is used to create wireless LANs.

802.11

22 Which of the following are wireless security protocols? (Choose all that apply.)

    A WiMAX

    B WPA

    C WAP

    D WEP

23 Which of the following utilities can you use to verify IP addressing information?

    A Tracert

    B Ipconfig

    C Ftp

    D Telnet

24 Which of the following utilities can you use to verify basic network connectivity between a computer and another network device?

A Ping

B Telnet

C Ipconfig

D Nslookup

25 What's one important consideration when using network scanning technologies?

Probably the most important consideration is the permissions assigned to the user account of the user of the network scanning features. Without the right permissions, a user can't access shared network folders, e-mail servers, or ftp servers.

Independent practice activity

Ensure that students have access to a printer and a scanner and to the cables needed to connect them to a computer. Also ensure that there's a shared printer on the network.

In this activity, you'll connect a scanner and a printer to your computer; then you'll connect to a shared network printer.

1 Obtain a printer and the cables used to connect it to a computer.

2 Connect the printer and install the drivers for it. Print a test page to ensure that the printer's working.

3 Obtain a scanner and the cables used to connect it to a computer.

4 Connect the scanner to the computer and install drivers for it. Scan a document and a photograph to ensure that the scanner's working.

5 Browse the network for a shared printer. When you find a shared printer, connect to it. Print a test page.

Unit 4
Maintenance and troubleshooting

Unit time: 210 minutes

Complete this unit, and you'll know how to:

A Perform routine maintenance.

B Troubleshoot printer and scanner problems.

Topic A: Maintenance

This topic covers the following CompTIA PDI+ exam objectives.

#	Objective
4.4	**Demonstrate the proper and safe use of tools**
	• Toner Vacuum and toner rags
	• Service documentation (i.e.: theory of operation, block diagram and wiring /circuit diagram)
	• Lubricants and cleaning solutions
	• Test chart
	• Chip puller / EEPROM puller
4.5	**Demonstrate and follow recommended maintenance guidelines and practices**
	• Define the reasons and benefits for adhering to maintenance guidelines and practices.
	• Examine device log data and previous service history
	• Scheduled preventative maintenance
	• Replacing parts based on parts life counters
	• Check firmware version and update as necessary
	• Clean, lubricate and perform adjustments per device specifications
	• Unscheduled service calls
	• Perform preventative maintenance during service calls
	• Examine device for potential future problems
	• Clean, lubricate and perform adjustments per device specifications
	• Verify device functionality
8.1	**Demonstrate and apply safety procedures**
	• Demonstrate proper use of cleaning solutions and sprays
8.2	**Demonstrate an awareness of environment and environmental considerations**
	• Describe effects of temperature and humidity on media and supplies

Printer maintenance

Explanation

Sometimes simple maintenance is all that's needed to keep a printer running smoothly. Check the manufacturer's documentation for each device you're supporting. The manufacturer recommends if and when you should perform scheduled maintenance, especially on laser printers. Also check the device log data and previous service history to see what other maintenance or repairs other technicians have performed.

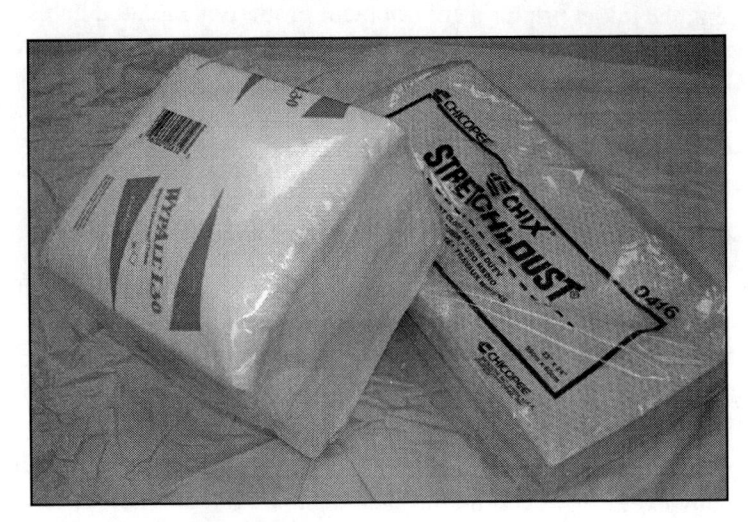

Exhibit 4-1: Cleaning cloths

Some common maintenance tools to have with you when performing routine maintenance include:

- Cleaning solutions and sprays, including isopropyl alcohol and denatured alcohol
- Cleaning equipment, including soft cloths, such as those shown in Exhibit 4-1, and cotton swabs
- Lubricants
- Compressed air
- Toner vacuums and toner rags, or extension magnet brushes
- Screwdrivers (to open compartments)
- Chip puller, for removing memory chips or EPROM and EEPROM chips, in case the chips need to be reseated or replaced

In the following sections, you'll learn how to perform routine maintenance on inkjet and laser printers. When working with printers and scanners, remember to take certain safety precautions. These include practicing ESD safe practices, keeping dangling jewelry and neckties out of the printer, and handling components so as not to damage them. And remember the main rule of thumb for printer and scanner maintenance: Always follow the manufacturer's recommendations. When maintenance is complete, document the steps you took in the device's service log.

Inkjet printers

Inkjet printers don't need as much maintenance as laser printers. To keep an inkjet printer working properly, the main thing you need to do is change the cartridge when the ink gets low. You usually have a visual warning from lights on the printer, a software utility, or just poor quality output. Always use recommended supplies when replacing ink supplies.

Sometimes, you might have to clean the print nozzles and recalibrate the printer. You can do this by following the manufacturer's instructions, which typically have you use the printer's control panel or a software utility. Then print a test page to verify functionality. You should also clean the small well that holds the ink that's dispersed during a cleaning cycle. The well may have a sponge or absorbent pad that needs to be replaced periodically.

Keeping the inkjet printer's environment properly ventilated helps the printer last longer as well. Adequate ventilation keeps the printer from overheating. Another environmental concern is keeping dust out of the printer. Most inkjet printers have a very open design, which allows dust to gather inside. The accumulation of dust can result in the following:

- Stray marks on the paper, if the dust gets caught on the print cartridge
- Overheating of elements, if dust blocks the airflow around them

You can use a dry cloth to remove dust or paper dander, or if recommended by the manufacturer, a vacuum cleaner. Clean the outside of the unit with a damp cloth or with any recommended cleaning solution.

Laser printers

Laser printers require more maintenance than inkjet printers, and the maintenance is more involved. However, regular maintenance can prevent service calls for poor quality print output and paper jams. Generally, there are two times when you should perform preventative maintenance on laser printers:

- Scheduled maintenance: Clean, lubricate, and perform adjustments based on the manufacturer's recommended schedules.
- Unscheduled service calls: During service calls, check the counters, such as the one shown in Exhibit 4-2, and the manufacturer's recommendations for preventative maintenance, and clean, lubricate, and adjust components, or replace components as recommended. Before you complete the service call, examine the printer for any potential future problems, and resolve those before you leave.

Exhibit 4-2: Counter

Laser printer maintenance routines may include:

- Replacing toner cartridges.
- Cleaning and lubricating internal components. (Be sure to follow safety procedures, as well as the manufacturer's guidelines for cleaning components.) For example, clean rollers are less likely to slip and cause paper jams.

- Replacing components as recommended by the manufacturer, such as the ozone filter, fuser assembly, or transfer roller. Often the components come in a special *maintenance kit* that you can obtain from the manufacturer. To keep the printer operating smoothly, some manufacturers recommend installing maintenance kits after a specified duration of use or a specified number of printed pages, tracked by counters. (Other printers have their counters displayed on the printer's control panel or onboard monitors.) After installing the maintenance kit, you may have to reset the page count. Check with the manufacturer.
- Checking the printer's firmware version and the manufacturer's Web site to see if there's a newer version available. Newer firmware can provide better interoperability with newer operating systems and improved print quality. Check the printer's documentation to see how to access the firmware utility (usually through the printer's administrative software or by connecting to the printer using a Web browser).

Depending on a company's financial and service contracts with the manufacturer, it might receive toner and maintenance kits automatically. Some newer large laser printers can contact the manufacturer directly to report page counts. This contact, generally for financial purposes, can then trigger the automatic shipment of maintenance kits and replacement parts. Your company or client may have a similar arrangement; ask about it before you order any supplies.

When replacing components, take some time to clean out any accumulated toner and paper dust inside the printer. Doing so prevents this debris from hindering printer operations, and it keeps a clean printing environment. Often manufacturers' maintenance kits include cleaning materials.

When removing toner, don't use a regular vacuum cleaner or even an anti-static vacuum cleaner; use only a special toner-certified vacuum. You can also use an extension magnet brush to remove toner. If you get any toner on your hands or clothes, use cold water and soap to remove it (hot water can set the toner).

Be sure the printer is well ventilated and situated securely on a flat surface, and keep the printer trays full. Try to use only recommended supplies. Remember to follow appropriate safety precautions when working with the laser printer.

After you've completed maintenance, print a few test pages to verify functionality. You don't want to leave an inoperable printer after you've completed your service routine.

Consumables

You should always keep a sufficient supply of consumables—paper, ink cartridges, and toner cartridges—on hand. If you must order these supplies from another person who's in charge of ordering supplies for the company, ensure that your requests are submitted in a timely fashion and that you follow up on their status.

All consumables should be kept in their original packaging; in a cool, dry location, out of direct sunlight; and in a room with low humidity. If paper is too moist because of high humidity, the toner might not adhere properly. Conversely, dry paper can create static electricity, which can cause the paper to stick together, resulting in paper jams. Toner cartridges stored out of their packaging in a humid environment can cause the toner to clump.

A-1: Performing inkjet and laser printer maintenance

Do it!

Provide students with the documentation for each printer that they'll be working on.

Here's how	Here's why
1 Turn off and unplug your inkjet printer	You're going to perform some routine maintenance on your inkjet printer.
2 Obtain the appropriate manufacturer's documentation	
Read through the documentation to find the maintenance recommendations	
3 Follow necessary electrical and ESD safety procedures to prepare to open the printer	
4 Open the printer and remove the ink cartridges	
Remove any dust or debris in the compartment and on the outside of the printer	Use recommended cleaning solutions.
5 Follow the manufacturer's instructions to clean the print heads	(Plug in the printer, if you're using a Windows-based utility. Connect to your computer, if necessary.)
If necessary, reinstall the ink cartridges and download and install printer software	
6 Make sure there's enough paper	
Print a test page and recalibrate the printer, as necessary	Follow the instructions to print a page and adjust settings.
7 Obtain a laser printer and its documentation	
Follow necessary electrical and ESD safety procedures to prepare to open the printer	
8 If you have a laser printer, follow the manufacturer's cleaning and maintenance instructions	(Check the counters.) This can include removing accumulated toner and dust and cleaning internal components. This step also includes replacing the ozone filter, which is important to prevent damage to printer components and to prevent the release of ozone into the environment around the printer.

Provide students with necessary cleaning materials and devices, according to manufacturers' instructions.

Maintenance and troubleshooting **4–7**

9	Check the printer's firmware version	
	Use a chip puller to remove and reseat any memory chips	Follow your instructor's directions, if necessary.
10	Close the printer and plug it in	
	If necessary, connect it to your computer	
11	Ensure that the printer has enough paper	
12	Print a test page	To verify that the printer is working properly.

Scanner maintenance

Scanner maintenance generally consists of ensuring that the glass on a flat-bed scanner is clean. Or if you're supporting a multifunction device, you need to ensure that the paper-feed path is clear of dust and debris and the glass surface over which the documents pass is clean and free of streaks. When cleaning printer glass, use a soft, dry cloth or a mild glass cleaner.

When you're done, make sure the glass is dry. Scan a test page or a *test chart*, which is used to provide a more objective measure of a scanner's image-reproduction ability, and make adjustments to the scanner's settings as necessary.

Do it!

A-2: Performing scanner maintenance

Here's how	Here's why
1 Obtain a scanner and its supporting documentation	
2 Unplug the scanner	
3 Use a soft cloth or a mild glass cleaner to clean the glass	
4 Ensure that the glass is dry	
Plug the scanner in	
5 Use a test chart or other document or photo to scan test pages	To determine scan quality.

Topic B: Troubleshooting

This topic covers the following CompTIA PDI+ exam objectives.

#	Objective

3.1	**Describe and apply general troubleshooting methodology**
	• Observation – gather information and validate the symptoms
	• Establish theory of probable cause based on information gathered
	   • Attempt to isolate the problem by eliminating non-causes
	   • Use tools and service documentation as needed
	• Test or Analyze – try to recreate the problem and validate theory
	• Once theory is validated, determine next steps to resolve the problem
	• Implement solution, validate solution and document actions and results

3.2	**Identify and isolate printing hardware issues using available tools**
	• Image quality issues
	   • Dark images, light images, weak images, repetitive image defects, ghosting, smearing, banding, focus, shadows, voided areas, jitters, registration issues, skew, misaligned color registration, weak color, missing color, vertical and horizontal black/white lines, black pages, blank pages, incorrect consumables
	• Causes of image quality issues
	   • Fuser, charging components, laser/LED component, developer assembly, consumables, photoconductor, print head, drive components, media transport/feed system, environment
	• Transport/feed issues
	   • Media jamming, skewing, creasing, wrinkling, folding, tearing, multifeeding, burning, misfeeding
	• Causes of common media transport/feed issues
	   • Media feed, fusing, media exit, registration, delivery, duplex, damaged media, separation, media feed timing, foreign objects
	• Service error messages
	   • Critical operational failures (service code)
	• Common user informational messages
	   • Add media, add supplies, add toner, regular maintenance, paper jam, incorrect media
	• Testing tools
	   • Print test page, event logs, configuration pages, paper path test, parts life counters, user setting list, engine test page

#	Objective
3.3	**Identify and isolate printing software issues using the following methods**
- Verify use of appropriate drivers by checking driver type/version
- Verify driver port setting
- Print driver test page
- Proper driver accessory/option configuration
- Application settings vs. driver settings
- Installing and uninstalling drivers
- Confirm driver settings: "offline vs. online"
- Print from multiple applications and workstations
- Print different files from the same application
3.5	**Identify and isolate scanning software issues**
- Verify use of appropriate drivers by checking driver type/version
- TWAIN, WIA, ISIS
- Verify and configure application settings
- Resolutions, color depth, single sided vs. duplex, media size, exposure levels, file format, reduction and enlargement, ADF vs. flatbed, monochrome vs. color
3.6	**Identify and isolate basic connectivity issues using available tools**
- Connectivity issues
- Slow printing, intermittent activity, communication errors, unexpected output, no activity
- Common causes of wired and wireless connectivity issues
- Loose, broken, damaged, improperly wired cables, broken network devices (hubs, switches), incorrect protocol / network settings, incorrect TCP/IP settings, bad network card, firmware, interference, line of site, EMI
- Service or informational messages
- Refer to manufacturer documentation for error codes and messages
3.7	**Identify and isolate faxing issues**
- Common fax issues
- Cannot send, cannot receive, random disconnections, speed, reception/send image quality
- Common causes of faxing issues
- Bad fax card, noise on the line, line levels, non-analog line, bad cable, wrong port, inappropriate document orientation, DSL interference, call-waiting, line share devices, firmware, no dial tone
- Identify similarities between faxes and scanners as it relates to image quality issues when transmitting faxes or copying
- Identify similarities between faxes and printers as it relates to image quality issues when receiving faxes or printing
8.1	**Demonstrate and apply safety procedures**
- Demonstrate proper use of cleaning solutions and sprays

Troubleshooting

Explanation

Troubleshooting is the process of determining the cause of and, ultimately, the solution to, a problem. By applying a logical, consistent method to the troubleshooting process, you make your job easier and shorten the time it takes to discover the root of a problem.

There are several popular models that you can follow when troubleshooting printer and scanner problems, but all models incorporate basic troubleshooting theory. The stages of basic troubleshooting theory are described in the following table.

Stage	Description
Observe	Gather information and validate the symptoms. Verify all aspects of the problem. Be sure not to overlook the obvious problems; remember never to make assumptions.
Establish theory of probable cause	Assess the problem systematically. Attempt to isolate the problem by eliminating non-causes. If it's a large or widespread problem, divide the problem into smaller components to be analyzed individually. Determine whether the problem is something simple. Use tools and service documentation as needed.
Test and analyze	Try to recreate the problem and evaluate the theory you established in the last stage. Validate the theory.
Determine next steps	Establish priorities for resolving the problem.
Implement and validate	Implement the solution and validate its effectiveness.
Document	Document your findings. This includes the actions you take and the outcomes of your actions, both for those solutions that worked and for those that didn't.

Documentation

Documentation is the key to the success of any troubleshooting model you choose to follow. Documentation takes two forms: that which is provided by others and that which you create yourself.

You'll find product manuals, service documentation, manufacturer Web sites, and technology-related databases to be invaluable sources of information when troubleshooting. You should consult these references early in the troubleshooting process to determine if you're dealing with a known problem with a previously published solution. Service documentation includes the theory of operation, which describes in detail the printer's internal components and function, block diagrams, and circuit/wiring diagrams, such as the example shown in Exhibit 4-3.

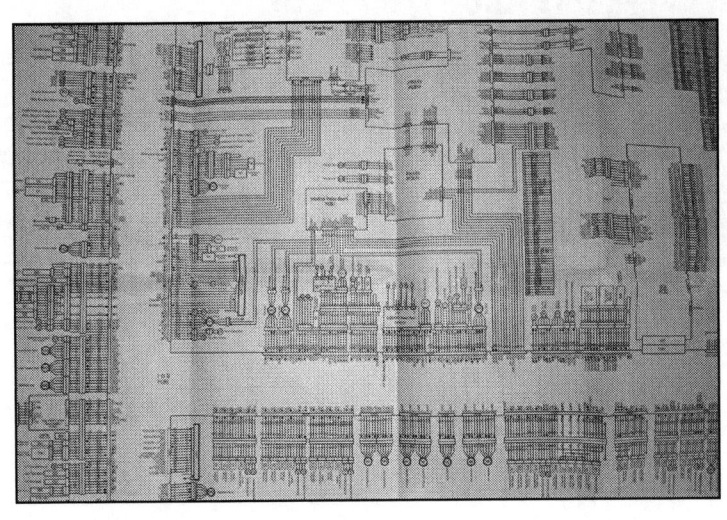

Exhibit 4-3: Point-to-point diagram

Problems that you must solve are often specific to your customers' combinations of hardware and software, as well as to how they use their systems. Your notes are the best reference for future problems, because they apply specifically to your customer's environment.

You must consider the factors described in the following table when determining the best documentation solution for your needs.

Item	Description
Paper or software	You must determine which is best for your needs, a paper-based or software-based record of problems and solutions. Paper logs are well suited for one- or two-person troubleshooting teams. You probably need to turn to software solutions for larger or distributed troubleshooting teams. If you use a software-based system, you must consider how to maintain the information and make it available during a computer outage or after a disaster.
Organization scheme	How you organize your log information determines how you can find the data later. If you're using software, it determines which scheme or schemes you must use. If you're using paper, you could organize your notes by hardware component, by software application, by problem symptom, by user or department, by location, or other scheme.
Level of detail	Only you and your troubleshooting team can determine how much information to record. If you don't record enough detail about the problem and its solution, the documentation is useless for solving future similar problems.

The Microsoft Knowledge Base

When you're having a problem with a computer running a Microsoft operating system, an excellent troubleshooting reference is the *Microsoft Knowledge Base*. This Web site contains problem and solution references for Windows 2000 Professional, Windows XP Professional, and Windows Vista. Sometimes, it provides a hyperlink to an FTP site, where you can download patches, new releases, or updated drivers. The Knowledge Base explains many Microsoft error messages. You can enter the specific message in the Search box and retrieve a description of the error's cause and a solution for resolving the problem.

To access the Microsoft Knowledge Base:

1. Using Internet Explorer or another Web browser, go to `support.microsoft.com`
2. Click Search the Knowledge Base.
3. Type a keyword or words for the search.
4. To find more results, click the Back button in your Web browser, and select a larger number of articles in the Results list.
5. Click an article to read it.

You can print articles or save them to your hard disk for later reference.

TIPS: Microsoft doesn't always code its Web sites to work well with other browsers. If students are having a problem using the site, they should switch to Internet Explorer.

Do it!

B-1: Troubleshooting problems

Questions and answers

1. Hector reports that his scanner doesn't work. Describe the first step you would take to fix his problem.

   First, you should gather information and identify the exact problem through a series of open-ended questions. For example, "What isn't working?" or "Can you describe the problem to me?"

2. Isabelle calls you to say she can't print from Microsoft Word but can print fine from other applications. She has a complex system with a scanner, two printers, a fax device, and dual monitors. What would your first steps be?

   After acquiring exact information, such as the applications being used and any error codes, you should simplify her system. Disconnect any devices that aren't being actively used and see if the problem remains.

3. What documentation should you record once you've found the solution to Hector's and Isabelle's problems?

   Answers will vary, but should include:
   - *The error symptoms*
   - *The components you removed from the computer*
   - *The solutions you tried and whether they were successful*
   - *A fully documented resolution for later reference*
   - *Any significant or obvious solutions that turned out not to be the cause of this problem, so that you can avoid dead ends in the future*

Do it!

B-2: Using Microsoft Knowledge Base to research a problem

Questions and answers

1 A user calls to report that, when she tries to print her PowerPoint presentation, she receives an error message that tells her there's "no printer installed." What might you search for on the Microsoft Knowledge Base to help resolve this problem?

   You can search for "no printer installed" or "PowerPoint printer" or even "printer error." However it's best to start your search with the text of a specific error message, if that's the problem reported.

2 If necessary, log on to your computer as **PDIADMIN*XX*** with a password of **Pa$$321**

3 Access the Microsoft Knowledge Base at **support.microsoft.com**

4 Click **Search the Knowledge Base**

5 Enter keywords in the For text box   Try searching for the text of the error message.

   Examine the results

6 Try more generic searches for printer and scanner problems

Problem and resolution tracking

Explanation

It's important to maintain information about the problems you need to resolve and the resolutions to those problems. You must keep track of all open issues, so you and your support technician teammates don't let customers slip through the cracks. Having a record of past resolutions can assist you when you encounter similar problems in the future.

Tracking options

The options for tracking problems and resolutions are nearly endless. You can do something as simple as a pen-and-paper-based system in a 3-ring binder to an off-the-shelf problem-tracking and resolution database system to a custom-built application. It all depends on the size of the user base you're supporting and the needs of the organization.

Whichever system you use, it's recommended you maintain a backup copy in a secure location so, if something happens to the original, you have access to the copy from another location. A system on a server could be unavailable due to server problems, network problems, or computer workstation problems. Any system could be unavailable due to fire or natural disaster problems.

Important information you should consider tracking in your system includes:

- User name
- User location
- Operating system
- Hardware platform
- Date call was received
- Date user was visited
- Time spent on problem
- Date problem was resolved
- Detailed description of the problem
- Detailed description of steps to resolve the problem
- Summary of problem (using keywords or a one-line summary)
- Summary of resolution (using keywords or a one-line summary)

Help desk software

Many vendors offer software to help manage problem-tracking and help desk functions. Companies such as IBM, Computer Associates, and others offer large-scale commercial problem-tracking applications.

Many smaller companies offer similar packages aimed at smaller company needs or for targeted vertical markets. For example, you can find applications designed specifically to support the tracking needs of Web site hosting companies or software developers.

Visit www.helpdesk.com/software-helpdesk.htm for a long list of help desk software publishers and their web sites. Further information, particularly on the smaller vendor products, is also available at http://linas.org/linux/pm.html.

Do it! **B-3: Tracking problems and resolutions**

Here's how

1 Use Internet Explorer to search the Web for a problem-tracking system

2 List the features in the solution you found.

Answers will vary

3 Are there any features you'd like that aren't included in this solution?

Answers will vary

4 Would your organization be more likely to develop its own database to track problems or to purchase some type of problem-tracking system? Would it be very basic or an integrated solution with modules for tracking assets as well as problem-tracking? Explain your reasons.

Answers will vary

Printer troubleshooting

When troubleshooting printer problems, which can include failed, distorted, and defective print jobs, you can employ the general troubleshooting steps described earlier to isolate the problem to one of the following areas:

- The application trying to print to the printer
- The printer
- The operating system and drivers
- The connection, either a printer cable or the network adapter, network cable, and the network between the computer and printer

The application

To troubleshoot the application, first restart the application. If that doesn't solve the problem, try printing other files from the same application.

- If you can print other files from the same application, troubleshoot the file that wouldn't print.
- If the other files won't print either, then try printing from another application, especially a simple text editor, such as Notepad.
- If you can print from another application, troubleshoot the application that's causing problems, using the manufacturer's documentation or Web site.
- If you can't print from any applications, move on to test the printer.

The printer

To verify that the printer is online and working, check its control panel or onboard screen. Look for any service error messages, which can indicate critical operational failures. (Service messages might also appear on the user's screen, if the printer or print server is configured to display messages to users.) If the printer displays a service or error code, refer to the manufacturer's documentation or Web site for a description of the error and the recommended solutions. Some common error and informational messages include:

- "Add media," which indicates empty paper trays or cassettes, or if the paper supplies are full, a possible sensor problem.
- "Add supplies" or "Add toner," which can indicate a low toner supply or a sensor problem.
- "Regular maintenance," which can indicate that a part's life counter has reached a number where regular maintenance is suggested for a specific component, such as the drum.
- "Paper jam," which indicates an obstructed paper path or a problem with a sensor.
- "Incorrect media," which can indicate a problem with the media in the trays or a problem with driver and option settings.

If there are no error codes, print an engine test page by using the printer's control panel, touch-screen, or a engine-test button located somewhere on the printer (refer to the manufacturer's documentation). If the test is successful, assume the printer is working properly. Then, on the computer, troubleshoot the operating system and drivers and the connection.

Finally, you can also print a user setting list, which details the all the settings you can modify directly on the printer (not through the operating system). You can check to see if these settings are correct before continuing on to troubleshoot the operating system and drivers.

Operating system and drivers

If the printer is online, and you can print a test page using the printer's control panel, try to print a test page from the printer's Properties dialog box in Windows.

- If the test page prints from the Properties dialog box, you can stop troubleshooting the printer and the connection, the operating system, and the drivers. Go back and troubleshoot the application and verify that the application settings aren't conflicting with the driver settings.
- If the test page doesn't print from the Properties dialog box, try these options:
  - In the Printers window, verify that the printer status is "Ready." If the printer status is "Offline," put the printer into the "Ready" state.
  - Use the printer's Properties dialog box to verify the most current version of the correct driver is installed. If necessary, update the driver, or uninstall and then reinstall the drivers.
  - Verify the driver port settings, using the printer's Properties dialog box.
  - Verify that accessories and options, such as duplex printing, configured for the print job are supported by the printer driver.
  - Check the Windows event logs for any error messages related to printing. (You might have to consult with a technician who's experienced in operating system troubleshooting.)

The connection

To test a network connection, use TCP/IP utilities to verify that the computer is connected to the network and can communicate with other devices. You might need to work with a network technician.

To test a local connection, verify that the cable is securely connected at both ends, and then try printing a test page. If the test page won't print, try printing from the computer with a different cable:

- If the test page prints, the problem was probably with the cable.
- If the test page won't print, try printing from another computer using the original cable:
  - If you can print the test page, the problem is with the original system and the drivers.
  - If you still can't print a test page using another printer with the same connection, the problem is likely with the printer, the cable, or the drivers.

When troubleshooting the connection, look for any of the following possible causes of connectivity issues, including slow printing, intermittent activity, communications errors, unexpected output, and no output at all.

In some cases, you might need to consult with a network administrator or technician or refer to the manufacturer's documentation for error codes and messages, not just for printers but for any network devices, such as hubs, switches, routers, and print servers.

- Loose, broken, damaged, or improperly wired cables. You can probably check the printer cable and network cable attached to the computer and printer, but you might need assistance to check cables elsewhere in the network or the cable attached to a printer server locked in a server room.
- Broken or malfunctioning network devices. This step is likely to involve a network technician. Check for blinking LEDs or link lights on network devices such as routers or hubs to verify network activity.
- Incorrect protocol, network settings, or TCP/IP settings on the computer that's experiencing problems, and on network devices, such as print servers or on the network printer itself.
- Bad network card on the problem computer, the network printer, or the print server. Check for a blinking LED light on the network card to verify network activity.
- Firmware on network printers and other network devices, such as routers.
- Electromagnetic interference (EMI) or other interference from nearby electrical devices. While this isn't usually a big problem, sometimes network cables that are too close to electrical devices can cause intermittent connectivity problems.
- Wireless connection problems, including obstacles within the line of site of a wireless device and wireless access point. Obstacles can include walls and other structural components, and devices that can cause interference with radio waves, including other wireless devices.

Printer issues

When you've ruled out the application, the operating system, the drivers, and the connection, you've isolated the problem to the printer. Use the following sections to find a cause and solution for the specific print issue.

Dark images

The following table lists possible causes of and solutions for text or graphics that are too dark.

Cause	Solutions
Application settings; printer settings	Adjust settings to lighten the text and graphics.

Light or weak images

The following table lists possible causes of and solutions for light or weak text and graphics.

Cause	Solutions
Low toner	Remove toner cartridge and shake horizontally, or per manufacturer's instructions, to redistribute toner. Replace toner cartridge as necessary.
Laser failing	Test and replace the laser assembly.
Incorrect paper	Replace paper according to manufacturer's specification.

Repetitive image defects

The following table lists possible causes of and solutions for repetitive image defects.

Cause	Solutions
Drum defect	Clean drum, if possible. Replace drum.
Faulty registration rollers	Clean or repair rollers and gears. Replace, as necessary.
Debris on heated fusing roller	Unplug printer and allow the heated roller to cool for at least 15 minutes. Clean roller following manufacturer's recommendations. Replace roller or fuser assembly, if necessary.

Ghosting and shadows

The following table lists possible causes of and solutions for ghosting and shadows on printed pages.

Cause	Solutions
Residual toner on the drum	Repair or replace cleaning blade and discharge lamps. Replace drum if necessary.
Drum not discharging properly	Repair or replace drum.
Primary corona not putting adequate conditioning charge on drum	Repair or replace primary corona.

Smearing

The following table lists possible causes of and solutions for smeared or smudged text and graphics.

Cause	Solutions
Dirty or worn registration rollers	Clean debris from rollers. Clean rollers. Clean and replace damaged gears.
Dirty or worn registration assembly	Clean, reinstall, or replace.
Dirt or debris on polygon mirror	Clean the mirror and optical components.
Damp or moist paper	Replace paper supply with fresh paper. Store all consumables in a dry, cool location.
Incorrect paper	Replace paper with paper recommended by the manufacturer.
Fuser not at correct temperature	Inspect thermistor and thermistor cable. Test and replace fuser assembly. Replace worn or missing cleaning pads in fuser assembly.

Banding

The following table lists possible causes of and solutions for banding.

Cause	Solutions
Paper feed problem	Inspect paper path and remove any obstructions or paper scraps.
Specially coated paper	Replace paper with paper recommended by the manufacturer.
Registration roller worn or dirty	Clean rollers. Clean and replace damaged gears.
HVPS ground loose (heavy banding)	Check that HPVS harness isn't crimped or shorted by other assemblies.
Laser/scanner assembly failure (white horizontal lines)	Check connectors on main logic board and mechanical control boards. Replace boards. Replace laser assembly.

Focus

The following table lists possible causes of and solutions for unfocused text and graphics.

Cause	Solutions
Not enough toner on drum	Remove toner cartridge and shake to redistribute, or replace empty toner cartridge.
Loose or improperly mounted laser assembly	Remount the laser assembly.
Incorrect paper	Replace paper with paper recommended by the manufacturer.
Fusing temperature or pressure too low	Replace worn or missing pads is fuser assembly. Adjust roller pressure.
HVPS failing	Troubleshoot and replace HVPS.

Voided areas

The following table lists possible causes of and solutions for blank or voided areas.

Cause	Solutions
Paper entering printer too early	Check registration rollers and registration roller clutch. If clutch is jammed in on position, repair or replace.
Damaged drum	Examine drum surface and replace, if necessary.
Limited memory	Try printing simpler print jobs to see if they're successful. Install more memory, if possible.
Slipping gear/failing motor drive	Repair or replace gears or motor drive assembly.

Registration, jitters, skew

The following table lists possible causes of and solutions for printed pages that show registration errors and jitters, and text and graphics that are skewed.

Cause	Solutions
Problems with pick-up roller or separation pad	Verify that the pick-up roller is operating properly. Clean and remove any obstructions. Replace components, as needed.
Faulty rollers or roller assembly	Replace worn rollers or roller assemblies.
Drive train worn or clogged	Check for proper operation of gears in drive train; remove debris, if necessary.
Paper path obstructions	Check for and remove paper path obstructions.
Damaged paper tray	Verify the paper tray isn't worn or defective. Check paper guide tabs.
Special paper	If a heavyweight or paper is used, try printing with plain 20lb paper or the paper recommended by the manufacturer.
Paper in paper path at wrong angle	Check for loose or bent paper guide tabs. Check for obstructions or debris buildup in paper path.

Misaligned color registration

The following table lists possible causes of and solutions for misaligned color registration.

Cause	Solutions
Misaligned print heads on inkjet printers	Print color registration test page and recalibrate print heads, following manufacturer's instructions.
Misaligned or worn transfer belt	Recalibrate or replace transfer belt.

Weak or missing color

The following table lists possible causes of and solutions for weak or missing colors.

Cause	Solutions
Low toner supply (EP printer)	Remove toner cartridges and shake horizontally to redistribute toner. Replace cartridges, as necessary.
Low ink supply (inkjet printer)	Replace ink cartridges
Dried ink in nozzles (inkjet printer)	Follow the manufacturer's directions to clean print head manually or using printer's software.
Incorrect paper	Replace paper with paper recommended by the manufacturer.

Vertical and horizontal black/white lines

The following table lists possible causes of and solutions for horizontal or vertical black and white lines on printed pages.

Cause	Solutions
Misaligned beam detector (horizontal black lines)	Remount beam detector. Remount laser assembly. Replace beam detector. Replace laser assembly.
Dirty transfer corona (vertical white lines)	Clean transfer corona.
Blocked laser beam or LED (vertical white lines)	Remove dust and debris from laser aperture, LEDs, or other optical components.
Failed or failing beam sensor (horizontal white lines)	Reseat or replace cables from beam sensor. Replace laser assembly.
Debris in toner cartridge (vertical white line)	Check for debris (tape, staples, etc.) in the cartridge where the magnetic roller lifts the toner out of its trough. Remove debris.

Black or blank pages

The following table lists possible causes of and solutions for black or blank pages.

Cause	Solutions
Damaged primary corona (black pages)	Replace primary corona.
Faulty drum (blank pages)	Replace drum.
Defective logic board (black pages, banding)	Replace logic board.
Defective toner cartridge	Replace toner cartridge.

Transport/feed issues

Transport and feed issues, some of which have already been described above, include the following:

- Media jamming
- Skewing
- Creasing, wrinkling, folding, and tearing
- Multiple sheets feeding in at one time (multifeeding) and misdirected media (misfeeding)
- Burning

To troubleshoot any of these issues, look for and correct the following causes:

- Foreign objects: Check for foreign objects, such as staples, paper clips, and tape. Clear away any jammed paper, paper scraps, or other debris.
- Damaged media: Verify that all media conforms to manufacturer's recommendations and isn't damaged, warped, wet, or too dry. Damaged or incorrect media can cause burning or scorching when it reaches the fuser assembly.
- Media feed problems: Check for problems with the pickup roller, separation pad, and registration assembly. Check any roller that's involved in moving the paper through the printer or multifunction device, including the rollers in any automatic document feeder. Make sure paper is fresh and matches the manufacturer's specifications.
- Media feed timing: Check the pickup rollers and registration assembly.
- Separation: Ensure that the transfer corona is working properly, so the media doesn't stick to the drum, and check the heated fusing roller to ensure that the media isn't sticking to it.
- Duplex: Check the duplex assembly if a duplex print job is causing problems in the printer.
- Fusing: Make sure the media is properly separating from the heated roller in the fusing assembly. Make sure the fuser is at the proper temperature, and, to prevent burning and scorching, check that the assembly doesn't contain any debris.

- Media exit and delivery: Make sure the exit rollers aren't blocked or jammed with any debris or foreign objects, and ensure that they're working properly. Check any finishing assemblies, such as staplers or collators, for wear or malfunction.
- Faulty sensors: If there are no foreign objects or debris in the paper path, and you can't find any other problems, check for malfunctioning sensors that could be giving false paper jam errors.

You can also perform a paper path test using the printer's control panel or onboard screen. This test pulls paper through the printer. If the print ejects the paper, there's no paper path obstruction. If the paper jams, the printer informs you of the specific location in the paper path. You can then examine that location for paper, debris, foreign objects, or failed sensors. If the printer has multiple paper trays, you can perform the test on each tray to help isolate the problem to a specific tray.

Do it!

B-4: Troubleshooting printer problems

You must set up this activity according to the Troubleshooting Labs Setup section of the Course Setup instructions.

Here's how	Here's why
1 Determine if you can print a document from within Notepad	One or more problems were introduced into your system. You need to resolve them.
2 Determine if you can successfully print a Test Page	From the printer's Properties dialog box.
If possible, print an engine test page or a user setting list	Follow the instructions in the documentation.
3 Determine if the print quality of the page is acceptable	You might need to perform some printer maintenance to resolve print quality problems.
4 Document the problem(s) you find	**Answers will vary, based on the problems introduced into the system.**
5 Use the concepts in this topic to take the appropriate steps to resolve the problem(s) you encountered	
6 Document the steps you took to resolve the problem(s):	**Answers will vary, based on the problems introduced into the system and on the steps taken to resolve them.**
7 Test the system	To verify that the problems were completely resolved.

Repeat this activity multiple times to provide students with the opportunity to troubleshoot multiple problems on more than one type of printer.

Scanner troubleshooting

When troubleshooting scanner and multifunction device problems, you can employ the same troubleshooting steps you use to troubleshoot printers. You want to isolate the problem to one of the following areas:

- The application
- The operating system and drivers
- The connection, either the cable connecting the scanner directly to the computer, or the network adapter, network cable, and the network between the computer and printer (or fax card or modem, phone cord, and phone line for faxes on multifunction devices)
- The scanner

On the computer connected to the scanner or on the multifunction device's control panel, look for any service error messages, which can indicate critical operational failures. If the scanner displays a service or error code, refer to the manufacturer's documentation or Web site for a description of the error and the suggested solutions. Some common error and informational messages for multifunction devices include:

- "Add media"
- "Add supplies" or "Low ink"
- "Media jam"

If your scanner is receiving power and is recognized by Windows but won't actually scan an image, the problem could be with an engaged *carriage lock*. The carriage lock keeps the mechanism that physically scans images from moving and being damaged when you transport the scanner. Typically, you find the lock underneath or in the back of the scanner. You should check to see if a scanner has a carriage lock before you set it up for the user and disengage it. If the user tries to scan an image when the carriage is locked, the scanner won't scan. Instead, the user hears loud grating noises, and the scanner's internal lamp might flash, as the carriage tries to move but can't. Repeatedly attempting to scan images on a scanner with a carriage lock engaged can do serious damage to the scanner's components.

The application

First try restarting the application to reinitialize it. If that doesn't work, verify the scanning application's settings to determine if they're the cause of the problems. Scanning settings include:

- Resolution
- Color depth
- Single-sided versus double-sided (duplex) scans
- Media size
- Exposure levels
- File format
- Reduction and enlargement
- Monochrome versus color
- ADF versus flatbed scanner

Many scanners come with application software to scan images using either controls within the operating system interface or manual buttons on the front of the device. Typically, these buttons need software from the device manufacturer to function correctly. If a scanner is working correctly using the operating system interface controls but not when you use the buttons on the front of the device, you should verify that the software from the device manufacturer has been installed. You might want to check the manufacturer's Web site for any updates as well.

Operating system and drivers

Verify that you're using the appropriate driver and driver version for the scanner or multifunction device. The scanner probably uses a TWAIN, WIA, or ISIS driver. If the scanner driver you have installed isn't compatible with the scanner or the operating system, install the correct driver and test the scanner. If the problem still isn't resolved, or if image problems persist, continue troubleshooting using the guidelines below.

Connection

To test the connection, try using a different cable between the scanner and the computer. If the scanner works, suspect the cable as the problem.

If the scanner still doesn't work, test the scanner and the original cable on a different computer. If the scanner works, you can focus on the original computer by troubleshooting the operating system and drivers.

If the scanner or multifunction device is on the network, troubleshoot the network card on both the computer and the scanner, and the network cables and devices. You might need to consult with a network technician to troubleshoot network connectivity. If you can't find any problems with the network connection, focus on the computer's operating system and drivers.

Many scanner problems are caused by improper USB connections. If your scanner doesn't work at all:

- Make sure the scanner is plugged into a built-in USB port and not a secondary USB port, such as a keyboard connection. If you have to plug the scanner into a USB hub, make sure the hub has its own power supply.
- Check the cable's length between the scanner and the computer. USB cables should be as short as possible. A USB cable that's more than 6 feet long has trouble transferring data, especially in an environment where there's considerable electrical interference.
- Verify that you're using the correct USB cable and that it's plugged into the correct ports.
- If the scanner works when you first boot up Windows but then stops working, check the power management features within Windows. The operating system could be turning off (putting to sleep) the USB port due to inactivity.

Finally, some older scanners connect to the computer via a parallel cable. If the computer has a single parallel port that both a scanner and a printer must share, each time the user wants to switch between the printer and the scanner, they must restart the computer after connecting the new device.

Image quality issues

When troubleshooting image quality issues, refer to the following table, which describes some common issues and suggests possible causes. If you can replace a part, be sure to contact the manufacturer or authorized reseller for a replacement. In some cases, you might find that it's more cost-efficient to replace the entire scanner or multifunction device than it is to replace a part. In some cases, it might not be possible to replace scanner or multifunction device components.

When testing and calibrating scanner settings, you can use a test or target chart or calibration strip, all of which provide an objective standard that can be used to measure scanner performance better than user documents or photographs.

Issue	Cause	Resolution
Dark images	Scan lamp; glass contamination; scanner settings	Repair or replace scan lamp; clean glass; adjust scanner settings.
Light or weak images	Scan lamp; glass contamination	Replace scan lamp. Clean glass.
Banding and vertical/horizontal black/blank lines	Glass contamination	Clean glass.
Out of focus	Dirty or defective mirrors, lens, or CCD	Clean, repair, or replace components, as necessary.
Shadows	Alignment; defective rollers	Repair or replace rollers.
Voided areas	Limited memory; rollers; ADF; alignment; cables	Add more memory, if possible. Repair, clean, or replace rollers inside the multifunction device or in the ADF to correct alignment. Reseat cables, and replace as necessary.
Jitters, skew, and registration errors	Rollers; ADF	Repair, clean, or replace rollers inside the multifunction device or in the ADF.
Misaligned color registration	Rollers; improper calibration; scanner software settings	Repair, clean, or replace rollers. Recalibrate scanner or multifunction device. Verify and reconfigure scanner software settings.
Weak or missing color	Scan lamp; CCD; contaminated glass	Repair or replace scan lamp and CCD. Clean glass.
Vertical stripes that are brighter than the surrounding image	White *reference plate* (also known as a *calibration strip*) is dirty	If possible, clean the strip. (This might be impossible, if it's sealed under the scanner glass.) Adjust driver settings.
Image incomplete or distorted	Defective storage device	Make sure the storage device has sufficient storage space for scanned files. Check with a network administrator about file size and space restrictions.

Faxing issues

Typically, problems you encounter when you send faxes are similar to those you might encounter when using a scanner to create an image file. The same components that create the image for faxing also create the image file when you scan a document. Likewise, when receiving a fax, you might encounter problems similar to those you encounter when printing, because the same components are responsible for producing a printed page.

The following table describes the causes of and the solutions for common fax problems you might encounter in a multifunction device.

Issue	Cause	Solution
Fax won't send	Bad fax card; non-analog line; bad cable; wrong port; no dial tone	Replace fax card. Connect device to analog phone line. Replace phone cable. Insert connector into correct port. Ensure that phone line is operable.
Can't receive faxes	Bad fax card; non-analog line; bad cable; wrong port	Replace fax card. Connect device to analog phone line. Replace phone cable. Insert connector into correct port. Ensure that phone line is operable.
Random disconnections	Noise on the line; line levels; bad cable; call-waiting; line share devices; firmware	Contact the telephone company for line testing and service, if necessary. Replace cable. Disable call-waiting. Remove other devices from the same phone line. Upgrade firmware.
Slow speed	Noise on the line; line levels; DSL interference	Contact the telephone company for line testing and service, if necessary.
Poor quality sent fax	Bad fax card; bad cables; line levels; noise on the line; inappropriate document orientation	Replace fax card. Replace cables. Contact the telephone company for line testing and service, if necessary. Resend document.
No dial tone	Bad fax card; bad cable; wrong port	Replace fax card. Replace phone cable. Insert connector into correct port. Ensure that phone line is operable.

Maintenance and troubleshooting **4–29**

Do it!

B-5: Troubleshooting scanner and multifunction device problems

🗗 *You must set up this activity according to the Troubleshooting Labs Setup section of the Course Setup instructions.*

Provide students with a test chart or other material to scan.

Here's how	Here's why
1 Determine if you can successfully scan a test page	One or more problems were introduced into your system. You need to resolve them.
2 Determine if the quality of the output is acceptable	
3 Document the problem(s) you find	*Answers will vary, based on the problems introduced into the system.*
4 Use the concepts in this topic to take the appropriate steps to resolve the problem(s) you encountered	
5 Document the steps you took to resolve the problem(s):	*Answers will vary, based on the problems introduced into the system and the steps taken to resolve them.*
6 Test the system	To verify that the problems were completely resolved.

Repeat this activity multiple times to provide students with the opportunity troubleshoot scanner and fax problems.

Unit summary: Maintenance and troubleshooting

Topic A   In this topic, you learned how to maintain printers and scanners. You learned the steps you should perform during **routine maintenance** of inkjet and EP printers, including replacing **consumables**, removing accumulated dust and toner, replacing parts based on **parts-life counters**, and ensuring a well-ventilated environment. Finally, you learned that scanners typically, require little maintenance other than ensuringthat the scanner glass is clean and dry.

Topic B   In this topic, you learned to troubleshoot printers and scanners. You learned how to isolate problems in printers and scanners, and you learned to troubleshoot problems with **image quality**.

Review questions

1. True or false? You may use any vacuum to clean accumulated toner from inside a printer.

    True (but not recommended)

2. What are some of actions you should perform during routine maintenance of inkjet printers?

    Answers will include replacing ink cartridges, removing accumulated dust, and cleaning the purge unit.

3. What are some of the actions you should perform during routine maintenance of EP printers?

    Answers will include replacing toner cartridges or any components based on the parts-life counters, cleaning and lubricating internal components, replacing filters, removing accumulated toner, and checking for firmware updates.

4. What should you always do when you've completed maintenance on a printer?

    Print a test page to ensure that the printer is working correctly.

5. What should you always do when you've completed maintenance on a scanner?

    Scan a test chart to ensure that the scanner is working correctly.

6. What are the general steps you should employ when troubleshooting printer and scanner problems?

    Observe; establish a theory of probable cause; test and analyze; determine next steps; implement and validate; and document.

7. Microsoft _____ is a Web site that contains problem and solution references for Microsoft applications and Windows operating systems.

    Knowledge Base

8. True or false? When troubleshooting a print job from an application, the first thing you should troubleshoot is the printer cable.

    False

9 When might you have to consult with a network technician or administrator when troubleshooting a network printing issue?

When you've isolated the problem to the network or a network component.

10 Which of the following is the name given to network interference from electrical devices?

A API

B EPI

C EMI

D ECI

11 True or false? Low toner is a likely cause of repetitive image defects.

False

12 Why might improperly stored paper cause smearing?

The toner won't adhere to the paper properly.

13 Which of the following is the most likely cause of ghosting or shadows on printed page?

A Accumulated toner on the transfer corona

B Broken paper guides

C Faulty sensor in registration assembly

D Residual toner on the drum

14 Which of the following are possible causes of smudged print? (Choose all that apply.)

A Low toner

B Damp paper

C Debris on the laser scanning mirror

D Limited memory

15 What problems might you see if the temperature of the fuser is too low?

Answers will include smearing and unfocused text and graphics.

16 What's the likely culprit when you have printed copies that are skewed or misaligned?

A problem in the paper path, including rollers and registration assembly.

17 What problem should you suspect if you have weak or missing color on printed pages?

The color toner supply or incorrect paper.

18 List some likely problems you'd see on pages printed in a laser printer with a faulty drum.

Answers will include repetitive image defects, blank pages, light or weak text and graphics, voided areas, and ghosts or shadows.

19 How can a paper path test help you isolate a problem in a laser printer?

It can show you where there's a problem in the paper path, from the paper tray to the exit rollers.

20 What problems might you suspect when a scanned image is too light?

Problems with the lamp or glass contamination.

21 What problem should you suspect when you try to send a fax, but there's no dial tone?

Answers will include defective fax card, defective cable, or the cable is plugged into the wrong port on the multifunction device.

Independent practice activity

In this activity, you'll obtain maintenance information for a printer and then troubleshoot it.

1 Obtain the manufacturer and model of a laser printer in your classroom, training center, or school, or at your place of business. Go to the manufacturer's Web site and find the documentation for the printer.

2 How often does the manufacturer recommend service? Detail the maintenance steps recommended at each different page-count threshold.

Answers will vary by manufacturer.

3 What kind of maintenance kits are available and what do they contain?

Answers will vary by manufacturer.

4 Are there updated firmware or drivers available for download?

Answers will vary by manufacturer.

5 Work with another student to introduce a problem into a printer.

6 Try to print a test page from the printer.

7 Examine the output, if any, to determine if it's acceptable quality.

8 Document any problems you encountered along with the steps you took to resolve the problem.

Unit 5
Professional conduct

Unit time: 120 minutes

Complete this unit, and you'll know how to:

A Communicate effectively with clients.

B Maintain a safe work environment.

Topic A: Communication

This topic covers the following CompTIA PDI+ exam objectives.

#	Objective
7.1	**Define and demonstrate effective communication and relationship building skills** • Use appropriate introduction • Use active listening skills • Probing: Asking open ended and closed ended questions • Show empathy for the customer • Speak clearly and concisely at all times • Use appropriate terminology for the audience • Clarify and confirm the customer's expectations and/or concerns • Provide closure the for the client at the end of the service call • Communicate status of repair and/or open issues – follow up calls when necessary • Use articulate and legible written communication
7.2	**Define and demonstrate effective communication skills with technical support** • Follow appropriate escalation procedures • Call from onsite and have appropriate reference materials available when speaking with technical support • Describe the problem, service history and troubleshooting steps accurately with appropriate terminology • Clarify and confirm technical support recommendations • Follow further escalation procedures if necessary
7.3	**Display and practice professional conduct with internal and external customers/contacts** • Maintain a positive attitude concerning the manufacturer of the product • Treat the customer with courtesy and respect, including the customer's property • Act as liaison between internal and external customers • Take ownership of the issues and follow through to its conclusion

Effective communication

Explanation

Effective communication involves both verbal and nonverbal techniques. How you use your voice says a great deal about you. Listeners take note of your vocal characteristics and form opinions about your sincerity, enthusiasm, and even your knowledge of the topic being discussed. Your body language also clues listeners into your state of mind. Your posture, the firmness of your handshake, and your willingness to make eye contact all tell listeners something about your personality and character. You need to make sure you're communicating the same message with both your voice and your body language.

Verbal communication

Your voice often indicates whether you're nervous, which might affect how a listener perceives your credibility. Being able to control your voice and communicate in a pleasing way attracts and maintains listeners' attention. There are three vocal characteristics you can control to become a more effective speaker: volume, rate, and pitch.

- *Volume* is a vocal characteristic you need to tailor to the environment. Room size, number of listeners, and external noise should all influence the volume of your voice. Make sure your listeners can hear everything you say.
- *Rate* is the speed at which you speak. Every person has an individual natural rate, so it's important to adapt your rate to the topic and listener. Nervous speakers tend to speak rapidly. If you feel anxious about the message you're delivering, you should try to maintain a slow, even rate of speech, so that the listener hears the actual message instead of being distracted by your nervousness. Conversely, you shouldn't let your speaking rate drop much below 120 words per minute, or you risk losing the listener's attention. Stay enthusiastic about your message to maintain an appropriate rate.
- *Pitch* is the highness or lowness of your voice. When your vocal muscles are taut, your voice has a high pitch; when your vocal muscles are relaxed, your voice has a low pitch. If you're nervous, your vocal muscles tighten and your voice rises above its natural pitch.

Rate and volume also affect your pitch. When you speak rapidly, your muscles are tense, which causes your pitch to rise. Speaking loudly also causes your pitch to rise. Although pitch variations might be useful in emphasizing certain points, generally it's best to maintain an even and natural pitch in most situations.

Negative language

Negative language can be expressed in a variety of ways, but the main concern with negative language is the word "no." The word "no" delivers a blunt, end-of-conversation attitude, regardless of the rest of the message. If at all possible, avoid using the word "no" and any other negative language such as "can't," "won't," and "don't." Also, avoid criticizing specific manufacturers or vendors, and don't criticize a previous support technician, if his or her work didn't completely fix the problem at a previous service call.

Inflammatory language

Inflammatory language is meant to stir intense negative emotions in the listener. It's often prejudicial against someone because of gender, ethnicity, or physical attributes. Inflammatory language is always inappropriate in the workplace or at customer locations.

Powerful language

Powerful language involves the use of clear, direct statements of fact and feeling, rather than dancing around an issue. A powerful speaker lets you know exactly what the situation is and how to handle it efficiently and effectively.

A powerless speaker uses "hedge phrases," such as, "I guess…"and "Maybe we should…." Often, powerless speakers form their ideas as questions, such as, "Shouldn't we start the meeting?" instead of stating, "We should start the meeting." Powerless speakers tend to be disappointed with the results of their ambiguity.

Keep in mind that speaking powerfully doesn't mean being blunt, abrupt, or rude. An effective powerful speaker combines politeness with directness so as to be clear and concise.

Name times three

Dale Carnegie's How to Win Friends and Influence People is recommended reading for anyone who interacts with people.

According to Dale Carnegie, "the sweetest sound in any language is the sound of one's own name." People feel that you respect them and believe in their importance when you use their names. The common recommendation is "name times three," which means that you should use a person's name at least three times in any conversation.

Take care to use the other person's name properly. In most business settings, you should start with Mr. ('mist-ər), Ms. (miz), or Mrs. ('mis-əz). If the other person shows less formality or directly requests that you use his or her first name, then do so.

Do it!

A-1: Using effective verbal communication

Questions and answers

1 Identify the characteristics of negative language.

    A Dull, discourages conversation

    B Bold, encourages conversation

    C Blunt, ends conversation

    D Timid, ends conversation

2 Which of the following phrases defines inflammatory language?

    A Inflammatory language is appropriate and insignificant.

    B Inflammatory language stirs negative emotions and is prejudicial.

    C Inflammatory language is angry and prejudicial.

    D Inflammatory language is intense and always appropriate.

Nonverbal communications

Explanation

You're constantly communicating with those around you. You express fear, anger, happiness, sadness, enthusiasm, and many other emotions without even saying a word. It's important to be aware of the signals you are communicating to those around you. It's also important to be able to recognize the nonverbal signals that others are communicating to you.

When meeting with someone, nonverbal communication gives each of you clues about the other's personality, attitudes, and feelings. The five types of nonverbal communication that have the most impact on your conversations are:

- Handshakes
- Expression and eye contact
- Proximity
- Touch
- Gestures and posture
- Physical appearance

Keep in mind that the following recommendations are based on North American customs. If you're working elsewhere in the world, local customs might dictate a different type of behavior. Be sure to ask colleagues about the customs in your locale.

Handshake

A firm handshake is the foundation of any business interaction. Some people carry firmness to an extreme—you aren't out to crush the other person's hand with your handshake. Of course, you don't want to give a "limp rag" handshake either.

A good firm handshake starts with a dry palm; carry a handkerchief if you need to wipe damp palms before entering a situation where you expect to shake someone's hand. Grasp the other person's palm, not just the fingers. Give a positive squeeze but not so firm as to cause discomfort. Use one hand; don't clasp both hands around the other person's hand.

Your handshake should last a couple of seconds, no longer. People are sensitive to being touched and restrained. Too long a handshake makes the other person feel caught in a trap. Of course, the handshake should last long enough to appear deliberate and sincere.

Look the other person in the eye. Introduce yourself with a greeting, such as "Hi, I'm (say your first and last name). Nice to meet you." Let go of the other person's hand and then listen intently as s/he greets you back. Remember the person's name; repeat it to yourself a couple times, if you need to. Then use the "name times three" guideline to help you remember the name.

Expression and eye contact

A friendly expression and direct eye contact send a message that you're open, honest, and enthusiastic. When coming into a meeting or interaction, smile and look into the eyes of the other person as you're introduced. You can show interest in the other person by maintaining eye contact as s/he speaks. When you tilt your head toward the speaker, you give the impression that you're an interested listener. These cues encourage the other person to relax and help open the lines of communication.

Proximity

Personal space is an important element to keep in mind when communicating. Typically, people of a higher status tend to keep more than the normal four to six feet between themselves and their subordinates. Close friends and romantic partners usually keep approximately 18 inches of distance. While you don't want to give the appearance of invading an acquaintance's personal space, too great a distance sends a message that you aren't totally involved in the conversation. Three to five feet of distance evokes feelings of closeness, trust, and parallel status between acquaintances.

Touch

Touch in the workplace must be dealt with carefully. Touching in the workplace is more common between women than men. Appropriate touching can convey openness, trustworthiness, and interest. It can also result in self-disclosure and compliance. Appropriate touching includes a good handshake or sometimes a light touch on the shoulder or arm of an acquaintance.

Inappropriate touching conveys disrespect to the recipient. It might also demonstrate hostility. Inappropriate touching includes lingering contact and caresses or contact to inappropriate areas of the body. When determining the appropriateness of a touch, you should also consider the pressure used in the touch, the body part that does the touching, what body part receives the touch, and if anyone else is present when contact is made.

Many people are easily bothered by touching. Such folks can be offended by a hand on the shoulder or a touch to the arm. When in doubt, don't touch!

Gestures and posture

Although most people are aware of the hand gestures that flow naturally throughout the course of communication, many people are less aware of the messages that hand, leg, and foot activity send. Restless hands or legs can suggest nervousness, which might make people question your honesty or integrity. Fidgeting might also indicate impatience and concealed anger. To ease nervousness, take deep, calming breaths and practice keeping your hands, feet, and legs still.

Keep in mind that there are regional differences in hand gestures. A thumbs up sign can deliver an affirmation of a job well done or can be a vulgar insult depending on where you are in the world. Avoid pointing at people—they can feel they're being accused or reprimanded.

Similarly, your posture can affect the impression you make on someone. Standing or sitting straight signals that you're ready for open communication. Sitting or standing hunched over gives the impression that you're uninterested in conversation or contact.

Appearance

How you dress and look sends a message. Compare your first reaction to these two fictitious technicians:

- Technician A wears dress slacks, a white button-down shirt, and shoes, not sneakers. He keeps his hair short and neatly combed.
- Technician B wears faded blue jeans and a T-shirt advertising a hard rock band. His hair is shaved short on the sides and spiked in the middle. He wears dirty-looking sneakers.

Without judging one look to be better than the other, these two technicians send different signals with their appearance. Which is appropriate for you depends on your industry, company dress code, region, and the expectations of your customers.

Do it!

A-2: Using nonverbal communication effectively

Here's how	Here's why
1 With another student, practice your handshake and greeting. Provide constructive and friendly feedback to your fellow student and accept his or her advice graciously.	
2 With another student, determine your personal space.	Some people are comfortable communicating within a couple feet of another person. Others need more space.
3 With another student, try different postures. Have one person pose while the other guesses at mood and intention. Reverse roles.	
4 Compare your appearance with the expectations of your business, company dress code, region, and customers. Do you look and dress appropriate for those expectations? If not, what should you change?	*Answers will vary.*

Professional service

Explanation

A support technician is often involved in tense situations. When a user needs to print a document for a meeting in five minutes and the printer isn't working, his or her anxiety level can be quite high. As a printer support technician, you have to remain calm and focus on the task at hand.

Introductions

Let the customer know when you've arrived. Introduce yourself and be sure that the customer contact person knows you're there. Don't just check in with one employee or the receptionist without contacting the person who called in the problem.

Ask the client where the problem device is. If there's more than one problem, ask the customer in which order they'd like them fixed. Sometimes one device is more important to the business than another. Be sure to respect the customer's business needs.

Speak professionally

Ask clarifying questions until you're sure both you and the customer agree that you understand the problem. Ask both open-ended and closed-ended questions. Show empathy to the customer when he or she explains the problem. Take ownership of the issue.

Often users don't know exactly what the problem is. They know only that, when they try to do X, Y happens. Their descriptions might not accurately explain the problems. A caller also might not directly answer the question; he or she might dance around it, leaving you to figure it out from the various clues given.

If the user tried to fix the problem on his or her own and covered up the original problem with their attempted fixes or made the problem worse, he or she isn't likely to want to admit this to you. If he or she tells you that they already tried a particular fix when you attempt to perform a step in your troubleshooting, calmly tell the user that, in order to fix the problem you yourself need to go through all of the mostly likely possibilities that could fix it in an orderly manner, even if the user has already performed some of the necessary steps. If you do something that was already tried, then it's possible that some step in between has altered the outcome of trying that fix again.

If you discover that the user has created a problem through a misunderstanding of how things work, be sure to explain to the user how to perform the task, so the problem doesn't recur. You might recommend an online course or classroom course that the user could consider enrolling in to learn more about using the device.

Stay focused

Many times, customers pay for your time on a per-minute or per-hour basis. Some are quick to take offense if you "waste" time with idle chit-chat. They perceive you to be wasting their money. Stick to the task at hand, fix the problem, and move on.

Of course, if you're just watching files copy during the support call, and the user is interested in talking about last night's game or the new restaurant that just opened, that would be a fine time to engage in some pleasantries. You should be friendly and engaging, but not too talkative.

Avoid sensitive topics. Politics, religion, parenting, and relationships are all topics that you should avoid discussing with customers. When all else fails, you can always fall back on the old standby, the weather.

Competence

You must match your communications level with your customer's abilities. You need to judge the customer's competence level and deliver the message appropriately. Consider how you might give a different answer to a three-year old and high school student when he or she asks why the sky is blue. The same must be true with customers, though you should certainly never provide inaccurate or incorrect information just because a customer lacks a technical background.

Keep in mind that most people overstate their understanding or imply they have a higher level of understanding than they actually possess. Ask clarifying questions to judge comprehension and explain your message in various ways to ensure that the customer understands what you're saying.

Avoid using jargon where plain language suffices. You aren't out to impress the user with all the "technobabble" you picked up at the latest conference or training you attended. You need to speak clearly about the issue and implement the appropriate solutions. Explain any acronyms and abbreviations you use.

Many users like to think of themselves as computer-savvy and find it difficult to admit that there are some situations that they just can't resolve on their own. Other users refuse to admit that they understand anything about computers and just throw up their hands when the least little problem occurs. It's up to you as the support technician to determine at what level the user can understand what the problem is and give you the information you need about the problem. Be sure not to talk down to the user, but don't talk over the head of the user either.

Respect the customer

It's critical that you respect the customer and his or her property. For example, when in a customer's office or cubicle, you shouldn't read the customer's papers, look through desk drawers, open computer files (unless required for the troubleshooting task at hand), and so forth. You should refrain from making personal phone calls or text messaging. Don't eat or drink in the customer's space. Avoid surfing the Web and other non-work activities in the customer's office.

Don't use the customer's printer, fax machine, phone, or other devices unless needed as part of your troubleshooting. Don't adjust the customer's chair, monitor, keyboard and mouse location, and so on, unless the current configuration makes your troubleshooting tasks impossible.

Never interrupt the customer while he or she is speaking. Listen attentively, showing interest and involvement in the conversation. Be sure to look at the customer while listening—avoiding eye contact suggests that you don't care about what the customer is saying.

Don't argue with the customer. Even if the customer did something blatantly foolish, never be judgmental or insulting. Don't belittle the customer or minimize the importance of his or her computer problems. Obviously, you should *never* insult the customer, swear and curse, or call him or her names.

You show respect for the customer when you honor his or her privacy and confidentiality. If the customer receives a call or visitor while you're there, excuse yourself or make it clear that you won't eavesdrop or interrupt. Never discuss or distribute information that you learn while at a customer's premises.

Match delivery to the customer

Technology, when abused, can prevent or hinder communication. The pitfalls that organizations should avoid when they use technology to communicate include:

- Using technology for technology's sake
- Over-reliance on or unrealistic expectations of technology
- Mismatching a technical solution to users' needs or expectations

You must match the communications channel to the customer. Many customers prefer phone calls to e-mail. Others want an instant message solution, prefer e-mail, or want to see you in person for face-to-face communications. Make sure you use the channel that your customer prefers, not the one that you're most comfortable with.

Internal and external customers

You might find yourself working to support both internal and external customers, especially when problems arise during projects where both types of customers are working together. When troubleshooting problems in this type of situation, act as a liaison between the internal and external customers, coordinating support and an appropriate resolution to the problem.

Contacting technical support

You might experience a problem that requires you to contact technical support for the product you're servicing. You should follow appropriate procedures to escalate the call to technical support when you realize that you can't resolve the problem yourself.

Before you call, be sure to gather appropriate documentation and the device's service history. Call from onsite at the service location, preferably as close to the device as possible, so you can refer to it during your phone call. Using appropriate technical language (considering your audience), describe the problem, the service history, and any troubleshooting steps you've taken so far. Clarify any recommendations and confirm the next steps. If the problem still isn't resolved, you might need to escalate the call to the next level of technical support.

Provide closure

When you end the service call, inform the customer of the status of the repair. If you've fixed the problem, tell the customer the problem has been fixed and provide a brief description of how you solved it. If the customer can take steps in the future to prevent the problem, clearly outline those steps.

If you need to return with a part or you need to find documentation before you can complete the repair, let the customer know you'll return at a specific time, and then be sure to keep to that schedule. Speak clearly and use articulate oral and legible written communication, such as e-mails, text messages, and service reports, when possible. To demonstrate ownership of the issue, consider making a follow-up call after an appropriate time has passed to ensure that you resolved the problem. A problem isn't resolved until both the technician and the user agree that the problem is resolved.

Guidelines for effective communication

In summary, there are several basic guidelines that help you communicate effectively:

- Speak clearly — It helps your listener understand the message and prevent decoding problems.
- Avoid jargon — Define jargon whenever necessary to ensure that your message is accurately interpreted.
- Keep messages concise — Avoid using unnecessary words, stories, and irrelevant topics.
- Be specific — Keep your message to the point, rather than broad and general.
- Make sure the message is understood — Question your receiver to ensure that the message has been understood as intended.
- Listen actively — Maintain eye contact, focus on the message, and use nonverbal cues to indicate interest. These actions help focus the sender and facilitate easier decoding. Good nonverbal cues include nodding your head in agreement and leaning slightly toward the source. Other cues, such as affirmative comments, noises, and uncrossed arms, also indicate openness to the source. It's important to remember that communication is an exchange.
- Paraphrase messages — Paraphrasing helps you clarify a sender's message and confirms your understanding to the sender.

Pitfalls to avoid in communication

These are some pitfalls you should avoid when communicating:

- Jumping to conclusions — When decoding messages, listen to the entire message before planning your response. If you jump to conclusions, you might miss information that would change your response.
- Becoming distracted — It's important to remain focused on the speaker so that you don't miss important parts of the message.
- Exaggerating — Although exaggeration can function as a tool for humor and other nontechnical purposes, it might send incorrect information.
- Using negative words — Negative messages can be sent without belittling or offending the receiver. For example, replace "I can't" statements with "I can" statements. Focus on what you can do.
- Sending conflicting messages — When the symbols and language of your message don't match, you weaken your credibility. Avoid telling someone you're listening when you're watching something out the window. Active listening incorporates eye contact, appropriate body language, and verbal assurances. By listening actively, you can avoid sending conflicting messages and focus on receiving information accurately.

Stay up to date

It's important for hardware technicians to keep up to date on the hardware they support, as well as learning about new equipment on the market that could benefit their companies and users. Sources to monitor on a regular basis for current information include:

- Magazines
- Forums
- Newsgroups
- Web sites

Do it!

A-3: Maintaining professionalism

Here's how

1. A user calls, distressed that the report he's been working on all day for a meeting in five minutes won't print. Prepare a script describing how you would respond to the user, and then role-play it with a partner. Be sure to include details about how you'd follow up with the user after the service call.

   Answers will vary.

2. You receive a trouble ticket for a user who has had a string of problems with a scanner. When you call the user, he's quite upset that the scanner still won't work when connected to his computer. Prepare a script describing how you would respond to the user, and then role-play it with a partner.

   Answers will vary.

3. A technically savvy user calls the support hotline about a problem with the multifunction device she's using. She's been using it for only a week but is an experienced user who's comfortable around technology. Prepare a script describing how you'd respond to the user, and then role-play it with a partner.

   Answers will vary.

4 You receive a call from a customer named Joe and visit his cubicle to provide assistance. Joe believes himself to be pretty computer savvy and tells you all the steps he's taken to solve his printing problem. In fact, he becomes irate when you try to send a test print job to the queue before doing any further troubleshooting. What's the best way to respond to Joe?

   A Tell him that you're the expert and you'll solve the problem.

   B Tell him that you want to make sure that a problem really exists.

   C Tell him that you're trying to follow a methodical troubleshooting plan, and the first step is to try printing.

   D Tell him that, before arriving, you degaussed the fuser and primed the piezoelectric elements so that the print device should be operational.

5 List at least three activities that you shouldn't engage in while in a customer's cubicle or office.

   Answers might include making personal calls on your cell phone, reading their papers, eating or drinking, opening their computer files, browsing the Internet, and so forth.

6 While troubleshooting Jill's scanner, you find that she spilled coffee onto her desk and some of it got inside the scanner, causing it to fail. How might you inform Jill of the problem?

   A Sternly tell her that it's against corporate policy to consume food or drink near company equipment.

   B Tell her the source of the problem and suggest she keep food and drink more than an arm's reach from her computer and devices.

   C Replace the scanner without telling her why it failed.

   D Tell her boss what she did.

7 You've spent hours working to repair a laser printer located in a client's office, but you aren't able to resolve the problem. You need to escalate the call to the manufacturer's technical support hotline. Prepare a script describing how you'd work with tech support, and then role-play it with a partner.

   Answers will vary.

Service level agreements

Many companies develop a Service Level Agreement (SLA) that specifies how clients and support personnel are to interact, what to expect from each other, and timeframes for the resolution of issues. The following are just some of the important concerns that an SLA should cover.

Item	Description
How to contact tech support	Phone, Web-based application, e-mail, or some other method. It might also specify contact methods that aren't to be used. For example, some companies might not accept e-mail requests for assistance or stopping techs in the hallways to ask for support.
How soon the user can expect a response	This is usually just an e-mail or other correspondence to let the user know that the request has been received and queued up for resolution.
How soon the user can expect a tech to attempt to fix the problem	The tech might need to do something behind the scenes to resolve the problem, might be able to walk the user through the problem over the phone, or might need to meet with the user in person. In some companies, the response time is in minutes or hours. In others, it's in days.
What happens if the tech can't initially fix the problem	This often includes how much time the tech is allowed to spend trying to resolve the problem before escalating it. It also might specify whether the user gets a loaner system (to use if his or her system is completely down) or other workarounds to the problem.
Escalation of the problem	Usually there are three tiers of support. This often starts with a help desk (via phone or e-mail), then a deskside hardware technician, and finally a backroom technician who works at a bench making repairs. Each tier of support usually has more experience, as well as access to additional resources to help resolve the problem.

The course, "A Guide to Customer Service Skills for the Help Desk Professional, 2nd edition," is available if you'd like more in-depth coverage of this topic.

Do it!

A-4: Ensuring customer satisfaction

Here's how

1 Working in groups, determine what you'd include in your SLA for a small workgroup that needs support for printing and document imaging devices.

Answers will vary but should include information that shows respect for the customer's needs and property and a timely response.

2 Compare your SLA with those of other groups.

Topic B: Safety

This topic covers the following CompTIA PDI+ exam objectives.

#	Objective

8.1	**Demonstrate and apply safety procedures**
	• Use proper ESD (Electrostatic Discharge) practices and proper grounding techniques
	    • Wrist straps, static mats, unplugging / lockout / tagout
	• Identify potential safety hazards
	    • Heated rollers, electricity, sharp edges, airborne toner, moving parts (be aware of clothing, jewelry, hair)
	• Adhere to and follow MSDS (Material Safety Data Sheet) guidelines
	• Define and demonstrate proper laser safety practices
	• Follow manufacturer safety documentation for:
	    • Transportation and handling of units, appropriate placement of unit and unit operation
	    • Appropriate power source and power protection
	    • Routing of power cords and network cables

8.2	**Demonstrate an awareness of environment and environmental considerations** • Proper disposal/recycling of devices and consumed supplies according to local regulations • Adhere to and follow MSDS (Material Safety Data Sheet) guidelines • Describe the need for ozone filters and their replacement at regular intervals • Describe effects of temperature and humidity on media and supplies • Follow manufacturer safety documentation for appropriate place of unit (ie: temperature, humidity, dust considerations, sun light, etc)

Office hazards

Explanation

Part of keeping your printing and scanning devices safe is making sure that the environment in which they're used is free of potential hazards and operationally safe. Let's take a look at some of the factors you should consider when examining office hazards.

Floor surfaces

Follow the following guidelines for floor surface safety:

- Floors should be level and dry.
- Carpets should be secured to the floor.
- Cables and power cords shouldn't cross walkways.
- Static protection should be provided using antistatic floor mats, and if necessary, static mats under the user's keyboard and/or computer.

Fire safety

Follow the following guidelines for fire safety:

- Keep papers orderly, so that, if fire does break out, loose papers don't catch fire easily. It's best to store papers in metal filing cabinets whenever possible.
- If hot pots, coffee makers, personal heaters, and other such small appliances are used, keep combustibles away from them and be sure they're used properly. These appliances not only produce heat that can ignite materials but, if left on for prolonged periods of time, they can possibly catch fire themselves.
- Keep working smoke detectors in all areas of the building.
- Fire extinguishers for each type of equipment you have should be readily available.

Some fire extinguishers use chemicals that shouldn't be used on certain types of equipment. The fire extinguisher lists the types of combustible materials it's designed to handle. The *Material Safety Data Sheets (MSDS)* for materials and equipment list the type of fire extinguisher that should be used for fires involving that equipment or material. Newer fire extinguishers have a picture on them that indicates the types of fires they're designed to put out. Older extinguishers use color-coded shapes with a letter to designate on which types of fires they may be used. Some fire extinguishers are made to put out fires on multiple types of flammable materials. The following table describes them. An example of the label for a fire extinguisher is shown in Exhibit 5-1.

Class	Use for	Description
A	Ordinary combustibles	Designed to put out fires involving wood or paper. The label shows either a green triangle with the letter A inside it or a wastebasket and a pile of logs on fire.
B	Flammable liquids	Designed to put out fires involving grease, oil, gasoline, or similar liquids. The label shows either a red square with the letter B inside it or a gas can on fire.
C	Electrical equipment	Designed to put out fires involving electrical equipment. The label shows either a blue circle with the letter C inside it or a plug and cord on fire.
D	Flammable metals	Designed specifically for certain types of flammable metals. The label shows a yellow star with the letter D inside it. There's no picture label for this class of extinguisher.

Exhibit 5-1: Fire extinguisher label

Fire extinguishers are filled with one of four substances for putting out fires. These are described in the following table.

Type	Description
Dry chemicals	These are designed for putting out fires from multiple types of flammable materials using an extinguishing chemical along with a nonflammable gas propellant.
Halon	Halon gas interrupts the chemical reaction of burning materials. It's designed for use on electrical equipment.
Water	Class A fire extinguishers use water along with compressed gas as a propellant.
CO_2	Carbon dioxide fire extinguishers are designed for Class B and Class C fire extinguishers. CO_2 cools the item and the surrounding air.

More information about fire extinguishers, including how to use them, can be found at `http://hanford.gov/fire/safety/extingrs.htm`.

Electrical safety

Follow the these guidelines for electrical safety:

- Avoid overloading electrical circuits, which can lead to tripped breakers and potential fires.
- Label the breakers in the electrical box so you know which outlets are serviced by that breaker.
- Use surge protectors and Uninterruptible Power Supplies (UPS), as appropriate, to protect equipment from surges and spikes. The delicate connections in a circuit board or many other electrical components can easily be damaged by the surges and spikes related to inadequate electric circuits. Follow manufacturer's recommendations for power source and power protection.
- Avoid stringing together power strips, as shown in Exhibit 5-2.

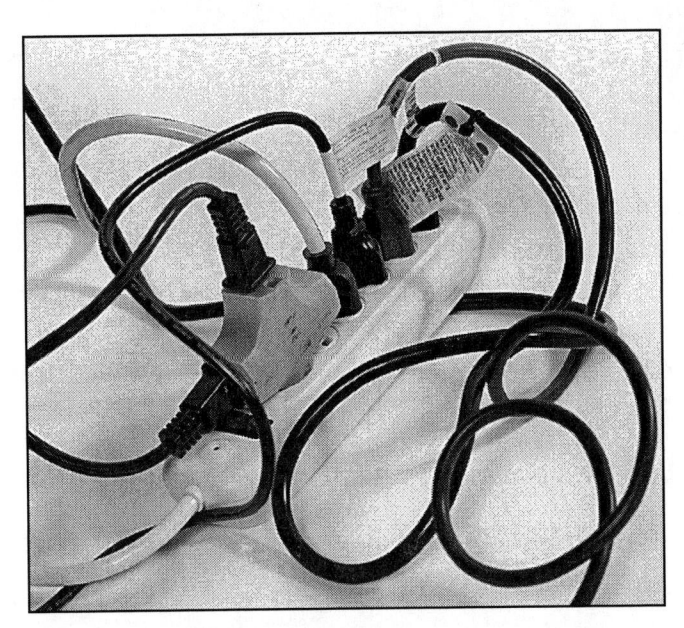

Exhibit 5-2: Overloaded circuits

- Don't run electrical cords or network cables across walkways. If the wires inside the cable or cord become frayed, power cords don't work properly and network cables fail as well. Follow manufacturer's safety instructions for routing of power cords and network cables. If there's no alternative, and power cords and network cables must be run across a walkway, they should be encased in a cord protector. These are most often made of a rubber or plastic strip through which the cords and cables can be easily inserted. The top of the strip is slightly domed, so that people don't trip over it as they're walking, and it contains ample room for the cords and cables to be protected from being damaged.

Some components—notably laser printers—contain high voltage components. Take special care when working around these pieces of equipment by following these guidelines:

- Always use care when working with any electrical equipment. Be sure that it's turned off and unplugged before beginning to make repairs. Use lockout procedures to prevent the device from being re-energized while you're still working on it. Use tagout procedures to warn others of potential electrical hazards with plastic and paper warning tags.
- Visually inspect wiring of equipment for defects, such as faulty insulation or loose connections before each use.
- Don't use damaged or frayed electrical cords.
- Remove metal jewelry, watches, rings, etc., before working on printer components.
- Don't place containers of liquid, including beverages, on or near equipment.
- Always know the electrical ratings of the equipment in your work area, so that you don't overload electrical circuits in your workspace.

Only specially trained technicians should attempt to make repairs to the inside high-voltage components within a laser printer. Such training is beyond the scope of this course.

Air quality

Devices function best in clean air environments, but they're often used in less than ideal conditions, such as on factory floors and other locations where dust, dirt, and particulate matter abound. Use the following guidelines for maintaining air quality:

- Provide good ventilation for computer equipment, so that it doesn't overheat, which can lead to melted components.
- Use fans to keep the air as clear as possible, if necessary.
- Avoid smoking around computers. The pollutants from cigarette smoke adhere to computer components and can cause them to fail.
- Install working carbon monoxide detectors throughout the building. This precaution is more important for the users than for the computer equipment, but it's an important thing to monitor in air quality. An example of a carbon monoxide detector is shown in Exhibit 5-3.

Exhibit 5-3: Carbon monoxide detector

Physical hazards

Some equipment can be heavy and bulky, especially laser printers. Use care and follow manufacturer safety documentation when lifting and moving equipment, not only for the sake of the equipment, but also for your back and other muscles. When lifting equipment, take a balanced stance. If the item is on the floor, squat close to it and use your leg muscles to lift it as you stand up. Keep your back straight with your chin tucked in. Grip the equipment, using your entire hand rather than just your fingers, and bring the equipment close to your body, keeping your elbows close to your body as well. Also, make sure that you can see where you're going with the equipment! Crashing into another person, a wall, or other equipment can also be hazardous.

When working inside a laser printer, you must be aware of hot surfaces, such as the fuser, sharp edges, and moving parts. Keep hair, jewelry (necklaces and bracelets), ID badges, and clothing (especially long sleeves) away from internal components.

When choosing where to place a printer or scanner, follow the manufacturer's recommendation to choose a safe location. Typically it's best to position expensive equipment on a flat, dry, level surface, in an area where humidity and temperature are controlled, and where the unit won't be exposed to physical knocks and jolts, contaminants (such as dust), and exposure to excessive amounts of direct sunlight.

Toner

Toner particles are about 10 microns or smaller in size. Toner dust can irritate your respiratory tract, causing you to cough or sneeze. You can protect yourself from inhaling airborne dust by wearing a protective face mask. In addition, the components in toner can cause an allergic reaction, if they come in repeated contact with your skin. The symptoms of the allergic reaction include skin rashes and burning sensations in your eyes. To prevent exposure, you should handle toner cartridges with disposable gloves and facemasks and always wash your hand after you handle a toner cartridge or work on a photocopier or laser printer.

You should clean up spilled toner with a vacuum specially designed to clean up material so small; other vacuums can let the toner through the bag onto the motor, where it can melt onto it or release dust particles into the air.

Always send used toner cartridges to a recycler for proper disposal. You should never send them to the landfill. Chemicals in the toner cartridges can contaminate the environment. Also, be sure to follow local laws and regulations concerning hazardous materials disposal.

Laser

While the laser in laser printers can't burn the skin, it can damage the eyes, especially with prolonged exposure. Most laser printers enclose the laser diode in the laser assembly, surrounded by shutters to prevent it from emitting any light unless the printer is closed during normal operation. Don't tamper with the security features in the laser assembly.

Ozone

Some EP printers, create ozone as part of the printing process. These printers can have a negative impact on the air around them. As a result, you need to ensure that ozone filters in laser printers with a primary corona are changed at regular intervals and disposed of properly.

Incident reporting

Students can search the Web and examine incident-reporting policies for various organizations.

An organization should have policies in place for how to handle accidents. These policies should detail the method by which incident reporting is handled. Proper documentation in a timely manner is necessary for OSHA, workers compensation claims, and insurance purposes.

Do it!

B-1: Identifying typical office and computer-related hazards

Questions and answers

You've been called in to repair a printer in a small office. When you arrive, you can barely get to the printer, due to the piles of papers surrounding it, along with the network and power cords crossing from desk to desk across the walkway. You find that toner has been spilled inside the printer. That happened when the table the printer had been sitting on collapsed under the weight of the printer and papers. You find that the printer is plugged into a power strip along with a scanner, a fax machine, a lamp, and a portable heater. The power strip is plugged into another power strip. There's a fire extinguisher in the office located behind the printer table.

1 What physical hazards are present in the office?

   Answers might include: Piles of papers around the printer and near a personal heater; cords and cables crossing the walkway; a weak table; and overloaded circuits.

2 What electrical hazards are present in this scenario?

   Answers might include: Inadequate power to the equipment can lead to equipment problems, and this is a possibility if so many electrical devices are plugged into a single outlet. The spilled toner needs to be cleaned up properly.

3 What changes need to be made to this office?

   Answers might include: Papers should be filed in a metal filing cabinet. Cords and cables, if they must cross the walkway, should be placed in conduits. It would be better to reroute the cables and cords so that they don't cross walkways. Also, it seems as if additional electrical outlets need to be installed. A sturdy enough table or desk needs to be found on which to place the printer; if you decide to move the printer, be sure to follow the manufacturer's safety documentation. The fire extinguisher should be placed in a location where it can be easily reached if it's needed.

4 If a physical injury were sustained during the service call, what would the policy be at your company for reporting the incident?

   Answers will vary.

MSDS

Explanation

A *material safety data sheet (MSDS)* is a document that lists the proper procedures for handling and working with a particular substance. An MSDS includes information such as:

- Physical data (melting point, boiling point, flash point, etc.)
- Toxicity
- Health effects
- First aid
- Reactivity
- Storage
- Disposal
- Protective equipment
- Spill/leak procedures

These sheets are designed to give emergency personnel, employees, and employers information about the dangers of products.

MSDSs are available for a huge range of substances. There's even an MSDS for water.

An MSDS should indicate what first aid measures should be taken if a person ingests or comes into contact with the material (depending on the material and what happens if a person does encounter it), the fire extinguishing measures including which types of fire extinguishers can be used on it, handling and storage procedures, as well as any other information needed.

OSHA requires that MSDS information be made available to anyone who might be exposed to toxic or hazardous materials. The MSDS is created by the manufacturer of the product. It's available upon request from the manufacturer and should be sent with the first order of a product and any time an update is made to the product or to the MSDS. Many MSDSs are available on the Internet.

Many MSDSs include a Hazard Rating section. This is a summary of the top, most important hazards that might be posed by the product. There's a code associated with each hazard. The following table lists the ratings that you might find.

Rating	Description
None	No potential hazard in this category
0	Least hazardous
1	Slightly hazardous
2	Moderately hazardous
3	Highly hazardous
4	Extremely hazardous

An MSDS might also include further codes indicating items of personal protection (such as gloves) that should be worn or used when handling the product. An example is shown in the following table.

Rating	Description
A	Wear goggles when using this product.
B	Wear goggles and gloves when using this product.
C	Wear goggles and gloves and other protective wear when using this product.

There are many Web sites with links to MSDSs. Manufacturers post them somewhere on their Web sites. One location you might check is http://msdssearch.com/find.htm. You can search by manufacturer or for a specific MSDS.

Do it!

B-2: Reading a material safety data sheet

Here's how	Here's why
1 In your Web browser, open a search Web page, such as google.com or yahoo.com	You'll search for an MSDS and evaluate the product's level of hazard potential.
2 Search for toner MSDSs	Laser printer toner is one of the more common spills you might need to clean up.
3 View the MSDS for one of the toners found in the search	
4 How would you clean up a spill according to the MSDS?	**Answers will vary**
5 What type of fire extinguisher should be used on a fire with the toner involved?	**Answers will vary**

Try to have individual students look at various MSDSs, so that they can compare what they find.

Disposal of electronics

Explanation

It's often more cost-effective to replace a component or even an entire computer than to fix it or upgrade it. Home users and companies alike often end up with large piles of broken or outdated computers and other electronic equipment that need to be disposed of properly.

Electronic components and equipment can't just be sent to the landfill along with the ordinary trash. They contain many hazardous materials, a number of which can be reclaimed. In order to help prevent environmental damage and comply with local and national laws and regulations, hazardous materials need to be removed before items are sent for disposal. Be sure to check the MSDS for information on the correct handling and disposal of unwanted equipment.

Hazardous materials

Hazardous materials in electronic equipment often include lead. Lead is used in the solder joints in electronics. CRT monitors contain phosphorous. Both of these materials must be disposed of in accordance OSHA and EPA guidelines. The MSDS lists any hazardous materials in equipment, along with measures to take when disposing of them.

Disposing of used toner and ink cartridges

Toner cartridges aren't suitable for landfill disposal. The manufacturer has information on how they can be recycled. The cartridges are often refilled and reused, if the rest of the components in the cartridge are still in good condition. Some manufacturers include a shipping label with the replacement cartridge for returning the used cartridge to them for recycling or disposal.

Ink cartridges aren't usually as toxic as toner cartridges, but they still contain electronic and metal components that can be reclaimed. And although they can also be refilled and reused, some printer manufacturers don't honor the printer's warranty if you use recycled ink cartridges. Office supply stores and other locations often accept ink cartridges for recycling.

Disposal of computer equipment

Companies specializing in the disposal of electronic and computer equipment are increasingly common. They sort the equipment by type and then begin manually dismantling the equipment. They divide it into plastic, metal, electronic components, and CRTs. Circuit boards are then sent on for recapturing precious metals. A breakdown of the materials found in one ton of circuit boards can be found at `http://thegreenpc.com/the.htm`.

Reusing equipment

The first choice when your equipment no longer meets your needs should be to donate the equipment to an organization that can make use of it. This might be a local school or other charitable organization. Many recyclers attempt to send useable equipment back out for use rather than dismantling it for materials reclamation.

Methods of disposal

Some municipalities offer local electronic equipment recycling services. These might be available year round or offered periodically. There's often a small fee for disposing of the equipment. Considering the amount of manual labor involved in recycling these materials, the fees aren't exorbitant.

If no local service is offered, you can check the Web for recyclers. If you have pallet upon pallet of equipment, a recycler might be able to pick it up from you or arrange to have it picked up.

Do it!

B-3: Selecting the proper methods for equipment disposal

Here's how	Here's why
1 Open your Web browser	You're going to locate a computer recycler on the Web.
2 Search for computer recyclers	
3 Determine if the recycler you find offers equipment for reuse	
4 Determine if they recycle other electronic components or batteries	
5 Determine how to get the equipment to the recycler	

Try to have students research various companies, so that they can compare the services offered.

Unit summary: Professional conduct

Topic A In this topic, you learned that being professional, courteous, and respectful is critical to success as a support technician. You learned that a problem isn't resolved until both the technician and the user agree that the problem has been resolved. You learned to stay focused, speak professionally, respect the customer, and stay up to date, and you learned about verbal and nonverbal communication. You also learned about **service level agreements** that specify how clients and support personnel are to interact.

Topic B In this topic, you learned about office **safety**. You learned about **physical**, **electrical**, and **fire** hazards, and you learned how to stay safe. You also learned how to dispose of equipment safely and how to use a **Materials Safety Data Sheet**.

Review questions

1 List at least three activities you should avoid while in a customer's office.

   Answers might include making personal calls on your cell phone, reading their papers, eating or drinking, opening their computer files, browsing the Internet, and so forth.

2 You should _____ the customer and his or her property.

   respect

3 When speaking to a customer, you should speak simply and clearly and not use _____.

   jargon or "technobabble"

4 When a customer describes the problem, you should ask _____ to elicit complete details.

   clarifying questions

5 Never _____ the customer while he or she is speaking.

   interrupt

6 A problem isn't resolved until _____.

   both the technician and the user agree that the problem is resolved

7 How can you protect equipment from static electricity?

   By using static mats on the floor or under keyboards and computers.

8 Which type of fire extinguisher should be used on a computer that's on fire?

   Class C. (Carbon dioxide extinguishers are the best choice for extinguishing any electrical fires.)

9 True or False? Any vacuum cleaner can be used to pick up spilled toner.

   False. You should clean up spilled toner with a vacuum specially designed to clean up material so small; other vacuums can let the toner through the bag onto the motor, where the toner can melt onto it or put the dust particles into the air.

10 List some computer and office equipment that produces static charges.

   CRTs, televisions, laser printers, copiers, and computer and other equipment power supplies.

11 What's the purpose of an MSDS?

These sheets are designed to give emergency personnel, employees, and employers information about the proper uses and the dangers of products.

12 Where can you find an MSDS?

MSDSs are available upon request from the manufacturer and should be sent with the first order of a product and any time an update is made to the product or to the MSDS. Many MSDSs are available on the Internet.

13 Why shouldn't electronics devices be sent to the landfill?

They contain heavy metals that are damaging to the environment.

14 What can be done with outdated or inoperable electronic devices?

The outdated devices can be donated to organizations that can make use of them. If they're too old to be of use to anyone or if they're broken, recyclers can dismantle them and reclaim metals from the equipment. Components can then be sold back to manufacturers for use in making new materials.

15 True or False? Batteries, toner cartridges, and ink cartridges can be disposed of in landfills without any consequences.

False. Many batteries contain heavy metals that can't be sent to a landfill. Batteries in the equipment might contain nickel, mercury, or cadmium. Toners are usually a mixture of plastic resin, iron powder, and carbon black. Chemicals in the toner cartridges can contaminate the environment. Ink cartridges are usually less toxic than toner cartridges, but they still contain electronic and metal components that can be reclaimed.

Independent practice activity

In this activity, you'll practice applying safety practices to a computer environment.

1 Practice lifting equipment using the proper technique and moving it from one desk to another.

2 Obtain the MSDS for the type of toner or ink cartridge used in your office.

3 Determine what to do if a piece of equipment is involved in a fire, as well as how to dispose of it.

4 Check your offices for unsafe or hazardous configurations.

5 Locate an electronics recycler and obtain a quote for disposing of outdated equipment in your office.

6 Compile a list of organizations to which you can donate used equipment.

Appendix A
Certification exam objectives map

This appendix provides the following information:

A CompTIA PDI+ exam objectives with references to corresponding coverage in this course manual.

Topic A: Comprehensive exam objectives

Explanation

This section lists all CompTIA PDI+ exam objectives and indicates where each objective is covered in conceptual explanations, activities, or both.

1.0 Print Engine Process and Components

Objective	Conceptual information	Supporting activities
1.1 Define, describe and demonstrate an understanding of the following commonly used printing processes		
Identify and describe basic steps of laser / LED printing		
• Photoconductor preparation, charging, writing, developing, transferring, fusing	Unit 2, Topic A	A-4
• Photoconductor preparation		
– Removal of residual toner by cleaning blade, brush or roller		
– Removal of residual charge by light or electrical charge		
• Charging	Unit 2, Topic A	A-4
• Supply uniform charge to the photoconductor surface by charge corona or charge roller		
• Writing	Unit 2, Topic A	A-4
• Laser or LED creates a latent image by discharging the appropriate areas of the photoconductor		
• Developing	Unit 2, Topic A	A-4
• Toner is attracted to the latent image		
• Transferring	Unit 2, Topic A	A-4
• Toner is transferred from the photoconductor to the media by using electrostatic charges		
• Fusing	Unit 2, Topic A	A-4
• Toner is fixed/fused to the media with heat and pressure		
Identify and describe basic steps of Ink dispersion printing		
• Purging, ink delivery, image application to media	Unit 2, Topic A	A-3
• Purging	Unit 2, Topic A	A-3
– Cleaning the heads and nozzles		
• Ink delivery	Unit 2, Topic A	A-3
– Ink is moved from reservoir to print head		
– Unidirectional and Bi-directional printing		
• Image application to media	Unit 2, Topic A	A-3
– Ink is delivered through the nozzles (print head) directly to media via heat/charge		

Objective	Conceptual information	Supporting activities
1.2 Identify and describe print process components and their functions		
Laser or LED image formation components		
• Photoconductor	Unit 2, Topic A	A-4
• Laser Unit (beam detector, polygon mirror / motor, laser diode, toner shield) or LED unit	Unit 2, Topic A	A-4
• Developer Unit (toner supply, mono component, vs. dual component)	Unit 2, Topic A	A-4
• Charge assembly	Unit 2, Topic A	A-4
• Cleaning Unit (residual toner removal)	Unit 2, Topic A	A-4
• High Voltage Power Supply	Unit 2, Topic A	A-4
• Low Voltage Power Supply	Unit 2, Topic A	A-4
• Transfer / separation	Unit 2, Topic A	A-4
Device fuser components		
• Heat roller / belt, pressure roller, lamps / heaters, thermistor, fuser cleaning components, pawls, thermal protection	Unit 2, Topic A	A-4
Ink dispersion image formation components		
• Print head, IDS (ink delivery system), carriage, carriage belt, ink supply, purge unit, absorption pads	Unit 2, Topic A	A-3
Media transport/feed components		
• Pickup roller, feed roller, separate roller/pad, torque limiter, transport rollers, registration assembly, sensors, media guides, exit rollers, gates/diverters/deflectors, static brushes	Unit 2, Topic A	A-4
Ventilation components		
• Fans, ozone filters, dust filters, ducts	Unit 2, Topic A	A-4
Accessories		
• Finishers, sorters, large capacity paper source, document feeders, stapler, duplexers, punch units, folders cutters, binders, stackers, inserter	Unit 2, Topic A	A-4

Objective	Conceptual information	Supporting activities
1.3 Describe the purpose of firmware	Unit 2, Topic A	A-4
1.4 Identify and describe print data flow and job processing		
Demonstrate awareness of the interaction between software application, driver, printer control languages, raster image processing, printing and image creation	Unit 2, Topic A	A-1, A-4
Identify the impact of memory on the printer	Unit 2, Topic A	A-1, A-4
	Unit 4, Topic B	B-4
1.5 Identify media types and explain their impact on print process, quality and device performance		
• Use appropriate media types based on device specifications	Unit 2, Topic A Unit 4, Topic B	A-5 B-4
• Identify and recognize paper weights, sizes and standards	Unit 2, Topic A	A-5
• Identify and recognize paper textures, brightness, grain, coatings	Unit 2, Topic A	A-5
• Identify and recognize other media types (ie: transparencies, envelopes, labels, card stock, raised letterhead, recycled paper)	Unit 2, Topic A	A-5
• Describe adverse affects of improper media storage on device performance	Unit 2, Topic A Unit 4, Topic B	A-5 B-4

2.0 Scan Process and Components

Objective	Conceptual information	Supporting activities
2.1 Identify and describe common hardware scanner components		
• Lamps, mirrors, CCD, CIS, CMOS, lens, glass, analog to digital converter, color filters	Unit 2, Topic B	B-1
• Differentiate between ADF (Automatic Document Feeder) and flatbed component	Unit 2, Topic B	B-1
2.2 Describe and summarize image capture in relation to scanning technologies		
Identify and describe common scanner technologies such as TWAIN and network scanning methods	Unit 2, Topic B Unit 3, Topic B	B-1 B-8
Identify the effects of using different image formats (ie: PDF, JPG, GIF, TIFF)		
• Impact on file size, quality, scan time, network bandwidth, storage, resolution, color, depth, reduction, enlargement, compression	Unit 2, Topic B	B-1
Define the image capture process		
• Light exposure, reflection, focus, filter, capture (CCD), Analog to Digital conversion, image processing	Unit 2, Topic B	B-1
Recognize the reasons for and potential impact of security and anti-counterfeiting features	Unit 2, Topic B	B-1

3.0 General Troubleshooting

Objective	Conceptual information	Supporting activities
3.1 Describe and apply general troubleshooting methodology		
Observation – gather information and validate the symptoms	Unit 4, Topic B	B-4, B-5
Establish theory of probable cause based on information gathered		
• Attempt to isolate the problem by eliminating non-causes	Unit 4, Topic B	B-4, B-5
• Use tools and service documentation as needed	Unit 4, Topic B	B-4, B-5
Test or Analyze – try to recreate the problem and validate theory	Unit 4, Topic B	B-4, B-5
Once theory is validated, determine next steps to resolve the problem	Unit 4, Topic B	B-4, B-5
Implement solution, validate solution and document actions and results	Unit 4, Topic B	B-4, B-5

Objective	Conceptual information	Supporting activities
3.2 Identify and isolate printing hardware issues using available tools		
Image quality issues		
• Dark images, light images, weak images, repetitive image defects, ghosting, smearing, banding, focus, shadows, voided areas, jitters, registration issues, skew, misaligned color registration, weak color, missing color, vertical and horizontal black/white lines, black pages, blank pages, incorrect consumables	Unit 4, Topic B	B-4
Causes of image quality issues		
• Fuser, charging components, laser/LED component, developer assembly, consumables, photoconductor, print head, drive components, media transport/feed system, environment	Unit 4, Topic B	B-4
Transport/feed issues		
• Media jamming, skewing, creasing, wrinkling, folding, tearing, multifeeding, burning, misfeeding	Unit 4, Topic B	B-4
Causes of common media transport/feed issues		
• Media feed, fusing, media exit, registration, delivery, duplex, damaged media, separation, media feed timing, foreign objects	Unit 4, Topic B	B-4
Service error messages		
• Critical operational failures (service code)	Unit 4, Topic B	B-4
Common user informational messages		
• Add media, add supplies, add toner, regular maintenance, paper jam, incorrect media	Unit 4, Topic B	B-4
Testing tools		
• Print test page, event logs, configuration pages, paper path test, parts life counters, user setting list, engine test page	Unit 4, Topic B	B-4

Objective	Conceptual information	Supporting activities
3.3 Identify and isolate printing software issues using the following methods		
• Verify use of appropriate drivers by checking driver type/version	Unit 4, Topic B	B-4
• Verify driver port setting	Unit 4, Topic B	B-4
• Print driver test page	Unit 4, Topic B	B-4
• Proper driver accessory/option configuration	Unit 4, Topic B	B-4
• Application settings vs. driver settings	Unit 4, Topic B	B-4
• Installing and uninstalling drivers	Unit 4, Topic B	B-4
• Confirm driver settings: "offline vs. online"	Unit 4, Topic B	B-4
• Print from multiple applications and workstations	Unit 4, Topic B	B-4
• Print different files from the same application	Unit 4, Topic B	B-4

Objective	Conceptual information	Supporting activities
3.4 Identify and isolate scanning hardware issues using available tools		
Image quality issues		
• Dark images, light images, weak images, banding, focus, shadows, voided areas, jitters, registration issues, skew, misaligned color registration, weak color, missing color, vertical and horizontal black/blank lines, black pages, blank pages	Unit 4, Topic B	B-5
Common causes of image quality issues		
• White reference plate, scan lamp, glass contamination, mirrors, lens, CCD, focus, alignment, cables, automatic document feeder, rollers, improper calibration, limited memory, defective storage device	Unit 4, Topic B	B-5
Service error messages		
• Critical operational failures (service code)	Unit 4, Topic B	B-5
User informational messages		
• Media jam	Unit 4, Topic B	B-5
Testing tools		
• Test / target chart, calibration strip	Unit 4, Topic B	B-5
3.5 Identify and isolate scanning software issues		
Verify use of appropriate drivers by checking driver type/version		
• TWAIN, WIA, ISIS	Unit 4, Topic B	B-5
Verify and configure application settings		
• Resolutions, color depth, single sided vs. duplex, media size, exposure levels, file format, reduction and enlargement, ADF vs. flatbed, monochrome vs. color	Unit 4, Topic B	B-5

Objective	Conceptual information	Supporting activities
3.6 Identify and isolate basic connectivity issues using available tools		
Connectivity issues		
• Slow printing, intermittent activity, communication errors, unexpected output, no activity	Unit 3, Topic B Unit 4, Topic B	B-5 through B-7 B-4
Common causes of wired and wireless connectivity issues		
• Loose, broken, damaged, improperly wired cables, broken network devices (hubs, switches), incorrect protocol / network settings, incorrect TCP/IP settings, bad network card, firmware, interference, line of site, EMI	Unit 3, Topic B Unit 4, Topic B	B-5 through B-7 B-4
Service or informational messages		
• Refer to manufacturer documentation for error codes and messages	Unit 4, Topic B	B-4
3.7 Identify and isolate faxing issues		
Common fax issues		
• Cannot send, cannot receive, random disconnections, speed, reception/send image quality	Unit 4, Topic B	B-5
Common causes of faxing issues		
• Bad fax card, noise on the line, line levels, non-analog line, bad cable, wrong port, inappropriate document orientation, DSL interference, call-waiting, line share devices, firmware, no dial tone	Unit 4, Topic B	B-5
Identify similarities between faxes and scanners as it relates to image quality issues when transmitting faxes or copying	Unit 4, Topic B	B-5
Identify similarities between faxes and printers as it relates to image quality issues when receiving faxes or printing	Unit 4, Topic B	B-5

4.0 Basic Electromechanical Components and Tools

Objective	Conceptual information	Supporting activities
4.1 Identify and explain the function of electromechanical components		
• Clutches	Unit 1, Topic A	A-3
• Solenoids	Unit 1, Topic A	A-3
• Motors (ie: stepper motors, AC/DC motors)	Unit 1, Topic A	A-3
• Relays	Unit 1, Topic A	A-3
• Sensors (ie: photo reflective, encoders, photo interrupters)	Unit 1, Topic A	A-3
• Switches (ie: micro switches, magnetic switches)	Unit 1, Topic A	A-3
4.2 Identify and explain the function of mechanical components		
• Drive components	Unit 1, Topic B	B-1
• Gears (ie: one way, gear trains)	Unit 1, Topic B	B-1
• Bearings	Unit 1, Topic B	B-1
• Bushings	Unit 1, Topic B	B-1
• Belts	Unit 1, Topic B	B-1
• Rollers (ie: rubber, teflon, steel, etc)	Unit 1, Topic B	B-1
• Cams	Unit 1, Topic B	B-1
• Cables	Unit 1, Topic B	B-1
• Pulleys / Idler	Unit 1, Topic B	B-1
• Springs	Unit 1, Topic B	B-1

Objective	Conceptual information	Supporting activities
4.3 Identify and explain the function of electrical components		
• Power supplies (ie: low and high voltage)	Unit 1, Topic C	C-1
• Fuses	Unit 1, Topic C	C-2
• Thermistors	Unit 1, Topic C	C-2
• Thermal switches/fuses	Unit 1, Topic C	C-2
• Lamps (ie: halogen, xenon, LED)	Unit 1, Topic C	C-2
• Grounding components (ie: screws, shields, points, straps, wires)	Unit 1, Topic C	C-2
• Cables (ie: copper wire harnesses, flat cable, fiber optics)	Unit 1, Topic C	C-2
• Connectors (ie: ZIF sockets, Molex, Ultrex, spade, pin connectors, spring contacts)	Unit 1, Topic C	C-2
• EEPROM and EPROM (ie: NVRAM)	Unit 1, Topic C	C-2
• Memory	Unit 1, Topic C	C-2
• Control PCBs (Printed Circuit Boards) (ie: I/O boards, drivers boards, logic boards, fax board, network card)	Unit 1, Topic C	C-2
4.4 Demonstrate the proper and safe use of tools		
• Multimeter	Unit 1, Topic C	C-1
• Polarity tester	Unit 1, Topic C	C-1
• AC line monitors	Unit 1, Topic C	C-1
• Toner Vacuum and toner rags	Unit 4, Topic A	A-1
	Unit 4, Topic B	B-4
• Service documentation (ie: theory of operation, block diagram and wiring / circuit diagram)	Unit 4, Topic A	A-1
	Unit 4, Topic B	B-4
• Lubricants and cleaning solutions	Unit 4, Topic A	A-1, A-2
	Unit 4, Topic B	B-4, B-5
• Test chart	Unit 4, Topic A	A-2
	Unit 4, Topic B	B-5
• Chip puller / EEPROM puller	Unit 4, Topic A	A-1

Objective	Conceptual information	Supporting activities
4.4 Demonstrate and follow recommended maintenance guidelines and practices. Define the reasons and benefits for adhering to maintenance guidelines and practices.		
• Examine device log data and previous service history	Unit 4, Topic A	A-1
• Scheduled preventative maintenance	Unit 4, Topic A	A-1
• Replacing parts based on parts life counters	Unit 4, Topic A	A-1
• Check firmware version and update as necessary	Unit 4, Topic A	A-1
• Clean, lubricate and perform adjustments per device specifications	Unit 4, Topic A	A-1
• Unscheduled service calls	Unit 4, Topic A	A-1
• Perform preventative maintenance during service calls	Unit 4, Topic A	A-1
• Examine device for potential future problems	Unit 4, Topic A	A-1
• Clean, lubricate and perform adjustments per device specifications	Unit 4, Topic A	A-1
• Verify device functionality	Unit 4, Topic A	A-1

5.0 Connectivity

Objective	Conceptual information	Supporting activities
5.1 Identify and describe basic network and communications technologies		
Protocols		
• TCP/IP	Unit 3, Topic B	B-2
Communication settings		
• 10/100/1000 Mbps	Unit 3, Topic B	B-1
• Dialog modes (ie: simplex, half/full duplex, auto negotiation)	Unit 3, Topic B	B-1
Physical connections		
• Port types (ie: RJ-45)	Unit 3, Topic B	B-1
• Cable types (ie: UTP, STP, CAT-5 crossover/standard cable)	Unit 3, Topic B	B-1
• Network interface card	Unit 3, Topic B	B-1
Wireless connectivity		
• 802.11x, SSID, WEP-WPA encryption, infrastructure vs. adhoc	Unit 3, Topic B	B-3
• Bluetooth, infrared	Unit 3, Topic B	B-3
Fax / modem		
• Port types (ie: RJ-11)	Unit 3, Topic B	B-1
• Analog phone line	Unit 3, Topic B	B-1
• Transmission speeds (ie: baud rates)	Unit 3, Topic B	B-1

Objective	Conceptual information	Supporting activities
5.2 Describe and demonstrate the use of the TCP/IP protocol and related tools		
Static addressing		
• IP address, Subnet mask, Default gateway, DNS	Unit 3, Topic B	B-2
Dynamic addressing		
• DHCP	Unit 3, Topic B	B-2
• APIPA	Unit 3, Topic B	B-2
Validate network connectivity using tools and utilities		
• PING, IPCONFIG, TELNET, NSLOOKUP, web browser, configuration page, cross-over cable	Unit 3, Topic B	B-5 through B-7
• Link lights (LEDs), Activity lights	Unit 3, Topic B	B-1
5.3 Identify the basics of network scanning technologies		
Requirements to utilize Scan to Email functionality		
• SMTP, authentication, POP3, LDAP, file size limitation	Unit 3, Topic B	B-8
Requirements to utilize Scan to Folder functionality		
• Shared folder on network, permission levels, SMB, UNC path	Unit 3, Topic B	B-8
Requirements to utilize Scan to File functionality		
• Application based, drivers, TWAIN, ISIS	Unit 3, Topic B	B-8
Requirements to utilize Scan to FTP functionality		
• FTP server, permissions	Unit 3, Topic B	B-8

Certification exam objectives map A–15

Objective	Conceptual information	Supporting activities
5.4 Identify the basic purpose and use of printer drivers		
• Install, remove and update drivers (using Windows 2000 and XP)	Unit 3, Topic A	A-5, A-6, A-7
• Verify driver versions	Unit 3, Topic A	
	Unit 4, Topic B	B-4
• Follow manufacturer documentation when installing USB devices (software vs. hardware install)	Unit 3, Topic A	A-5, A-7
• Basic features and settings of printer drivers	Unit 3, Topic A	A-5, A-6
• Duplex printing, tray settings, media settings, paper sizes, finishing, quantity, scaling	Unit 3, Topic A	A-5, A-6
• Printer control languages		
• PCL, Postscript, GDI, PJL	Unit 3, Topic A	A-5
• Demonstrate awareness of vendor specific drivers and languages	Unit 3, Topic A	A-5
• Spooling	Unit 3, Topic A	A-5, A-6
• Operation and configuration	Unit 3, Topic A	A-5, A-6
• Differentiate between shared printing and direct printing	Unit 3, Topic A	A-5, A-6
	Unit 3, Topic B	B-4
• Demonstrate awareness of the effect of application settings on driver settings	Unit 3, Topic A	
	Unit 4, Topic B	B-4
5.4 Identify common device ports		
Types of physical ports		
• LPT, USB, Serial, Firewire, Parallel, miniparallel, SCSI	Unit 3, Topic A	A-1 through A-4
Types of memory card slots		
• SD Slot, Compact Flash	Unit 3, Topic A	A-5
Type of network ports		
• LPR, RAW, port 9100, SMB – Simple TCP/IP, External print server port	Unit 3, Topic B	B-4
Assignment of printer driver to ports	Unit 3, Topic A	A-6, A-7

6.0 Color Theory

Objective	Conceptual information	Supporting activities
6.1 Identify and describe the basics of color theory		
• Differentiate between additive and subtractive color (RGB vs. CMYK)	Unit 2, Topic A	A-2
• Describe color gamut and its relationship to device limitations	Unit 2, Topic A	A-2
• Explain perception of color and what affects perception	Unit 2, Topic A	A-2
• Light, media, contrast, the observer	Unit 2, Topic A	A-2
6.2 Define and explain basic color management		
• Identify how color adjustments affects the quality of image output	Unit 2, Topic A	A-2
	Unit 4, Topic B	B-4
• Describe the need for color calibration	Unit 2, Topic A	A-2
	Unit 4, Topic B	B-4

7.0 Professionalism and Communication

Objective	Conceptual information	Supporting activities
7.1 Define and demonstrate effective communication and relationship building skills		
• Use appropriate introduction	Unit 5, Topic A	A-2, A-3
• Use active listening skills	Unit 5, Topic A	A-3
• Probing: Asking open ended and closed ended questions	Unit 5, Topic A	A-3
• Show empathy for the customer	Unit 5, Topic A	A-3
• Speak clearly and concisely at all times	Unit 5, Topic A	A-2, A-3
• Use appropriate terminology for the audience	Unit 5, Topic A	A-3
• Clarify and confirm the customer's expectations and/or concerns	Unit 5, Topic A	A-3
• Provide closure the for the client at the end of the service call	Unit 5, Topic A	A-3
• Communicate status of repair and/or open issues – follow up calls when necessary	Unit 5, Topic A	A-3
• Use articulate and legible written communication	Unit 5, Topic A	A-3
7.2 Define and demonstrate effective communication skills with technical support		
• Follow appropriate escalation procedures	Unit 5, Topic A	A-3
• Call from onsite and have appropriate reference materials available when speaking with technical support	Unit 5, Topic A	A-3
• Describe the problem, service history and troubleshooting steps accurately with appropriate terminology	Unit 5, Topic A	A-3
• Clarify and confirm technical support recommendations	Unit 5, Topic A	A-3
• Follow further escalation procedures if necessary	Unit 5, Topic A	A-3
7.3 Display and practice professional conduct with internal and external customers/contacts		
• Maintain a positive attitude concerning the manufacturer of the product	Unit 5, Topic A	A-3
• Treat the customer with courtesy and respect, including the customer's property	Unit 5, Topic A	A-2, A-3
• Act as liaison between internal and external customers	Unit 5, Topic A	
• Take ownership of the issues and follow through to its conclusion	Unit 5, Topic A	A-3

8.0 Safety and environment

Objective	Conceptual information	Supporting activities
8.1 Demonstrate and apply safety procedures		
• Use proper ESD (Electrostatic Discharge) practices and proper grounding techniques	Unit 1, Topic A	A-2
	Unit 1, Topic C	C-1
• Wrist straps, static mats, unplugging / lockout / tagout	Unit 1, Topic A	A-2
	Unit 1, Topic C	C-1
• Demonstrate proper use of cleaning solutions and sprays	Unit 4, Topic A	A-1, A-2
	Unit 4, Topic B	B-4, B-5
• Identify potential safety hazards	Unit 4, Topic A	A-1
	Unit 5, Topic B	B-1
• Heated rollers, electricity, sharp edges, airborne toner, moving parts (be aware of clothing, jewelry, hair)	Unit 4, Topic A	A-1
	Unit 5, Topic B	B-1
• Adhere to and follow MSDS (Material Safety Data Sheet) guidelines	Unit 5, Topic B	B-2
• Define and demonstrate proper laser safety practices	Unit 4, Topic A	A-1
	Unit 5, Topic A	
• Follow manufacturer safety documentation for:		
• Transportation and handling of units, appropriate placement of unit and unit operation	Unit 5, Topic B	B-1
• Appropriate power source and power protection	Unit 5, Topic B	B-1
• Routing of power cords and network cables	Unit 5, Topic B	B-1
8.2 Demonstrate an awareness of environment and environmental considerations		
• Proper disposal/recycling of devices and consumed supplies according to local guidelines		
• Adhere to and follow MSDS (Material Safety Data Sheet) guidelines	Unit 5, Topic B	B-2, B-3
• Describe the need for ozone filters and their replacement at regular intervals	Unit 2, Topic A	
	Unit 4, Topic A	A-1
	Unit 5, Topic A	
• Describe effects of temperature and humidity on media and supplies	Unit 2, Topic A	A-5
	Unit 4, Topic A	
	Unit 4, Topic B	B-4
• Avoid distractions and/or interruptions when talking with customers	Unit 5, Topic A	A-3
• Follow manufacturer safety documentation for appropriate place of unit (ie: temperature, humidity, dust considerations, sun light, etc)	Unit 4, Topic A	A-1
	Unit 5, Topic B	B-1

Course summary

This summary contains information to help you bring the course to a successful conclusion. Using this information, you'll be able to:

A Use the summary text to reinforce what students have learned in class.

B Direct students to the next courses in this series, if any, and to any other resources that might help students continue to learn about printing and document imaging.

Topic A: Course summary

At the end of the class, use the following summary text to reinforce what students have learned. It's intended not as a script, but rather as a starting point.

Unit summaries

Unit 1

In this unit, students learned to identify and explain the function of various electromechanical, mechanical, and electrical components that they'll encounter when working in printers, scanners, and multifunction devices. These devices include **clutches**, **solenoids**, **relays**, **sensors**, **gears**, **rollers**, **cams**, **fuses**, **power supplies**, **thermistors**, and **PCBs**.

Unit 2

In this unit, students learned the details of the Windows print process in Windows XP and Windows Vista. They also learned about **color theory** and how printers use the **subtractive method** to create color. Students then examined the components and steps involved in the **inkjet** and **EP** print processes, and they examined various types of **print media**. Finally, they examined the components and steps a **scanner** uses to create an image file.

Unit 3

In this unit, students learned about **ports** and **connectors**, including **serial**, **parallel**, **USB**, and **IEEE 1394**. Students also connected printers and scanners to their computers. They then learned basic networking concepts, including **TCP/IP** basics and **wireless** technologies. They also connected to a shared **network printer** and learned to identify requirements for **network scanning** functions.

Unit 4

In this unit, students performed **routine maintenance** on inkjet printers, EP printers, and scanners. They then learned to **troubleshoot** and resolve problems with **applications**, **connections**, **drivers**, and **image quality** for both printers and scanners.

Unit 5

In this unit, students learned how to **communicate** effectively using **verbal** and **nonverbal** communication skills. They also learned the importance of **customer satisfaction** and **professional behavior**. Finally, students learned the importance of **safety**, including how to avoid **electrical** and **fire** hazards. They learned how to read a **material safety data sheet** and how to **dispose** of unwanted equipment properly.

Topic B: Continued learning after class

Point out to your students that it's impossible to learn to use any software effectively in only two days. To get the most out of this class, students should begin working with printers and scanners to perform real tasks as soon as possible. We also offers resources for continued learning.

Next courses in this series

This is the only course in this series.

Other resources

For more information, visit www.axzopress.com.

Glossary

AC (alternating current)
Current that flows repeatedly back-and-forth through a circuit at a constantly varying voltage level.

Additive color method
The method of mixing color, using colored lights. Used in monitors and other display devices.

ADF (automatic document feeder)
A mechanical component that allows you to feed a multi-page document automatically into a scanner or multifunction device one sheet at a time.

Amps
A count of electrons passing a given point per second. (Also called amperes.)

Armature
A moveable component inside a solenoid or motor that transmits motion when the device is electrified.

Beam detector
Tracks the position of the laser beam in laser printers.

Bearing
A friction-reducing device between two contacting surfaces. Typically small steel balls enclosed in a ring-shaped sleeve.

Belt
A mechanical device made of a flexible material that transmits rotation between nonadjacent rotating shafts.

Bluetooth
A short-distance—up to 10 meters—radio communications technology, developed by the Bluetooth Special Interest Group.

Brightness
A paper's brightness indicates the amount of light reflected from its surface, on a scale of 1 to 100. General use printer paper has a brightness in the upper 80s or lower 90s.

Bus
The main communication pathway between various components of the PC.

Bushing
A disposable material used to support rotating shafts and reduce friction in place of bearings.

Cam
A mechanical component that converts rotation into a push or reciprocating motion.

CCD (Charge-coupled device)
A type of image sensor in some (typically high-end) scanners.

Charge roller
Component in some EP printers that applies an electrical charge to the photoconductive drum. Used in place of a primary corona.

CIS (Contact Image Sensor)
A type of image sensor in some scanners, especially inexpensive units.

Clutch
An electromechanical component that transmits rotation to aligned shafts. It can be engaged or disengaged as necessary.

CMOS (Complimentary Metal-Oxide Semiconductor)
A type of image sensor in some scanners. Consumes less power than CCD image sensors.

CMYK
The colors cyan, magenta, yellow, and black, used in most printers to create color output.

Color depth
Specifies how many bits are used to describe the color of a single pixel.

Color gamut
A term that describes the entire range of colors a device can produce.

Compact Flash card
A nonvolatile, removable storage card.

Conductor
A material that permits the flow of electricity.

Cover stock
Heavyweight paper, generally 65lb to 68lb.

Current
A measure of the flow of electrons past a given point.

DC (Direct current)
Current that flows in a single direction at a constant voltage through a circuit.

Demodulation
The process a modem uses to subtract the carrier analog wave electronically, revealing the digital signal it carries.

Developer
The unit in an EP printer that contains the toner.

DHCP (Dynamic Host Configuration Protocol)
Network service used to assign IP addresses automatically to computers on a network.

Doctor blade
Flat, blade-like component that scrapes toner into a thin, uniform layer on the magnetic roller that transfers toner from toner supply to the drum.

Dot matrix printer
An impact printer where small pins press the ink from a ribbon onto the page.

Driver
Software that enables communication between an operating system and a device.

Drum
Cylinder coated with a photoconductive material used in EP printing to apply toner to paper.

Duplex printing
The process of printing on both sides of a sheet of paper (double-sided printing).

EPROM (Erasable Programmable Read Only Memory)
Nonvolatile memory chip.

EEPROM (Electronically Erasable Programmable Read Only Memory)
Nonvolatile memory chip.

Electricity
The flow of electrons.

EP (Electrophotographic)
A printing method that uses light (laser or LED) to discharge a photoconductive drum. The discharged areas of the drum attract toner particles, which are then applied to paper.

Event Viewer
A Windows GUI utility that enables you to monitor events that occur on your system.

Fiber optic cable
Cable that transmits data using beams of light.

FireWire
See IEEE 1394.

Firmware
Software written permanently or semi-permanently to a computer chip. Printer firmware controls printer functions.

Flat cable
Cable in which the signal wires are side by side in a flat ribbon.

Fuse
A disposable, single-use electrical component that protects an electrical circuit from overload by opening the circuit if the flow of electricity exceeds the fuse's rating.

Fuser
Assembly in an EP printer that fuses (bonds) the toner to the paper using heat and pressure.

GDI (Graphics Device Interface)
A Windows component that renders graphics for output on a printer or monitor.

Gear
A mechanical device used to transfer rotation from one rotating shaft to another.

Gear train
A device with multiple gears.

GIF (Graphics Interchange Format)
A file format for scanned image files.

Grain
See Paper grain.

Grounding components
Components that protect technicians and sensitive electrical components from electrical charges by dissipating electricity.

Heated roller
Hot roller used to melt toner and fuse it to paper.

HVPS (High-voltage power supply)
Converts 120V, 60 Hz AC current into high-voltage electricity to power the primary corona in an EP printer.

IDS (Ink Delivery System)
In an inkjet printer, the ink cartridges, print head, and associated parts.

IEEE 1394
A high-speed peripheral interconnection bus.

Infrared
A wireless technology that uses pulses of invisible infrared light to transmit signals between devices.

Impedance
A force that opposes the flow of AC through a conductor. Measured in ohms (Ω).

Inkjet printers
Produce images by forcing ink through tiny nozzles and onto the paper.

Insulator
A material that prohibits the flow of electricity.

IP address
A 32-bit address, consisting of a series of four 8-bit numbers separated by periods, that identifies a computer, printer, or other device on a TCP/IP network.

Ipconfig
A TCP/IP utility that displays IP addressing information.

ISIS (Image and Scanner Interface Specification)
An open-standard image and scanner interface specification.

JPEG (Joint Photographic Experts Group)
A file format for scanned image files that combines a graphical format and a compression method.

Lamp
An electrical device that converts electricity into light. Used to illuminate documents or other objects in scanners.

Laser printer
Produces high-quality images using an electophotographic process where electrostatic charges, toner, and laser light are combined.

LPR (Line Printer Remote)
A protocol that provides network printing over TCP/IP.

MAC address
A unique address permanently embedded in a NIC.

MSDS (Material safety data sheet)
A document that lists the proper procedures for handling or working with a particular substance.

Memory
The hardware component that stores data as the CPU works with it.

Metering blade
See Doctor blade.

Modem
Device for connecting the computer to a phone line, which typically enables the computer to connect to the Internet.

Modulation
The process a modem uses to convert a digital signal into an analog signal.

Molex connector
A 4-pin power connector.

Monochrome
Black-and-white printed pages or image files.

Motor
An electromechanical device that converts electricity into a rotating mechanical force.

Multimeter
A meter that can be used to measure multiple electrical properties.

My Network Places
An icon in Windows used to display other computers and resources on your network.

Network adapter
Device for connecting the computer to a network.

Nonvolatile memory
Memory that retains its contents when power is removed.

OCR (Optical character recognition)
Software that uses a recognition engine to interpret scanned text.

Ohm
The measurement of resistance or impedance. Written as the Greek letter omega—Ω.

Ozone
Gas produced as a byproduct of the EP print process when the primary corona charges the drum.

Paper grain
The direction in which most of a paper's fibers lie.

Paper path
The path the paper takes through a printer.

Paper weight
The weight in pounds of an uncut basis ream of paper.

Parallel
A transmission technique in which one or more bytes is transmitted at a time, with each bit in a byte traveling over its own path in the transmission medium.

Pawls
Claw-like components that help guide paper to ensure that it doesn't wrap around the drum or the heated roller in the fuser.

Photo-interrupter
A sensor that uses a direct beam of light from the source to the transistor.

Photo-reflective sensor
A sensor that uses a continuous wavelength of light reflected off a target and onto a transistor.

Pickup roller
Roller that removes a sheet of paper from the paper tray or cassette and feeds it into the printer.

Piezoelectric technology
Print method that uses an energized piezo crystal to disperse ink from a print head.

Ping
A TCP/IP utility that verifies connectivity between two devices on a network.

Pixel
The smallest addressable unit of a picture.

Pixel depth
The bits per pixel devoted to each shade.

Port
A connector into which you can plug cables from external devices, or in some cases, plug in the devices themselves.

Portable Document Format (PDF)
A file format for scanned image files.

Pressure roller
Roller in the fuser assembly of an EP printer that, along with the heated roller, fuses the toner to the paper.

Primary corona
Component in EP printers that applies an electrical charge to the photoconductive drum.

Printer control language
Programming language that formats print jobs for a specific type of printer. Examples include PostScript and PCL.

Protocol
The language that computers and devices use to send data across a network.

Pulley
A motor-driven shaft that transmits rotation to another shaft, usually called an idler. The pulley and idler are connected by a cable.

Purge cycle
Cleaning cycle in an inkjet printer where the print head cleans itself.

Registration assembly
Series of rollers that keep paper flat and ensure that the paper is properly positioned to receive the image during the EP print process.

Relay
An electromechanical component that either opens or closes when energized by an electromagnetic field.

RAW
A network printing protocol.

Resistance
A force that opposes the flow of DC through a conductor.

Resolution
The number of pixels across and down that an adapter can create on a monitor.

RGB
A color system that uses red, green, and blue in various combinations to create the full range of colors produced on display devices such as monitors.

Roller
A smooth, axle-fitted cylinder, typically used to move paper through a printer.

SANE (Scanner Access Now Easy)
An open-standard scanner interface specification commonly used on Linux computers.

Scanner
A computer input device for converting pictures or documents to image data for storage and/or manipulation.

SD (Secure Digital) card
A nonvolatile, removable storage card.

Sensor
A device that transmits real-time information to a printer.

Separation roller/pad
Component that works with the pickup roller to ensure that just one sheet of paper is fed into the printer.

Serial
A transmission technique in which bits of data are sent one at a time across the transmission medium.

Skimming blade
See Doctor blade.

Solenoid
An electromechanical device that uses electromagnetic force to create a plunging motion using an armature.

Spring
A metal coil used to provide tension between components.

Static electricity
A phenomenon in which the charges on separate objects are unequal—one object has an excess positive or negative charge as compared to the other.

Stepper motor
A motor with toothed electromagnets around a central gear that allows the motor to turn at precise angles ("steps").

Subtractive color method
Method used in printing where color is created using ink or toner.

Surface tension
Liquid property that describes the elasticity of the unbroken liquid surface.

Switch
An electromechanical device used to change the flow of an electrical current.

TCP/IP (Transmission Control Protocol/Internet Protocol)
Predominant network protocol.

Thermal bubble technology
Print method that fires heat-dispersed ink from a print head.

Thermal fuse
A single-use electrical component that protects devices from excessive heat by cutting electrical power to the device when heat reaches a specific temperature.

Thermal switch
An electrical component that protects devices from excessive heat by temporarily cutting electrical power when heat reaches a specific temperature. When the temperature falls, the switch restores electrical power to the device.

Thermistor
An electrical device used to monitor temperature and regulate electrical current to a heated device.

TIFF (Tagged Image File Format)
A file format used for scanned image files.

Toner
Fine powder made of pigment and metallic particles, used to produce images on paper in an EP printer.

Torque limiter
A component in the separation roller that provides back-feed pressure to help keep paper straight in the paper path.

Transfer corona
A component in an EP printer that charges paper so that it attracts toner from the drum.

TWAIN
A protocol and API that defines and controls communication between a scanner and computer.

Ultrex connector
A block-shaped circuit-board pin connector.

USB (Universal Serial Bus)
A standardized peripheral specification that defines a serial architecture for buses, allowing connection of one or more peripherals, including printers and scanners.

UTP (unshielded twisted pair)
A type of network cabling in which four pairs of wire are twisted around each other. The twisted pairs are then twisted the other pairs and bundled together within a covering.

Viscosity
Liquid property that describes its ability to flow.

Volatile memory
Loses its contents when power is removed.

Voltage
Electrical pressure produced by differences in charge, or electrical potential, between two locations.

Volts
The measurement used to quantify electrical pressure caused by the difference in charge between two locations.

Watts
The derived measurement of electrical power calculated by multiplying the voltage times the current.

Weight
See Paper weight.

WIA (Windows Image Acquisition)
Microsoft's drive model for image-capture devices.

Wireless Internet connection
Used to connect users in hotspots where wireless Internet service is provided by an employer, business, or governmental unit, such as a city. Wireless connections can also be made over cellular telephone networks.

ZIF socket
A socket with a small lever, designed to ease the insertion of memory and other chips into a circuit board.

Index

:

:TCP/IP
   Troubleshooting, 3-40

A

Alternating current, 1-3
Ammeters, 1-24
Amperes, 1-3
Automatic Private IP Addressing (APIPA), 3-31

B

Baud rate, 3-27
Bearings, 1-15
Belts, 1-17
Bit depth, 2-37
Bluetooth, 3-35
Bushings, 1-16

C

Cables, 1-17
Cams, 1-18
Carriage locks, 4-25
Cassettes, 2-28
Circuits, 1-3
Clutches, 1-8
Color depth, 2-37
Color theory, 2-6
Communication
   Nonverbal, 5-5
   Verbal, 5-3
Conductors, 1-2
Connectors, 1-30
   FireWire, 3-9
   Serial, 3-3
   USB, 3-7
Current, 1-3
   Calculating, 1-4
   Measuring, 1-24

D

Demodulation, 3-26
Direct current, 1-3
Documentation, 4-10
Drums, 2-15
Duplexers, 2-26
Dynamic Host Configuration Protocol (DHCP), 3-31

E

Electricity
   Characteristics, 1-2
   Static, 1-6
Electromechanical components, 1-8
Ethernet, 3-24

F

Finishers, 2-26
FireWire, 3-9
Fuses, 1-26

G

Gears, 1-15
GIFs, 2-38
Graphics Device Interface (GDI), 2-4
Grounding components, 1-28

I

Impedance, 1-3
Infrared, G-2
Inkjet printers
   Installing, 3-15
Insulators, 1-2
IP addresses, 3-30

J

JPEGs, 2-38

L

Lamps, 1-27
Laser printers
   Installing, 3-18
Light Emitting Diodes (LEDs), 1-27
Logic boards, 2-9

M

Material Safety Data Sheets (MSDS), 5-17
Material safety data sheets (MSDSs), 5-23
Microsoft Knowledge Base, 4-12
Modems, 3-26
Modulation, 3-26
Motors, 1-9, 1-10
Multimeters, 1-22

N

Network interface card (NIC), 3-25
Networks
    Protocols, 3-30

O

Ohms, 1-3
Optical encoders, 1-12

P

Paper path, 2-24
Pawls, 2-21
PDFs, 2-38
Photoconductors, 2-15
Piezoelectric technology, 2-12
Ports
    FireWire, 3-9
    Parallel, 3-4
    Serial, 3-3
    USB, 3-7
Power supplies, 1-22
Print media, 2-28
Printed circuit boards (PCBs), 1-32
Printers
    Inkjet, 2-9
    Installing, 3-12
    Laser, 2-14
    Maintaining, 4-2
    Shared, 3-38
    Troubleshooting, 4-16
Printing
    Local, 3-2
    Network, 3-2
Printing processes, 2-4

R

RAM buffers, 2-4
Raster images, 2-5
Relays, 1-10
Release and renew, 3-31
Resistance, 1-3

    Measuring, 1-24
Rollers, 1-18

S

Safety considerations, 5-16
Scanners, 2-33
    Installing, 3-21
    Maintaining, 4-7
    Troubleshooting, 4-25
Sensors, 1-11
Service Level Agreements (SLAs), 5-14
Solenoids, 1-9
Springs, 1-19
Subnet masks, 3-31
Subnets, 3-30
Switches, 1-13

T

TCP/IP, 3-30
Thermal bubble technology, 2-12
Thermistors, 1-27
TIFFs, 2-38
Troubleshooting, 4-10
TWAIN, 2-35

U

Universal Serial Bus (USB), 3-6

V

Voltage, 1-2
    Measuring, 1-24

W

Watts, 1-3
WiMAX, 3-36
Win32 applications, 2-4
Wire harnesses, 1-29
Wireless local area networks (WLANs), 3-34